ESTHER

THE NIV
APPLICATION
COMMENTARY

From biblical text . . . to contemporary life

ESTHER

THE NIV APPLICATION COMMENTARY

From biblical text . . . to contemporary life

KAREN H. JOBES

ZONDERVAN.com/
AUTHOR**TRACKER**
follow your favorite authors

ZONDERVAN®

The NIV Application Commentary: Esther
Copyright © 1999 by Karen H. Jobes

Requests for information should be addressed to:

Zondervan, *Grand Rapids, Michigan 49530*

Library of Congress Cataloging-in-Publication Data

Jobes, Karen H.
      Esther / Karen H. Jobes.
         p. cm.—(NIV application commentary)
      Includes bibliographical references and indexes.
      ISBN-10: 0-310-20672-3 (hardcover : alk. paper)
      ISBN-13: 978-0-310-20672-9 (hardcover : alk. paper)
      1. Bible. O.T. Esther—Commentaries. I. Title. II. Series.
  BS 1375.3.J63 1999
  222'.9077—dc21   98–48164

This edition printed on acid-free paper.

Printed in the United States of America

10 11 12 13 14 15 • 15 14 13 12 11

To my family with love
and
in loving memory of my father,
Robert F. Hill Sr.
(1929 – 1996)

Contents

The NIV Application Commentary Series

When complete, the NIV Application Commentary
will include the following volumes:

To see which titles are available,
visit our web site at www.zondervan.com

NIV Application Commentary
Series Introduction

THE NIV APPLICATION COMMENTARY SERIES is unique. Most commentaries help us make the journey from the twentieth century back to the first century. They enable us to cross the barriers of time, culture, language, and geography that separate us from the biblical world. Yet they only offer a one-way ticket to the past and assume that we can somehow make the return journey on our own. Once they have explained the *original meaning* of a book or passage, these commentaries give us little or no help in exploring its *contemporary significance*. The information they offer is valuable, but the job is only half done.

Recently, a few commentaries have included some contemporary application as *one* of their goals. Yet that application is often sketchy or moralistic, and some volumes sound more like printed sermons than commentaries.

The primary goal of the NIV Application Commentary Series is to help you with the difficult but vital task of bringing an ancient message into a modern context. The series not only focuses on application as a finished product but also helps you think through the *process* of moving from the original meaning of a passage to its contemporary significance. These are commentaries, not popular expositions. They are works of reference, not devotional literature.

The format of the series is designed to achieve the goals of the series. Each passage is treated in three sections: *Original Meaning, Bridging Contexts*, and *Contemporary Significance*.

 THIS SECTION HELPS you understand the meaning of the biblical text in its ancient context. All of the elements of traditional exegesis—in concise form—are discussed here. These include the historical, literary, and cultural context of the passage. The authors discuss matters related to grammar and syntax, and

the meaning of biblical words. They also seek to explore the main ideas of the passage and how the biblical author develops those ideas.[1]

After reading this section, you will understand the problems, questions, and concerns of the *original audience* and how the biblical author addressed those issues. This understanding is foundational to any legitimate application of the text today.

THIS SECTION BUILDS a bridge between the world of the Bible and the world of today, between the original context and the contemporary context, by focusing on both the timely and timeless aspects of the text.

God's Word is *timely*. The authors of Scripture spoke to specific situations, problems, and questions. Paul warned the Galatians about the consequences of circumcision and the dangers of trying to be justified by law (Gal. 5:2–5). The author of Hebrews tried to convince his readers that Christ is superior to Moses, the Aaronic priests, and the Old Testament sacrifices. John urged his readers to "test the spirits" of those who taught a form of incipient Gnosticism (1 John 4:1–6). In each of these cases, the timely nature of Scripture enables us to hear God's Word in situations that were *concrete* rather than abstract.

Yet the timely nature of Scripture also creates problems. Our situations, difficulties, and questions are not always directly related to those faced by the people in the Bible. Therefore, God's word to them does not always seem relevant to us. For example, when was the last time someone urged you to be circumcised, claiming that it was a necessary part of justification? How many people today care whether Christ is superior to the Aaronic priests? And how can a "test" designed to expose incipient Gnosticism be of any value in a modern culture?

Fortunately, Scripture is not only timely but *timeless*. Just as God spoke to the original audience, so he still speaks to us through the pages of Scripture. Because we share a common humanity with the people of the Bible, we discover a *universal dimension* in the problems they faced and the solutions God gave them. The timeless nature of Scripture enables it to speak with power in every time and in every culture.

---

1. Please note that when the authors discuss words in the original biblical languages, the series uses the general rather than the scholarly method of transliteration.

Those who fail to recognize that Scripture is both timely and time-less run into a host of problems. For example, those who are intimi-dated by timely books such as Hebrews or Galatians might avoid reading them because they seem meaningless today. At the other extreme, those who are convinced of the timeless nature of Scripture, but who fail to discern its timely element, may "wax eloquent" about the Melchizedekian priesthood to a sleeping congregation.

The purpose of this section, therefore, is to help you discern what is timeless in the timely pages of Scripture—and what is not. For exam-ple, if Paul's primary concern is not circumcision (as he tells us in Gal. 5:6), what *is* he concerned about? If discussions about the Aaronic priesthood or Melchizedek seem irrelevant today, what is of abiding value in these passages? If people try to "test the spirits" today with a test designed for a specific first-century heresy, what other biblical test might be more appropriate?

Yet this section does not merely uncover that which is timeless in a passage but also helps you to see *how* it is uncovered. The author of the commentary seeks to take what is implicit in the text and make it explicit, to take a process that normally is intuitive and explain it in a logical, orderly fashion. How do we know that circumcision is not Paul's primary concern? What clues in the text or its context help us realize that Paul's real concern is at a deeper level?

Of course, those passages in which the historical distance between us and the original readers is greatest require a longer treatment. Con-versely, those passages in which the historical distance is smaller or seemingly nonexistent require less attention.

One final clarification. Because this section prepares the way for discussing the contemporary significance of the passage, there is not always a sharp distinction or a clear break between this section and the one that follows. Yet when both sections are read together, you should have a strong sense of moving from the world of the Bible to the world of today.

THIS SECTION ALLOWS the biblical message to speak with as much power today as it did when it was first written. How can you apply what you learned about Jerusalem, Ephesus, or Corinth to our present-day needs in Chicago, Los Angeles, or London? How can you take a message originally spoken in Greek and Aramaic and communicate it clearly in our own language? How can you take the eternal truths originally spoken in a different time and culture and apply them to the similar-yet-different needs of our culture?

In order to achieve these goals, this section gives you help in several key areas.

First, it helps you identify contemporary situations, problems, or questions that are truly comparable to those faced by the original audience. Because contemporary situations are seldom identical to those faced in the first century, you must seek situations that are analogous if your applications are to be relevant.

Second, this section explores a variety of contexts in which the passage might be applied today. You will look at personal applications, but you will also be encouraged to think beyond private concerns to the society and culture at large.

Third, this section will alert you to any problems or difficulties you might encounter in seeking to apply the passage. And if there are several legitimate ways to apply a passage (areas in which Christians disagree), the author will bring these to your attention and help you think through the issues involved.

In seeking to achieve these goals, the contributors to this series attempt to avoid two extremes. They avoid making such specific applications that the commentary might quickly become dated. They also avoid discussing the significance of the passage in such a general way that it fails to engage contemporary life and culture.

Above all, contributors to this series have made a diligent effort not to sound moralistic or preachy. The NIV Application Commentary Series does not seek to provide ready-made sermon materials but rather tools, ideas, and insights that will help you communicate God's Word with power. If we help you to achieve that goal, then we have fulfilled the purpose for this series.

The Editors

General Editor's Preface

ESTHER WAS A POWERFUL WOMAN. She rose to the top of her profession. She faced and helped avert the potential genocide of her people. She played "office politics" with the best of them. And she became rich beyond her wildest dreams. Although her beauty was the reason she became part of the king's harem, she achieved all this without any of the advantages of aristocratic birth, well-placed friends, inherited wealth, or social prestige. In fact, she did it in spite of being born a member of an outcast people whose future rested on the whims of rulers more interested in personal aggrandizement than serving their people well.

So reading the book of Esther should give us clues to becoming powerful, right? We should read Esther for the same reasons we read Katherine Graham's *Personal History* (Vintage, 1998) or Katherine Hepburn's *Me: Stories of My Life* (Ballantine, 1996). We should put out a popular version of the book of Esther—*Esther As CEO*—or someone should analyze Esther's story and create *The Five Rules of Business Success According to Esther*. In a day and age when women long for an equitable place in a society that values power and wealth, we should turn to this biblical model for guidance.

We could do that, of course. It wouldn't be the first time a biblical story has been used for secular ends: for example, King David as the prototype CEO. It wouldn't be the first time that cultural fashion turned to biblical models for inspiration: for example, Jesus Christ as superstar or political revolutionary. Esther's story seems ready-made for such adaptation.

But as Karen Jobes shows so well throughout the pages of this commentary, to use Esther in this way—Esther as ultra-feminist, Esther as politician par excellence, or even Esther as moral role model—would be to miss badly the real story of the book. Esther was at best an inconsistent feminist; her political skills and judgment have been repeatedly questioned, and her moral behavior simply will not pass muster when stacked against almost any modern moral theory.

Yet Esther *was* a powerful woman, and her story is without a doubt both an inspiration and one of the great teaching resources of the church. What is the key to unlocking the great lessons of this book? It is this: Read correctly, the lead character of the book of Esther is not even Esther, but God. Esther should definitely get an Oscar nomination as best supporting actress—but the conclusions one draws from the book don't work unless God plays the lead.

To be sure, this reading is a bit difficult to advocate since God is not mentioned anywhere in the book. Martin Luther, in fact, challenged the book's proper place in the canon because of this fact. But God is the lead character, no doubt. The great lesson of Esther is that it is the story of God's keeping promises in spite of the political configuration of the world. It is not an end-justifies-the-means argument. It is not a model of how a powerful woman should work her way up the corporate ladder. It is not a handbook on Christian leadership.

The story of Esther is perfect guidance for us "when we find ourselves in a situation where right and wrong are not so clearly defined and every choice we have seems to be a troubling mixture of good and bad" (p.114). It is perfect inspiration for us when we find ourselves in situations we never sought, never planned for, and don't think we have the gifts to succeed at. It tells us what to do: Trust these situations to the Lord and move on.

There are no books, secular or biblical, that give us one, two, three-step procedures for what to do in tough situations. But all sixty-six books of the Bible rest their cases on the fact that God is the lead character of the universe, and that our initial response to that and to all the situations confronting us is prayerful acknowledgment that God rules.

Terry C. Muck

Author's Preface

THREE YEARS OF LIFE have happened while writing this book. I have had major surgery, finished my doctorate degree, watched my father die of cancer, published my dissertation, moved from coast to coast, and assumed my first full-time faculty position. Many other joys and sorrows too personal or too trivial to mention have attended these life-changing events. Often during the three years of writing this book I have wondered at God's sense of timing (and sense of humor!) in giving me the opportunity to reflect on how his providence fulfills his promise just when I felt my life was in such turmoil. I am most grateful to him both for the opportunity to write and for the completion of this work. There have been moments when I doubted it would ever happen. My prayer is that this commentary will, in his providence, reach the hands of those who might find encouragement in it for their own lives and relationship to Jesus Christ.

I am also grateful to the people at Zondervan, especially Stan Gundry and Jack Kuhatschek, for allowing me to become one of the authors in the NIV Application Commentary series. I consider it a great privilege.

My editors, Jack Kuhatschek, Terry Muck, and Tremper Longman III, have read the manuscript at various stages and have provided generous encouragement and constructive criticism along the way. Andy Dearman and John Walton read early drafts of certain chapters and offered helpful comments. I have learned much from them, and this book is certainly better than it would have been without their insightful critique. My grateful appreciation goes to each of them. Many thanks are also due to Verlyn Verbrugge at Zondervan, whose skillful editing of the manuscript has made me sound in many places a better writer than I am. His thoughtful critique has provided me the opportunity to sharpen and clarify various points throughout the book.

No book is written without the reading of many others, and this one is no exception. I gratefully acknowledge the assistance of Grace Mullen, librarian at Westminster Theological Seminary in

Philadelphia, and the library staff at Westmont College. This book could not have happened without their help.

As the years pass, I continue to remember gratefully the faculty of Westminster Theological Seminary in Philadelphia (1987–1995), who trained me in biblical scholarship. My appreciation for what they taught me and the spirit in which they taught has deepened as I myself now teach students and engage contemporary issues of biblical scholarship. I am especially grateful to the late Raymond Dillard, who first aroused my interest in the book of Esther; to Tremper Longman III, who taught me the literary approach to biblical interpretation reflected in this commentary; and to Moisés Silva (now at Gordon-Conwell Theological Seminary), who supervised my doctoral dissertation on the Greek alpha-text of Esther and whose friendship and advice have been a continual source of encouragement.

Needless to say, much appreciation and love go to my husband, Forrest (Buzz), who has spent too many evenings and Saturdays alone in these last three years, always without complaint. He has taught me the true meaning of Ephesians 5:25, "Husbands, love your wives, just as Christ loved the church." I am grateful also for his assistance preparing the indices for this commentary. To him and to my family, this book is lovingly dedicated.

Karen H. Jobes
Santa Barbara, California
February 14, 1998

Abbreviations

AB	The Anchor Bible
BA	*Biblical Archaeologist*
BBR	*Bulletin for Biblical Research*
BHS	*Biblia Hebraica Stuttgartensia*
BSC	Bible Study Commentary
CT	*Christianity Today*
Gk.	Greek
Heb.	Hebrew
ICC	International Critical Commentary
JBL	*Journal of Biblical Literature*
JSOT	*Journal for the Study of the Old Testament*
JSOTSup	Journal for the Study of the Old Testament Supplement Series
LCL	Loeb Classical Library
NAB	New American Bible
NAC	New American Commentary
NCBC	New Century Bible Commentary
NCV	New Century Version
NASB	New American Standard Bible
NIV	New International Version (1984)
NIVAC	New International Version Application Commentary
NKJV	New King James Version
NLT	New Living Translation
NRSV	New Revised Standard Version
SBLDS	Society of Biblical Literature Dissertation Series
TOTC	Tyndale Old Testament Commentary
WBC	Word Biblical Commentary

Introduction

ON FEBRUARY 25, 1994, newspapers reported that fifty-five Palestinians had been killed and 170 more wounded at the mosque at Abraham's tomb in Hebron, Israel.[1] The assailant, Baruch Goldstein, was beaten to death by an angry mob immediately after the attack. Goldstein was an American physician who had emigrated to Israel in 1982. According to the newspaper, friends had seen him only hours before his assault on the Palestinians in his synagogue celebrating Purim, listening to the annual reading of the book of Esther. The book of Esther, which explains the reason for the Jewish holiday of Purim, has been read annually in the synagogue on Purim for more than two thousand years. The story tells how the Jewish people were themselves saved from annihilation, but killed 75,800 of their enemies in the Persian empire.

The Goldstein incident is only one recent example of why interpreters throughout history have found the book of Esther to be a somewhat troubling presence within the canon of the Old Testament. This book has next to nothing to commend it as a religious text, much less the inspired Word of God for the Christian church. The only textual link it has to the rest of the Old Testament is that the story it tells involves the Jewish people. If one went through the text and replaced every occurrence of the word "Jews" with the name of some other ethnic group, there would be no reason to think the story had anything at all to do with the Bible.

Other than the fact that the story is about the Jewish people, there is nothing Jewish about it in the religious sense. It contains neither the divine name *Yahweh* nor *ʾelohim*, the Hebrew noun meaning *God*. Although the events it records take place after the decree of Cyrus in 539 B.C., which allowed the Jews to return to Jerusalem from exile in Babylonia, there is no mention of Jerusalem or the temple. Unlike the book of Daniel, which is also set in the court of a pagan king, no one prays in the book of Esther. No one has an apocalyptic vision in the

---

1. "Gunman Slays 20 at Site of Mosque, Israel Reports Say," *New York Times* (late edition) (Feb 25, 1994), 1 (the final body count was larger than first reported); Russell Walter, "Massacre in a Mosque," *Newsweek* 123 (March 7, 1994): 34–37.

Hebrew book of Esther. There is no apparent concern for the law. And in this book there is not even one tiny miracle.

Beyond the fact that the book of Esther is conspicuously nonreligious, the two main characters, Esther and Mordecai, do not seem to reflect the character of other great biblical heroes and heroines. Unlike Daniel and his friends, Esther shows no concern for the dietary laws when she is taken into the court of a pagan king. Instead of protesting, she conceals her Jewish identity and plays to win the new-queen beauty contest. Esther loses her virginity in the bed of an uncircumcised Gentile to whom she is not married, and she pleases him in that one night better than all the other virgins of the harem. When Esther risks her life by going to the king, she does so only after Mordecai points out that she herself will not escape harm even if she refuses to act. Furthermore, Esther displays a surprising attitude of brutality. When she hears that the Jews have killed five hundred people in Susa, she asks that the massacre be permitted for yet another day and that the bodies of Haman's ten sons be impaled on the city gate. As a result, three hundred more Gentiles died.

And what about Mordecai? Mordecai is often described as a wise and insightful man who knew how to turn disaster into victory. He is celebrated among the Jews as a beloved national hero. But note that Mordecai was the one who insisted that Esther conceal her Jewish identity, even though it would mean compromising whatever faith she possessed and violating the Torah. Mordecai allowed his refusal to give Haman the due respect of his office to escalate into the political incident that jeopardized the entire Jewish people. When Mordecai told Esther that if she did not act to save her people, she herself would not escape harm even though she was in the palace, was he threatening to reveal her Jewish identity, or even worse?

The text is strangely silent about the motives and thoughts of Esther and Mordecai. We don't know what Esther thought about being taken into the king's harem or why Mordecai refused to bow to Haman. The author neither exonerates nor condemns Esther and Mordecai, and never evaluates their behavior as good or bad in the eyes of the Lord. The author's reticence to reveal their thoughts, motives, attitudes, and intentions may be frustrating to readers accustomed to modern techniques of characterization, where inner thoughts are usually described in detail. However, biblical authors stand in the literary tradition of Mesopotamia and Syro-Palestine, which was typically laconic in its description of characters.[2] In Hebrew narrative, character is often revealed only through action and speech, leaving the reader to draw inferences about motives and intentions. True to Hebrew narrative style, in the book of Esther the outward, observable events are stated without explanation or comment. The astute reader sees a disquieting moral ambiguity, at best, in the way Esther and Mordecai are portrayed.

Because of the absence of religious values and the presence of sensuality and brutality, the book of Esther has posed a problem for interpreters throughout its history. For the first seven centuries of the Christian church, not one commentary was produced on this book. As far as we know, John Calvin never preached from Esther nor did he include it among his commentaries. Martin Luther denounced this book together with the apocryphal 2 Maccabees, saying of them, "I am so great an enemy to the second book of the Maccabees, and to Esther, that I wish they had not come to us at all, for they have too many heathen unnaturalities."[3]

On the other hand, some Jewish rabbis have held the book in highest esteem. Among them, Moses Maimonides, the twelfth-century Jewish philosopher, ranked it equal to the Pentateuch: "When Messiah comes, the other books [of the Hebrew Bible] may pass away, but the Torah and Esther will abide forever."[4] Such sentiments may have been rooted in the eschatological hope that Jewish interpreters have found in Esther that the Jewish nation will survive any and all assaults throughout history. Just as God's law (i.e., Torah) stands forever, God's promise to deliver his people, illustrated so powerfully by the story of Esther, is everlasting.

In spite of the problems the book raises, the evangelical doctrine of Scripture does not permit us to dismiss any book of the canon as unworthy of our reverent attention. And Esther is undeniably a part of the canon for both synagogue and church. Although God himself is

---

2. See Robert Alter, *The Art of Biblical Narrative* (New York: Basic Books, 1981), esp. ch. 6, "Characterization and the Art of Reticence."

3. Martin Luther, *The Table Talk of Martin Luther*, trans. William Hazlitt (Philadelphia: United Lutheran Publication House, n.d.), 13.

4. Quoted in T. Witton Davies, *Ezra, Nehemiah, and Esther*, NCB (New York: Oxford Univ. Press, 1909), 294.

not mentioned in the story, because the book is in the Bible, in a sense God is telling us the story. He has inspired the biblical writer to narrate events for subsequent generations. As the apostle Paul writes in Romans 15:4, "For everything that was written in the past was written to teach us, so that through endurance and the encouragement of the Scriptures we might have hope." Thus, we can pick up the book of Esther with the assurance that, despite first appearances, God has here given us bread and not a stone.

Historical Issues

IN ORDER TO understand the message of the book of Esther, we must locate its place within biblical and world history. The Jews of Judah and Jerusalem were carried into exile by the Babylonian king Nebuchadnezzar when he sacked the city and burnt the temple in 586 B.C. This historical event had spiritual significance when viewed in light of Deuteronomy 28:15, 36, 64:

> However, if you do not obey the LORD your God and do not carefully follow all his commands and decrees I am giving you today, all these curses will come upon and overtake you .... The LORD will drive you and the king you set over you to a nation unknown to you or your fathers .... Then the LORD will scatter you among all nations, from one end of the earth to the other.

The destruction of Jerusalem was the fulfillment of the covenant curse for the disobedience and sin of the people. God's people did not obey the precepts of the covenant that set them apart as God's nation, but followed the same idolatrous and sinful practices as the pagan nations. Because of this, he scattered them among those nations. It was during this time of exile that God's people came to be called Jews, taken from the name of their homeland, Judah.

It is difficult to exaggerate the significance of the Exile and Restoration in shaping Judaism. The destruction of Jerusalem and the exile of its people was a break in a long and glorious history of a nation that had begun many centuries before when God called his people out of Egypt, entered into a covenant with them, and settled them in their own land. The magnificent temple in Jerusalem, conceived by King David and built by his son Solomon, symbolized the zenith of Israel's glory. All of God's promises to his people flourished in that time unequaled in Israel's history.

The destruction of the temple and Jerusalem and the subjugation of God's people to a pagan power signaled the end of the glory that was ancient Israel. Without the temple, the sacrifices, the priesthood, and the monarchy, God's people could not function as he had commanded. New religious practices, begun in the Exile, replaced those that had disappeared with the destruction of the temple in Jerusalem. Exilic Judaism centered on the study of the Torah, for the sacred scrolls could go wherever God's people found themselves. Modern Judaism, which also continues without the temple, the sacrifices, the priesthood, and the monarchy, stands in the same tradition as postexilic Judaism. The Exile was thus a turning point in biblical history that forever changed the character of Judaism.

But the punishment of God's chosen people was not without remedy. Before sending them into exile, he gave them his promise through the prophets that a remnant would one day return to Jerusalem. In one such oracle, the Lord said through Jeremiah: "'The days are coming . . . when I will bring my people Israel and Judah back from captivity and restore them to the land I gave their forefathers to possess,' says the LORD" (Jer. 30:3). Such prophecy was fulfilled through a pagan king, Cyrus the Great, who conquered the Jews' conquerors and set them free to return to their homeland.

Cyrus II (the Great) ruled in the succession of Achaemenid kings, whose lands met the northern and eastern borders of Babylonia.[5] He conquered the Babylonian empire without a battle when his army entered Babylon by wading up the Euphrates river and through the canals of the city on the night of October 12, 539 B.C. According to both Daniel 5 and the Greek historian Herodotus (ca. 450 B.C.), the Babylonian king Belshazzar was engaged in drunken revelry when his city was attacked and defeated. Cyrus was welcomed as a liberator by the inhabitants of Babylon, and the vast lands previously ruled by the Babylonian kings, including Jerusalem and Judah, became part of the expanding Persian empire. Nine years later, Cyrus died in battle at the age of seventy.

---

5. For a history of the Persian empire see A.T. Olmstead, *History of the Persian Empire* (Chicago: Univ. of Chicago Press, 1948). For Persian history as a background to the Bible see Edwin M. Yamauchi, *Persia and the Bible* (Grand Rapids: Baker, 1990).

Introduction

Cyrus ruled as perhaps the greatest king of the Achaemenid dynasty and was the founder of the Persian empire, which eventually stretched from what is modern Pakistan in the east to modern Turkey and the coastal islands of Greece in the west to northern Sudan in Africa. The Persian empire maintained its powerful hold over the ancient east for two hundred years, beginning with Cyrus's conquest of Babylon in 539 B.C. and ending when Alexander the Great conquered Persia in 330 B.C. at the battle of Issus.

Although he was a pagan king, Cyrus played an important role in biblical history. When he entered Babylon, the Jews of Judah had been living in exile in Babylon for forty-seven years. They were waiting for the time they would be allowed to return to their homeland, as predicted by the prophets Isaiah, Jeremiah, and Ezekiel. In 539 B.C., Cyrus issued a decree that the Jews be allowed to return to Jerusalem and to rebuild the temple, using the resources of Persia. The biblical account of his decree is found in Ezra 1:1–4:

> In the first year of Cyrus king of Persia, in order to fulfill the word of the LORD spoken by Jeremiah, the LORD moved the heart of Cyrus king of Persia to make a proclamation throughout his realm and to put it in writing:
> "This is what Cyrus king of Persia says:
> The LORD, the God of heaven, has given me all the kingdoms of the earth and he has appointed me to build a temple for him at Jerusalem in Judah. Anyone of his people among you—may his God be with him, and let him go up to Jerusalem in Judah and build the temple of the LORD, the God of Israel, the God who is in Jerusalem. And the people of any place where survivors may now be living are to provide him with silver and gold, with goods and livestock, and with freewill offerings for the temple of God in Jerusalem.'"

This biblical account of the return of the Jewish people to Jerusalem is one example of Cyrus's broader policy, documented in a sixth-century clay cylinder, inscribed with cuneiform, and currently housed in the British Museum.[6] The Cyrus Cylinder contains the

---

6. For a photograph and further details about the Cyrus Cylinder, see Yamauchi, *Persia and the Bible*, 87.

annals of Cyrus's rule. According to it, he released many people groups held captive by the Babylonian kings, and he organized and financed their return to their homelands. In it he states, "I (also) gathered their former inhabitants and returned (to them) their habitations."[7] In addition to the temple at Jerusalem, Cyrus restored and repaired pagan temples in Uruk, Ur, and Babylon.

Cyrus's motives were probably not entirely altruistic. He presumably adopted the policy to send exiles back to their homelands in order to strengthen his authority in those remote parts of his empire. By financing the rebuilding of ruined cities, such as Jerusalem, he established administrative centers throughout the empire from which Persian officials governed and through which taxes could be collected.

Nevertheless, because of his liberation of God's people, Cyrus is the only pagan king in the Bible to receive the title "my anointed," the same title used to refer to the Messiah. Through Isaiah the Lord announces the restoration of Jerusalem (Isa. 44:24–45:2):

I am the LORD . . .
who says of Jerusalem, "It shall be inhabited,"
    of the towns of Judah, "They shall be built,"
    and of their ruins, "I will restore them," . . .
who says of Cyrus, "He is my shepherd
    and will accomplish all that I please;
    he will say of Jerusalem, 'Let it be rebuilt,'
    and of the temple, 'Let its foundations be laid.'"
This is what the LORD says to his anointed,
    to Cyrus . . .
"For the sake of Jacob my servant,
    of Israel my chosen,
I summon you by name
    and bestow on you a title of honor,
    though you do not acknowledge me."

Because of Cyrus's decree, first Zerubbabel and then Ezra traveled to Jerusalem with a remnant of the people to restore the temple and the city. The books of Ezra and Nehemiah tell the story of the reestablishment of the Jews in their homeland. Ezra interpreted the beneficence

---

7. Ibid., 91.

of the Persian kings, starting with Cyrus, as kindness extended by God himself so that his people might have new life (Ezra 9:9). However, most of the Jews did not return, and Babylon continued to be a thriving center of Judaism for centuries thereafter. The situation today is similar to that of the postexilic period, in that the majority of Jews live outside of Israel, though they can immigrate if they wish. This fact creates certain tensions and dependencies in the relationship between the Jews who have chosen to return to the homeland and those who, for various reasons, have not.

The books of Ezra and Nehemiah show how the Jewish people who returned to the land were dependent on the resources of Persia. They rebuilt Jerusalem and reoccupied the land through hardship and toil, while for their compatriots who remained in Babylonia, life continued undisrupted. The book of Esther tells a story of the Jewish people who, about fifty years after Cyrus's decree, apparently had chosen not to return to the homeland.

The Bible focuses our attention during the sixth and fifth centuries B.C. on the rebuilding of the temple and the city of Jerusalem, but these events were not the center of attention in the rest of the world at that time. In fact, these events would seem relatively insignificant within the larger context of world history. While the Jews were pondering their relationship to God in light of Cyrus's decree, the Chinese philosopher Confucius (551–479 B.C.) was born in the Far East. To the west of Palestine, Greece was reaching its Golden Age. While Ezra and Nehemiah were busy rebuilding Jerusalem, Pericles (ca. 495–429 B.C.) was shaping a political system in Athens that would become the basis of modern democracy. Under his leadership, Athens reached the height of its cultural and intellectual influence. Among Pericles's close associates were Sophocles the playwright, Herodotus the historian, and Protagoras the philosopher. Sophocles wrote plays still considered masterpieces today, such as *Oedipus Rex*, *Electra*, and *Antigone*. Aristophanes, who wrote the great Greek comedies, lived at the same time. The historian Thucydides, who also wrote about the Greek-Persian conflict, was a contemporary of Pericles.

During the same century Esther lived, Socrates was born (ca. 470 B.C.). This great thinker left a legacy that early Christian apologists admired and defended. Pythagoras not only established a school of religion and philosophy about the time Cyrus issued his decree, but also formulated some of the foundational theorems in mathematics. The Pythagorean theorem is still one of the first equations learned by students of algebra and geometry today.

The Olympic games we enjoy today had their roots in ancient Greece. At the time the Jews returned from the Exile, the Olympian games already had a two-hundred year history. In 520 B.C., about the time Zerubbabel returned to Jerusalem, a new event was added, the footrace for men in armor. The heritage of our Western culture—its political systems, philosophies, mathematics, sports, art, and literature—had its origins in Athens of the sixth and fifth centuries B.C. To the educated person today, the names Pericles, Socrates, and Pythagoras are no doubt more familiar than those of Ezra, Nehemiah, and Esther. Nevertheless, it was in Jerusalem, not in Athens, that events of eternal significance were unfolding. God seems to work in unlikely places through seemingly insignificant events.

After Cyrus had encouraged the Jews to return to Judah, they began to recognize that perhaps the time of their punishment was indeed ending, as predicted by Yahweh's prophets. If so, what about the covenant that their ancestors had enjoyed with God while living in the land? What of the temple sacrifices, the law, and the feasts? Were the Jews returning to Jerusalem still bound to the ancient covenant with its blessings and curses? Would those Jews who decided not to return to the homeland nevertheless have a covenantal relationship with God?

During this postexilic period, the big theological question for God's people was their status with respect to the covenant they had broken. It was, after all, not a prophet of Yahweh who commanded the temple be rebuilt, but a pagan king. Furthermore, he was motivated not by reverence for Yahweh but by his own political agenda. This no doubt gave the Jews pause. How should they relate their relationship to God to the political situation in which they found themselves? The postexilic books of 1 and 2 Chronicles, Haggai, and Zechariah were written to encourage the remnant who had returned to the land, reconfirming Yahweh's covenant with his people. Ezra and Nehemiah tell the story of the rebuilding process and how the temple sacrifices required by the covenant were reinstituted with God's blessing. The book of Esther subtly addresses the question of the covenant from the perspective of those who did not, for whatever reason, return to Jerusalem.

The story of this book is set in Susa (located in modern Iran), in the court of the Persian king Ahasuerus, whose Greek name was Xerxes I. Because of the Greek historian Herodotus, who wrote his *History of the Persian Wars* only twenty-five years after the reign of Xerxes, we know a great deal about this Persian king (who ruled from 486–465 B.C.).[8] History remembers Xerxes as the Persian king who unsuccessfully led a major invasion of Greece.[9] Throughout its history, Persia was perennially at war with the Greek city-states. Despite repeated attempts, Persia never conquered the mainland of Greece, though they came threateningly close on several occasions.

It was during this period of struggle between Persia and Greece that the postexilic Jews reclaimed their homeland. Although the struggle between these two great powers dominated world history for centuries, the books of Ezra, Nehemiah, and Esther not once mention this great conflict. Almost all that we know about the history of the Persian-Greek wars comes from Herodotus, who considered Xerxes to be one of the three most formidable Persian kings. (The other two were his father, Darius, and his son, Artaxerxes.)[10] His reign ended when he was assassinated in his bedroom by close advisors. Herodotus characterizes Xerxes, the tallest and most handsome of the Persian kings, as an ambitious and ruthless ruler, a brilliant warrior, and a jealous lover.

Authorship and Date

THE BOOK OF Esther makes no claim about the identity of its author or the date of its composition, both of which remain unknown. Accord-

---

8. *Herodotus*, trans. A. D. Godley, LCL (New York: G. P. Putnam's Sons, 1922). Modern historians of ancient Persia are skeptical about the historical reliability of Herodotus and the sources he used (see H. Sancisi-Weerdenburg and A. Kuhrt, eds. *Achaemenid History II: The Greek Sources* [Leiden: Nederlands Instituut Voor Het Nabije Oosten, 1987]). Because Herodotus was Greek, he tells the history of the Graeco-Persian wars from the viewpoint of the victorious side, with perhaps a tendency to misrepresent the Persians. Nevertheless, Herodotus lived during the late Persian period and provides a wealth of information about the Persian empire that would otherwise have been lost. It is prudent to be cautious, but it is unwarranted to discount his writing completely.

9. For the story of this military campaign, see Charles Hignett, *Xerxes' Invasion of Greece* (Oxford: Clarendon, 1963).

10. LCL: *Herodotus* 6.98.

ing to the Jewish Talmud (*Baba Bathra* 15a) it was written by "the men of the Great Synagogue," who are believed to be anonymous teachers who lived in the period between the last prophets and the later rabbinical scholars. Josephus, the Jewish historian, and Clement of Alexandria, an early church father, claimed that Mordecai himself wrote the book. It was almost certainly written by a Jew who lived outside of Palestine under Persian rule and who was familiar with Susa and the Persian court.

The author writes from a temporal vantage point somewhat removed from the events he is recounting. The book opens with the phrase (1:1), "This is what happened during the time of Xerxes," suggesting that it was written long after Xerxes had been king. The phrase in apposition, "the Xerxes who ruled over 127 provinces," seems intended to distinguish Xerxes I of the Esther story from another king of the same name. The only other king with that name was his grandson, Xerxes II, who ruled for only forty-five days in 424 B.C. If the appositional phrase was included to distinguish Xerxes I from Xerxes II, it must have been written after 424 B.C. That phrase, however, may have simply been an oblique way of identifying Xerxes as a Persian king by specifying the extent of his empire. A modern author might pen a similar expression to describe Franklin D. Roosevelt as the man "who governed the forty-eight states from Maine to California." Such an expression would identify Roosevelt as an American president and situate him at a particular historical moment when there were only forty-eight states. But it would give no clue as to when the statement itself was written.

There is a wide range of opinion about when the book of Esther was written. Some scholars, such as Joyce Baldwin, date its writing in the latter half of the fifth or early in the fourth century B.C., not more than a hundred years or so after the events it records.[11] Baldwin gives several reasons for her conclusion. (1) The author's familiar knowledge of the geography of Susa and the palace is consistent with archaeological evidence. (2) There are many Persian loanwords in the text but few, if any, Greek words. This suggests that the book was written sometime before Greek became the lingua franca at the time Alexander the Great conquered Persia (ca. 323 B.C.). (3) The Hebrew in

---

11. Joyce G. Baldwin, *Esther*, TOTC (Downers Grove, Ill.: InterVarsity, 1984), 49.

which the text of Esther is written is similar to that of 1 and 2 Chronicles, which are also dated to the two-hundred-year Persian period (539–323 B.C.).

Most modern commentaries, however, put the composition of the book in the fourth or even third century B.C. Based on linguistic features of the Hebrew, Michael Fox dates the book in the third century B.C.[12] Because of the book's positive attitude toward a Gentile king, which Jon Levenson sees as unlikely during and after the Seleucid period (i.e., ca. 198 B.C.), he dates the book to the fourth or third century B.C.[13] Frederic Bush considers the story as it now exists to be the result of a redactional process that he dates to the fourth century B.C.[14]

An ancient Greek translation of the book was made in Jerusalem either in 114 or 78 B.C., which means the Hebrew text must have existed and have been highly esteemed by that time. A previous Greek version may have existed even earlier in the Hellenistic period.[15] All things considered, it is currently impossible to date the book more specifically than between the late fifth through third centuries B.C., that is, late in the Persian period or early in the Hellenistic.

Historicity of Esther

THE AUTHOR OF Esther opens the book with the same Hebrew formula (*wyhy*) that opens the historical books of Joshua, Judges, and Samuel, as well as the book of Ezekiel. The author apparently intends his readers to think of the story he is about to tell as events that really happened. Nothing in this book has been shown to be historically untrue, though a number of questions have been raised concerning its historical accuracy. Several problems usually raised against the book are the following:[16]

---

12. Michael V. Fox, *Character and Ideology in the Book of Esther* (Columbia, S.C.: Univ. of South Carolina Press, 1991), 140.

13. Jon D. Levenson, *Esther: A Commentary* (Louisville: Westminster/John Knox, 1997), 26.

14. Frederic W. Bush, *Ruth/Esther*, WBC (Dallas: Word, 1996), 297.

15. For a discussion of the relationship between these texts see Karen H. Jobes, *The Alpha-Text of Esther: Its Character and Relationship to the Masoretic Text* (Atlanta: Scholars, 1996), 223–33.

16. The issue of the historicity of the book and its historical problems is discussed in the introductions of most commentaries (see the annotated bibliography, below). In this commentary the historical problems will be discussed in the Original Meaning section of the relevant passages.

(1) The names of Vashti and Esther do not agree with Herodotus, who refers to Xerxes' wife by the name Amestris.

(2) If Mordecai was really taken into captivity with Jehoiachin as Esther 2:6 suggests, he would be over one hundred years old at the time of Xerxes.

(3) The number of satrapies (i.e., administrative regions) specified in Esther is inconsistent with the number found in other sources. The number given in 1:1 is 127, but Herodotus and inscriptions from the reign of Darius, Xerxes' father, give the number as 20 and 23–30 respectively. The inscriptions from Darius's reign do not agree on the number, but it is never close to 127. Daniel gives the number as 120 (Dan. 6:1).

(4) Persian kings collected their harem indiscriminately, but they usually took wives only from one of seven noble families; therefore, Esther's marriage to Xerxes' is believed to be unlikely.

(5) The practice of making the decrees of the king irrevocable is unknown in any of the extrabiblical texts from the period.

None of these problems is beyond explanation (see respective places in the commentary below), and some may result from the legitimate use of poetic license. Even when taken together they do not compel the conclusion that the story is entirely fiction.

Like other stories in the Bible, the book of Esther portrays history with all of the artistry of great literature. Some who wish to guard the historicity of the book are reluctant to acknowledge, much less appreciate, its literary qualities. Others argue that because it is literature, it does not matter if it really happened because like all great literature, its significance and value transcend the mundane facts of history.

Pitting literary achievement against historicity not only creates a false polarity, it also fails to resolve the question of what really happened.[17] Whether an event actually happened is independent of the style and genre in which an author chooses to write, although wise authors usually choose a genre appropriate to their subject. If we question whether a particular literary style and genre is appropriate to represent events that really happened, we end up judging ancient writing by modern expectations. Even if the biblical narratives were written in

---

17. For a cogent and thorough discussion of the relationship between history and literature see V. Philips Long, *The Art of Biblical History* (Grand Rapids: Zondervan, 1994).

the most straightforward, "factual" style of modern journalism familiar to us, we would still have to ask, "Did this really happen?" The answer one is willing to accept to the question of the historicity of Esther depends on one's attitude toward the Bible and ancient historiography in general, on one's understanding of the nature (or even possibility) of divine revelation, and perhaps most important, on one's own personal relationship to God.

While it is true that biblical narrative does not read like modern history, the style used by historians of our day is not found among any ancient writings. The writing of history as we know it simply did not exist back then. The conventions used by ancient writers for recounting history seem to be based on values different from those we have learned to appreciate in Western culture. When reading "history," our taste for the facts, and nothing but the facts, raises expectations that are sometimes disappointed by the ancient genres found in Scripture. The problem lies with our reading strategy, not with the ancient text. But to say simply that we possibly misread the text with modern expectations does not adequately address the issue of how biblical narrative is related to the events it describes.

Ancient Storytelling and the Book of Esther

TELLING HISTORY IN the form of story may be an unfamiliar approach by modern standards, but it is perhaps a particularly appropriate way for biblical truth to be told. The narrative form of a story is a natural and primary form of human thought. It has been observed that we "dream in narrative, daydream in narrative, remember, anticipate, hope, despair, believe, doubt, plan, revise, criticize, construct, gossip, learn, hate, and live by narrative."[18] From our earliest attempts to communicate using language, we tell stories about ourselves and others. When children first learn to read, they read stories, and only much later do they acquire the skills of abstraction required to read, for instance, a textbook in philosophy. Therefore, because narrative is a form of communication accessible to the most people, it is appropriate that God has revealed himself to us in stories.

---

18. Quoted in *Narrative in Teaching, Learning, and Research*, Hunter McEwan and Kieran Egan, eds. (New York: Teacher's College Press, 1995), vii.

Moreover, storytelling has two effects even apart from the story's content. Storytelling defines and builds relationship and has the power to change others' lives as they identify with the story. When we are getting to know someone, we ask, "Tell me about yourself." We expect to hear a story that narrates what that person considers to be significant events and characteristic experiences of his or her life. When our spouse or child comes home at the end of the day, we often ask, "How was your day?" expecting to hear a narrative of selected highlights of the day's events. Story is one way we use language to build relationships by getting to know another. Therefore, biblical stories written under God's inspiration tell us about God and his relationship with his people. We read biblical narratives with the implied request, "God, tell us your story."

Storytelling also defines community. The book of Esther was the story that resulted when someone reflected on the experiences and events that explained how Purim came to be celebrated. Those experiences of a previous generation had significance to subsequent generations. Those later generations who accepted Purim and the book of Esther as significant for themselves were thereby defined as a distinct group of people who shared ownership of the story.

Every family, society, or culture is defined, at least in part, by the stories of past experiences it shares. Families share common experiences unique to that group of persons, and their stories often have significance only for themselves. Americans share stories, such as those of George Washington, the Civil War, Pearl Harbor, and Neil Armstrong's first steps on the moon. By accepting these stories as our story, we are defined as a people, the American people. We may learn about others' stories, such as the Bolshevik revolution or Evita's role in Argentina's history, without identifying with them as our story. It is therefore appropriate that God gave us a Bible containing stories that both draw us into relationship with him and define us as God's people when we accept them as ours.

Narrative is particularly appropriate to the story of God's redemptive work in history culminating in Christ, because for those living after the events occurred, all knowledge of them is based on witness. Those who saw what actually happened told others about it. That witness resulted in the biblical writings. In his book *Models for Scripture*, John Goldingay extensively discusses the character of the Bible as narrative and its implications for knowing truth. As he points out, "witness characteristically takes the form of narrative" as the biblical authors attempt to draw readers into an understanding of reality where God promises to bless and redeem and overcomes all obstacles to fulfill his promise.[19] The resulting stories are much more than a statement of bare facts.

The biblical narratives that result from witness are "exercises in interpretation before they are objects of interpretation."[20] When we read the Esther narrative, we must understand it not as if it were a newspaper account from ancient Persia, but as an interpretation of the significance of what happened. Such interpretation must not be thought of as a bad thing that distorts the truth; to the contrary, the interpretive element introduced by the biblical authors, writing under the inspiration of the Holy Spirit, explains the true significance of events and makes demands on the reader. For example, history writes, "Jesus, called the Christ, died on the cross," whereas Scripture writes, "Jesus Christ died on the cross for our sins." Both are true statements, but the second makes a demand on the reader that the first does not. It is precisely the divinely inspired interpretation of what happened that distinguishes Scripture writing from history writing.

The authors of Scripture introduce interpretation into biblical stories first by being selective in what they tell, and second by presenting their material through rhetorically powerful literary techniques common in their ancient culture. This is simply the nature of writing stories. No author tells all the facts, just those that are significant for his or her purpose. By selecting what to tell, the author has made an interpretive decision. (Just think of how tedious it would be if your spouse decided to tell you every tiny detail of his or her day, including things like inserting the key into the car's ignition and opening the door to the office!)

An author also interprets by arranging and emphasizing the selected material in such a way as to make a point. This may mean telling events out of the order in which they occurred, or placing two events side by side for contrast that did not actually happen one right after the other.

---

19. John Goldingay, "Witness in the Form of Story," in *Models for Scripture* (Grand Rapids: Eerdmans, 1994), 61.

20. Ibid., 55.

Such interpretation is necessary for good, effective communication, for stories are unintelligible if they are a stream-of-consciousness account of the passing of time. The biblical writers do not just report the bare facts of what happened; rather, by selecting and arranging their material, they provide the divinely inspired, and therefore true, interpretation of its significance intended to evoke faith in the readers and draw them into right relationship with God. The author of Esther chooses the events he tells and then arranges them in such a way as to draw the reader to identify with one side of the conflict or the other, and by implication, to share in that ultimate destiny.

Literary genre and style are chosen by an author according to the degree of interpretation intended. Good journalism states only the facts without comment because it is intentionally noninterpretive (although even journalism is never completely uninfluenced by the reporter's interpretive bias). One method of interpretation is through employing literary artistry. Skillfully crafted narrative structure, repeated motifs, wordplays, and such literary techniques are effective methods for interpreting the significance of events. In contrast to journalism, poetry—perhaps the most artistic genre of written language—is also arguably the most interpretive.

Contrast and compare, for example: "For as high as the heavens are above the earth, so great is his love for those who fear him" (Ps. 103:11), to the equivalent statement, "God very much loves those who fear him." The integrity of truth is not compromised when it is expressed in poetic form. No one reads this verse and then asks, "How many miles (or kilometers) are there between the heavens and the earth?" Nor does one conclude that because we cannot actually measure the distance between the heavens and earth, God therefore does not love those who fear him. In other words, evangelical Christians have no trouble accepting and appreciating truth expressed in the form of divinely inspired poetry.

Similarly, the use of poetic license in biblical narrative to interpret the significance of the events told does not compromise the integrity of Scripture. Thus, some of the questions we have and "problems" we see with the book of Esther arise because we value historical accuracy and precision where the author valued poetic license for the purpose of interpretation. We who rightly insist on the historicity of biblical events must also fully appreciate the literary genre and the author's use of poetic license, and not press the story historically where the author did not intend his readers to do so.

Until recently, evangelical biblical scholars have tended to protect zealously the historicity of the biblical stories at the expense of fully appreciating the literary qualities of the ancient way of telling what happened. This zeal has usually been expressed in attempts to harmonize, or to explain, every detail of the text with historical information from other sources, especially when the two disagree. The results of such harmonization are sometimes more problematic than the problem they attempt to solve, and would no doubt make the original author laugh at how we have so misconstrued his intent and misread his literary devices.

Some of the apparent discrepancies that have been identified as historical problems by some, and that motivated harmonization by others, may instead be the legitimate literary use of poetic license in order to interpret the significance of what happened. In other words, some expressions in the story may have been intended for literary effect, not for historical accuracy as we define it today. This need not undermine the historical integrity of the book. For instance, the names of the characters in Esther have been questioned as historically problematic because they seem inconsistent with the names that would be expected, given the extrabiblical sources. Such problems have led some to conclude that the story is fiction. However, this may be one example of poetic license employed in the naming of characters, names that possibly have been assigned by the author to characterize the role each plays in the story.

For instance, Vashti's name is said to sound similar to the Old Persian expression for *beautiful woman* or *beloved*.[21] The Hebrew form of Xerxes' name (pronounced *Ahashwerosh*) sounds comical when pronounced in Hebrew and "would correspond to something like King Headache in English."[22] The name "Esther" sounds similar to *Ishtar*, the Babylonian goddess of love and war (see comments on 2:7). Haman's name pronounced in Hebrew sounds similar to the Hebrew word meaning "wrath." Of course, these phonetic wordplays do not

---

21. See Carey A. Moore, *Esther*, AB (New York: Doubleday, 1971), 8; L. B. Paton, *Esther*, ICC (Edinburgh: T. & T. Clark, 1908; repr. 1976), 66.

22. According to Yehuda T. Radday, "Esther With Humor," in *On Humour and the Comic in the Hebrew Bible*, JSOTSup 92 (Sheffield: Almond, 1990), 296.

come across in English translation. Instead of being the actual name of the historical person, these names may have been chosen or created by the author to characterize the people who nonetheless did actually exist in history with other names.

The relationship between biblical narrative and history is probably one of the most important issues in evangelical hermeneutics today. This is because Christianity and its parent, Judaism, consciously rest on the concept that God has in fact worked in history through events that really happened. Judaism and Christianity rest not on the inward, mystical journey of the mind and soul of the individual, but on events in history through which the Creator-Redeemer God revealed himself to his people. Biblical narratives such as Esther are the record of those events in the form of story. Purim would be a hollow religious celebration if the Jews of Persia had not truly been delivered from destruction. In the New Testament, the apostle Paul says that the Easter story would be a cruel farce if Jesus was not really raised from the grave (1 Cor. 15:19). The biblical stories that witness to these events tell us, with varying degrees of literary artistry and poetic license, why what happened so long ago is significant for us today.

Rather than deciding whether the book of Esther is history or literature, the real question is how to understand it as both. When reading the Esther story, it would be a shame to allow ourselves to be so distracted by the historical "problems" it raises that we completely miss the point of this wonderful book. Similarly, it would be a mistake to be so impressed by its literary qualities that we dismiss the book as pious fiction. This commentary will attempt to show how the literary artistry of the book is the key to understanding, and applying to life today, the divinely inspired message of what happened to God's people in Persia so long ago.

Literary Structure

THE ESTHER STORY is a literary delight told with irony, satire, and humor. Because the story is in the sacred canon of both the synagogue and the church, it must also be, in some sense, theology told with irony, satire, and humor. In order to appreciate fully the theological message of the book of Esther, its literary form and qualities must not be overlooked.

The book of Esther is a story that, like a parable, makes its point as a whole unit. Because parables are relatively self-contained and short, they make congenial preaching texts. Because Esther is much longer than a parable, the point it makes is multifaceted and invites deeper reflection. This also makes it difficult to preach Esther because when a manageable-sized portion of text is selected, the story as a unit recedes from view, and the part tends to lose its connection to the whole. For this reason, it is probably best to not try to preach or teach through Esther chapter by chapter. Instead, choose one of the book's major points for the sermon or teaching topic. Select as the sermon text a passage that illustrates or exemplifies that point and give a brief synopsis of the story, relating the selected passage to the meaning of the whole.

The major theological point of Esther is that throughout history God fulfills his covenant promises through his providence. The contemporary significance of this for application today is that God's will for an individual's life is unfolded through divine providence day by day. Some of the interweaving themes of the book of Esther include:

- the intriguing interplay of God's providence and human behavior:
  suggested text: 1:10–12; 2:17, 21–23; 4:14; 6:1–3.
- the self-deceptive and destructive nature of pride:
  suggested text: 6:4–14.
- identification with God's people as a defining moment in life:
  suggested text: 4:12–16.
- male and female partnership in God's providence:
  suggested text: 9:29–32.

To help the reader better understand the relationship of the parts to the whole, the overall literary structure of Esther that shapes the theological message of the book will be presented here. Within the commentary, the relationship of each scene to the larger structure will be explained. Often the contemporary significance of a given scene will be found in its contribution to the overall theme rather than being a direct application of the portion of text at hand.

To study any particular passage, the reader is encouraged to read through the entire book of Esther, preferably at one sitting, before using this commentary. The parts of the story can be understood only as they relate to the integrity of the whole literary structure, and, conversely, the point of the story in all of its complexity can be best understood by pondering the significance of each part.

Chapters 1 and 2 set the opulent stage in the Persian palace where Queen Vashti defies her husband and king, where all the beautiful virgins of the empire are gathered into the harem, where Esther alone pleases the king with her sensuous beauty, and where Mordecai foils an assassination plot against the king's life. Chapters 3 through 8 recount how the personal conflict between Mordecai and Haman escalates into the threat of genocide for the Jewish people, how Esther dares to seek an uninvited audience with the king at the risk of her life, how she entertains the king and Haman at two banquets, how Mordecai is honored after the king's sleepless night, and finally how Haman's plot is turned against him. The Jews are not only delivered from annihilation but are empowered. Chapters 9 and 10 explain how this great deliverance is commemorated by Purim, one of the two Jewish feasts not commanded by the Pentateuch.[23]

The book of Esther is treated as a literary unity in this commentary. If the author wrote much later after the reign of Xerxes, he obviously must have acquired his information from somewhere, unless one wishes to argue it is a fiction drawn completely from his imagination. His source(s) may have been written, such as the "annals of the kings of Media and Persia" (10:2), or oral, if the Esther story was repeatedly recited through the years before taking on written form. Some scholars see as many as three sources in the book—a Vashti source, a Mordecai source, and an Esther source.[24] Other scholars seek a preliterary source in Babylonian mythology.

Most theories of prior sources from which the book of Esther was composed are based on observing doublets in the story, such as the two banquets given by Esther (5:4–6; 7:1–2) and the two gatherings of virgins (2:2, 19). Source critics take this as evidence that originally two or more stories, each containing one occurrence of the doublet, were simply woven together to achieve the final form of the story. An

---

23. The other is Hanukkah, whose historical basis is recorded in the apocryphal book of 1 Maccabees.

24. For a discussion of possible sources see David J. A. Clines, *The Esther Scroll: The Story of the Story* (Sheffield: JSOT, 1984), 115ff.; Michael V. Fox, *The Redaction of the Books of Esther* (Atlanta: Scholars, 1991), 96ff.

alternate explanation is found by literary critics, who attribute such doublets to the deliberate intention of the author to use doublets as a literary device. Given the literary integrity of the book as it stands in its canonical form, it was carefully crafted by the author/redactor, regardless of how he came by his material.

The literary structure of this story is shaped by a dominant motif that is repeated throughout.[25] This motif is the "banquet" (Heb., *mišteh*), a term most often used to refer to eating and drinking on special occasions. This Hebrew word, usually translated "banquet" in the NIV, occurs twenty times in the book of Esther and only twenty-four times in the rest of the Old Testament.

This dominant motif of the banquet, or feast, is especially apt, since the Esther story explains the origin of Purim, a feast celebrated still today by the Jews.[26] Although this book explains the reason for the feast of Purim, Purim is not the theme of the book. The book tells a story that has its own literary form and message. The theme of the story is given by the author as the reason to celebrate Purim. Purim does not commemorate any one of the events found within the story, but the theme embodied by the story as a whole, which is the reversal of destiny. It is both implied by the literary structure of the book and stated explicitly by the author:

> On the thirteenth day of the twelfth month, the month of Adar, the edict commanded by the king was to be carried out. On this day the enemies of the Jews had hoped to overpower them, but *now the tables were turned* and the Jews got the upper hand over those who hated them. (9:1, emphasis added)

> ... the Jews got relief from their enemies ... *their sorrow was turned into joy and their mourning into a day of celebration.* (9:22, emphasis added)

This theme of the reversal of destiny is also built into the literary structure of the story, which is characterized by peripety. *Peripety* is a literary term used to refer to a sudden turn of events that reverses

---

25. A literary motif is a subject, idea, or referent that recurs throughout a work as a literary device.

26. Purim falls between mid-February and mid-March.

27. The term was first used by Aristotle; see Harry Shaw, ed., *A Dictionary of Literary Terms* (New York: McGraw-Hill, 1972).

the expected outcome of a story.[27] In Esther the recurrence of the motif of the *mišteh* focuses the reader's attention on the surprising event from which the great reversal of fortune proceeds (see comments on ch. 6).

The Esther story is about an event intended to harm the Jews, which, against all expectation, actually results in the opposite. Instead of being destroyed, the Jews are not only delivered but empowered through the agency of Esther and Mordecai. The empowered destroyer, Haman, not only loses his power but is himself destroyed. This structure of reversal operates at many levels throughout the story. The feast of Purim in the month of Adar celebrates this grand reversal—a "month when [the Jews'] sorrow was turned into joy and their mourning into a day of celebration" (9:22).

The use of peripety in Esther is not simply a literary device to produce an aesthetically pleasing story. This book is an example of how form and content mutually interact in a text. The structure of peripety deeply reflects the worldview of the author, and it provides the framework within which we can understand the theological implications of this story. The author is suggesting that beneath the surface of even seemingly insignificant human decisions and events, an unseen and uncontrollable power is at work that can be neither explained nor thwarted. Because this story is in the canon of the Jews, and subsequently the Christians, it is proper to construe that unseen power as God. What is the divinely inspired author of Esther trying to say to his readers about God?

The Theology of Esther

IT MAY SEEM inappropriate to speak of the "theology" of a book that does not mention God even once. It seems the author not only deliberately avoided mentioning God, but anything associated with religion as well (with the possible exception of fasting in 4:16). Christian theology, however, is concerned with the character of the unseen God, who manifests himself in the events of human history. The Esther story is an example of how at one crucial moment in history the covenant promises God had made were fulfilled, not by his miraculous intervention, but through completely ordinary events. Once the theological message of the book is understood, it is appropriate that God is not mentioned. In fact, the complete absence of God from the text is the genius of the book, from which its hope and encouragement flow to us today.

The appropriate application of the book is found in its theological message, which in turn is found in the historical setting of the book. For the Jews who returned to Jerusalem, the post-exilic books of Chronicles, Nehemiah, Ezra, Haggai and Zechariah explicitly answer in the affirmative the big theological question of that day: "Are we still God's people in covenant relationship with him?" The author of Esther answers that same question in the affirmative for the Jews living in the Diaspora, where they had no temple, prophet, or city.

The reversal so prominent in the literary structure of Esther is driven by the conflict between Haman the Agagite and Mordecai the Jew. The tiny detail that identifies Haman as an "Agagite" is the key that links the Jews of the Diaspora to the ancient covenant God made with their ancestors at Sinai, reassuring them of its continuing efficacy (see comments on ch. 3).

Agag was the king of the Amalekites at the time Saul was Israel's first king (1 Sam. 15). The Amalekites had the dubious distinction of being the first people to attack God's people and attempt to destroy the newly formed covenant nation just after the Exodus. As a result, God promised Moses that he would be at war with them from generation to generation until their memory was blotted out (Ex. 17:8–16; Deut. 25:17–19).

The Esther story is another episode of that ancient war between Israel and the Amalekites, and by every indication it looks as if God's people will be destroyed. They have no king, no army, no prophet, no land, no temple, no priesthood, and no sacrifices. They are but a small, defenseless minority living at the mercy of a ruthless and powerful pagan monarchy. Moreover, they find themselves in this predicament because their sin has been just as bad as that of the pagan nations. They can expect only the worst. The reversal dethroning Haman and empowering Mordecai shows that, despite their sin and despite their location away from Jerusalem, God's promise to Israel made at the beginning of their nation still stands. He will still destroy those who want to destroy his people, no matter where they are living. The book of Esther shows that the Jews living in the Persian empire are still under God's covenantal care.

These Jews are still under that protection even though they are living outside of the borders of the place where God promised to live with his people. The explicit absence of God in this story is particularly appropriate for its historical moment, because this book focuses on those Jews who have not returned to Jerusalem, the place where Yahweh lives. Nevertheless, these Jews turn out to be the ones who protect and preserve those who have returned to the land in order to rebuild the temple. That remnant who returned are equally at risk of destruction under a decree of death that reaches to the farthest ends of the Persian empire.

The message of the book can also be considered from the viewpoint of systematic theology. The book of Esther is perhaps the most striking biblical statement of what systematic theologians call *the providence of God*. When we speak of God's providence, we mean that God, in some invisible and inscrutable way, governs all creatures, actions, and circumstances through the normal and the ordinary course of human life, without the intervention of the miraculous.

The book of Esther is the most true-to-life biblical example of God's providence precisely because God seems absent. Even in the most pagan corner of the world, God is ruling all things to the benefit of his people and to the glory of his name. Even when his own people, like Esther and Mordecai, make decisions that come from ambiguous motives at best, or perhaps even outright disobedience, God is still providentially working through those very things to fulfill his covenant. Surely Romans 8:28 is a New Testament summary of the theological message of Esther: "And we know that *in all things* God works for the good of those who love him, who have been called according to his purpose" (emphasis added).

However, we can read a theological message of God's providence in Esther only by interpreting Esther within the larger context of the biblical canon. Other biblical books teach us explicitly that God is the unseen power behind world history (e.g., Dan. 4:35). If we did not have the teaching of these other books, we would have no reason to see a statement of God's providence in this story. We must be careful, then, to distinguish what we can learn from Esther by bringing other biblical concepts to our reading of it from what the author actually says, or (more to the point) he does not say within the book itself.

The author's silence about God's role in the Esther story should be allowed to stand and its significance carefully considered. The events in this book are deliberately left uninterpreted by the divinely inspired author, resulting in a purposeful ambiguity. That interpretive uncertainty is not a hermeneutical problem to be overcome; rather, it is itself an important part of the historical context in which the Jews of Susa lived and against which the events of the story should be viewed. Is God present or is he absent? From reading just Esther alone, we cannot be sure. Nor could the Jews of Susa who first experienced these events. This uncertainty aptly reflects the big question facing the Jews in the postexilic period: "Are we still the people of the covenant? Is God still with us or has he abandoned us to our sin and the judgment of exile?"

Looking back into history, we now know the answer, but those who lived through that time did not. The uncertainty can be resolved only by reading Esther within its larger canonical context. No amount of exegesis of the text apart from the rest of the canon can resolve the uncertainty since it is a deliberate part of what the author was trying to communicate.

The explicit absence of God in Esther, even though the book is divinely inspired, makes it difficult to interpret as we do other books of the Bible. But the uncertainty that results from his absence in the text teaches by example the most basic principle of biblical hermeneutics: Without divine revelation, the human experience is inherently ambiguous and cannot be rightly understood. Historical events can always be construed either for or against God's existence and activity. Elsewhere the Bible interprets historical events as ultimately caused by God. For instance, the Cyrus Cylinder mentioned above documents Cyrus's decree allowing the exiles of many nations to return to their homeland. The book of Ezra documents God's involvement in that event and relates it specifically to his intentions for his people (see Ezra 1:1):

> In the first year of Cyrus king of Persia, in order to fulfill the word of the LORD spoken by Jeremiah, the LORD moved the heart of Cyrus king of Persia to make a proclamation throughout his realm and to put it in writing.

Without God's own interpretive commentary on the events of history given to the other biblical authors, the whole Bible would read like the book of Esther, and we would have no certainty about God's involvement in the events of Israel's history or that of any people. In other words, God's verbal, interpretive self-revelation is essential if we are to know him. We can read the present story for theology only because of its place in the biblical canon. When all is said and done, lack of God's interpretive revelation in a book that is itself the Word of God is its genius. This book is a canonical example of how ambiguous life and history would be if God had only acted but had not also spoken.

Contemporary Significance

THE BOOK OF Esther is still treasured by Jews today and read annually in the synagogues on Purim because they find in it the reassurance that they will survive as a people against powers that want to destroy them. Its contemporary significance for the Jewish people is captured in the words of Robert Gordis,

> Anti-Semites have always hated the book, and the Nazis forbade its reading in the crematoria and the concentration camps. In the dark days before their deaths, Jewish inmates of Auschwitz, Dachau, Treblinka, and Bergen-Belsen wrote the Book of Esther from memory and read it in secret on Purim. Both they and their brutal foes understood its message. This unforgettable book teaches that Jewish resistance to annihilation, then as now, represents the service of God and devotion to His cause. In every age, martyrs and heroes, as well as ordinary men and women, have seen in it not merely a record of past deliverance but a prophecy of future salvation.[28]

Moreover, like the rest of the Hebrew Bible, the book of Esther has become the spiritual heritage of Christians, bequeathed to us by Jesus Christ (e.g., Luke 24:27, 44–45). The New Testament teaches that the Old Testament promises of future salvation were ultimately secured by the death and resurrection of Jesus Christ. The deliverance of God's people from Haman's death decree assured the continuance of the Jewish nation from which their Messiah would come. That Messiah brought a deliverance from death not limited to escaping the holocausts of history, but a deliverance from the grave that inevitably awaits each of us, both Jew and Gentile alike.

The theme of the reversal of destiny takes the form of peripety in the book of Esther. However, the reversal of destiny is a major theme

---

28. Robert Gordis, *Megillat Esther* (New York: Ktav, 1974), 13–14.

in biblical theology, spanning the entire Bible. God's plan to redeem a people from death is a reversal of expected outcomes for those he saves. Therefore, the cross of Jesus Christ is the pivot point of a greater peripety that spans all of history.

Because of our sin, we, like the Jews in exile in Persia, should expect only death and destruction. Our fate was reversed by the seemingly insignificant death of one man, Jesus of Nazareth. Dragging a cross through the streets to his death was not the outcome one expected when the long-awaited Messiah finally appeared in Jerusalem. Such a destiny was so unexpected that it has precluded in many minds even the possibility that Jesus was the Messiah. While the world may see the birth and death of Jesus as ordinary events, through that one man God was fulfilling the promises of his life-giving covenant. Against all human expectation, Jesus Christ took the death that was our destiny so that we could have the life that was his.

Christ's resurrection from the grave is the ultimate reversal of expected outcomes. Because of this great peripety, we who could expect only death have been given life, a life that is imperishable and eternal. There is no power that can wrest it from us. The episode in Israel's history from the Persian period is an illustration of the reversal of an expected outcome in history that resulted in life instead of death for God's people. Moreover, this deliverance from death was itself a necessary link in the chain of events that led centuries later to the ultimate peripety accomplished on the cross of Jesus Christ.

The major theological point of the book of Esther is that God fulfills his covenant promises through his providence. The major point of contemporary significance is that God unfolds his will for individual lives through that same providence. God continues to work through providence, through seemingly insignificant events, to call people in every age to himself. How did you come to know Christ? Perhaps someone invited you to a church service, or by chance you heard a radio program, or you picked up an evangelistic tract. God sovereignly controls events of history and flawed human decisions to fulfill his promise to save for himself a people. Once in Christ, God promises that we will "be conformed to the likeness of his Son" (Rom. 8:29). He uses the ordinary events of life, some happy, some quite tragic, to form Christ in us.

I remember being almost obsessed with trying to find God's will for my life when I became a Christian twenty-five years ago. I and my other recently converted Christian friends in college talked endlessly about how we would know God's will, whether we could possibly miss God's will, and what would happen to us if we did. God's will is, of course, important to the Christian seeking seriously to live for Christ. But as a young and uninformed Christian I had a flawed understanding of how to know God's will for my life. I was looking for something to happen, for some sign, that would clearly tell me where God wanted me to be and what he wanted me to be doing. I was sure (but wrong) that God would test my commitment to Christ through something like sending an angel to tell me to do something I dreaded in a place I would not want to go. I failed to realize that God's will for my life was being revealed day by day in the unfolding of ordinary events.

The true test is living for Christ at this present moment, in the place where one happens to be, in whatever situation one finds herself or himself. As I tried to search out God's will and plan to change my life accordingly, God was leading me silently, yet inexorably, from decision to decision, from situation to situation. One thing leads to another in the chain of unbreakable time. As the saying goes, "Life is what happens while you're making other plans." Although I never did get that certain "sign" of God's will I sought as a new Christian, God has undeniably worked in the ordinary moments of my life to take me from being a babe in Christ who had never read the Bible to a professor of New Testament studies twenty-five years later. And some of the ordinary moments along the way were, in fact, quite extraordinary.

However, all this is not to say that we can look at circumstances at any moment and know exactly what God is up to. When we look at current events in the world—and more personally, events in our own lives—we often find their meaning ambiguous. A given event in our life might be good or it might be bad, and it is most often a mixed blessing. Often we cannot evaluate the significance of an event until years later, if ever. To confuse us further, bad decisions may nevertheless produce good things, and what start out as good intentions may end up in heartbreak. That's peripety in operation! So often our carefully laid plans are frustrated and we are forced to admit that we are not in control of our lives, no matter how hard we try to be.

Even when we are the most confused, life goes on and we have to make decisions. The irony and the ambiguity of the story of Esther are so true to life. Esther must decide to risk her life by going to the king, unsummoned or not. She had no word from God, she had no prophetic vision. She had no promise of Scripture that she could claim for her personal safety. She was responsible for making a decision with serious consequences. In other words, she was just like us. She couldn't see the happy ending of the story from the frightening middle. What a picture of the interplay between God's omnipotent providence and human responsibility!

The role of "coincidence" is prominent in the plot of Esther. By coincidence Mordecai learns of the assassination plot. By coincidence the king's timely insomnia results in Mordecai's exaltation on the day we expect Mordecai's death. Is this not how God providentially directs the course of human events? The story of Esther illustrates that human action is essential to divine providence, yet God's triumph in history ultimately does not depend on what we do, but on what he does. It depends not on our character, but on his character.

Therefore, the story of Esther is of great relevance to Christians, particularly Christians living after the end of the apostolic age. For we live, like Esther and Mordecai, in a completely pagan world. Like the Jews of Persia, we have no earthly king, no earthly prophet, and no earthly kingdom. Like them, we live in an age where we cannot depend on miracles.

Like Esther and Mordecai, we face difficult ethical and religious questions in a highly political world, one that is hostile to our most fundamental Christian convictions. We struggle to respond wisely and faithfully to difficult circumstances that come our way and over which we sometimes seem to have little or no control. Like Esther and Mordecai, we Christians are also a morally ambiguous people at our best. Our motives are mixed; our hearts are not always devoted to covenant obedience. Because of our sin, we are not living in the Garden of Eden, where the Lord walks and talks with us in the coolness of the day. We live in the exile of history, in a world where God is unseen.

We should expect nothing but death from such a world, but we have seen the ultimate peripety, the ultimate reversal of expected ends, in the cross of Jesus Christ. God has guaranteed Christians life even though we face certain death. He reverses our lot, not because of the merit of anything we do, but because he has chosen us in Christ. God is working providentially, in the completely secular and ungodly course of human events, to save his people against all expectation and to bring all of history to culmination in Christ. There is no plot, no plan that can thwart God's purposes that stretch from Genesis to Revelation. Esther lies between the two.

The great paradox of Esther is that God is omnipotently present even where God is most conspicuously absent. Jesus' last words were, "Go and make disciples of all nations. . . . And surely I am with you always, to the very end of the age" (Matt. 28:19–20). And then, ironically, he left! Nevertheless, our Lord is omnipotently present even where he is most conspicuously absent.

Outline

Annotated Bibliography

Commentaries and General Studies

Baldwin, Joyce G. *Esther: An Introduction and Commentary*. TOTC. Downers Grove, Ill.: InterVarsity, 1984. A passage-by-passage commentary on the history, theology, and structure of the book.

Breneman, Mervin. *Ezra, Nehemiah, Esther*. NAC. Nashville: Broadman & Holman, 1993. An exegetical and theological exposition that reads Esther as historical narrative. Verse-by-verse commentary of the NIV text.

Bush, Frederic. *Ruth/Esther*. WBC. Dallas: Word 1996. A literary analysis, drawing on genre and discourse structure that divides the book into acts, scenes, and episodes. Includes notes on the Hebrew text and extensive bibliography.

Clines, D. J. *Ezra, Nehemiah, Esther*. NCBC. Grand Rapids: Eerdmans, 1984. Verse-by-verse commentary based on RSV text with introductory discussion, including canonicity, historicity, and the influence of other literature on the Esther story.

Dillard, R. D., and T. Longman III. "Esther." Pp. 189–97 in *An Introduction to the Old Testament*. Grand Rapids: Zondervan, 1994. Discusses the historical background, literary structure, and theological message of the book.

Fox, Michael V. *Character and Ideology in the Book of Esther*. Columbia, S.C.: Univ. of South Carolina Press, 1991. More than a commentary, this excellent work by a Jewish scholar includes a discussion of each character in the story, the major motifs, the three versions of the Esther story, as well as philological-textual notes on the Hebrew.

Gordis, Robert. *Megillat Esther: Introduction, New Translation and Commentary*. New York: Ktav, 1974. An English translation of the Esther scroll, with introduction and commentary, intended for use in the home and synagogue. Also includes the synagogue *Ma'ariv* service for Purim. A valuable look at how Esther is appreciated by Jewish people today.

Levenson, Jon D. *Esther: A Commentary*. Louisville, Ky.: Westminster/John Knox, 1997. A Jewish scholar brings the best of recent scholarship to bear on the book of Esther, including commentary on the six major additions found only in the Greek version.

Luter, A. Boyd, and Barry C. Davis. *God Behind the Seen: Expositions of the Books of Ruth and Esther*. Grand Rapids: Baker, 1995. A popular exposition of Esther written in a fun-to-read, anecdotal style.

Moore, C. A. *The Anchor Bible: Esther*. New York: Doubleday, 1971. An English translation of Esther with brief commentary and textual notes. The introduction includes discussions of the historicity and canonicity of the book, the style and syntax of the Hebrew text, and the two Greek versions. A valuable, but dated, bibliography.

———. *Studies in the Book of Esther*. New York: Ktav, 1982. An anthology of valuable journal articles on various topics concerning the book of Esther.

———. "Eight Questions Most Frequently Asked About the Book of Esther." *Bible Review* 3 (Spring 1987): 16–32. A concise response to questions on the more puzzling aspects of the book of Esther. Includes a gallery of photographs of scenes from the Esther story as depicted in fine art.

Pagán, Samuel. *Esdras, Nehemivas y Ester*. Comentario Biblico Hispanoamericano. Miami: Editorial Caribe, 1992. Commentary on sections of the book of Esther with essays on modern political issues such as the abuse of power, the problem of vengeance, and the relationship of Christians to secular authorities. Written in Spanish.

Paton, L. B. *A Critical and Exegetical Commentary on the Book of Esther*. ICC. New York: Charles Scribner's Sons, 1908; repr. 1976. An oldie but goodie that includes philological and historical information not found elsewhere. Also includes material from the Aramaic Targums of Esther.

Vos, Howard F. *Ezra, Nehemiah and Esther*. BSC. Grand Rapids: Zondervan, 1987. An amplification of the Esther story written for the popular audience.

Historical Issues and the Persian Period

Ackroyd, Peter R. *Israel Under Babylon and Persia*. Oxford: Oxford Univ. Press, 1970. This source only mentions the book of Esther in passing, but it provides historical information about the exilic and postexilic period that illuminates the biblical texts of that period.

Boyce, Mary. "Persian Religion in the Achaemenid Age." Pp. 279–307 in *Cambridge History of Judaism*. Ed. W. Davies and L. Finkelstein. Cambridge: Cambridge Univ. Press, 1984. An encyclopedic-style work providing valuable historical information on the religious ethos in which the Jews of Persia lived.

Heltzer, Michael. "The Book of Esther: Where Does Fiction Start and History End?" *Bible Review* 8 (February 1992): 24–30. A brief overview of the historical problems scholars have found with the book of Esther. Illustrated, including a photograph of a *pur* unearthed by archaeologists.

Moore, Carey A. "Archaeology and the Book of Esther." *Biblical Archaeologist* 38 (Sept. & Dec. 1975): 62–79. Surveys the archaeological evidence that informs the historical character of the book of Esther.

Olmstead, A. T. *History of the Persian Empire*. Chicago: Univ. of Chicago Press, 1948. The classic, but dated, history of Persia.

Yamauchi, Edwin M. *Persia and the Bible*. Grand Rapids: Baker, 1990. Extensive survey of the archaeological and historical evidence from the Persian period of relevance to the biblical texts.

Literary Structure and Characteristics

Berg, Sandra Beth. *The Book of Esther: Motifs, Themes and Structure*. SBLDS. Missoula, Mont.: Scholars, 1979. A literary analysis of the composition of Esther. Includes a comparison of the themes of Esther with the Joseph story.

Clines, David J. A. "Reading Esther from Left to Right: Contemporary Strategies for Reading a Biblical Text." Pp. 31–52 in *The Bible in Three Dimensions: Essays in Celebration of Forty Years of Biblical Studies in the University of Sheffield*. W. E. Fowl, D. J. A. Clines, and S. E. Porter, eds. Sheffield: JSOT, 1990. Considers the book of Esther in light of modern literary theories, including formalism, structuralism, feminism, and deconstruction.

Day, Linda. *Three Faces of a Queen: Characterization in the Books of Esther*. Sheffield: Sheffield Academic Press, 1995. Compares the characterization of Queen Esther as she is portrayed in the Hebrew and the two Greek versions.

Goldman, Stan. "Narrative and Ethical Ironies in Esther." *JSOT* 47 (1990): 15–31. Explores the ethical implications of the Jewish attack on the Persians by considering the use of irony woven throughout the plot.

Gordis, Robert. "Studies in the Esther Narrative." *JBL* 95 (1976): 43–58. Examines a number of passages and exegetical questions, such as the second gathering of virgins, Mordecai's role at the city gate, and various lexical issues.

McClarity, Wilma. "Esther." Pp. 216–29 in *A Complete Literary Guide to the Bible*. L. Ryken and T. Longman III, eds. Grand Rapids: Zondervan, 1993. Discusses narrative plot, characterization, and literary setting of the book.

Radday, Yehuda T., and Athalya Brenner, eds. *On Humour and the Comic in the Hebrew Bible*. JSOTSup 92. Sheffield: Almond, 1990. Points out the humor and irony in the Hebrew text that has been largely lost in translation.

Ryken, Leland. *Words of Delight: A Literary Introduction to the Bible*. Grand Rapids: Baker, 1987. A good introduction to appreciating the literary qualities of Scripture. Contains a brief discussion of the narrative structure and characterization in Esther.

Sasson, Jack M. "Esther." Pp. 335–42 in *The Literary Guide to the Bible*. R. Alter and F. Kermode, eds. Cambridge, Mass.: Harvard Univ. Press, 1987. A synopsis of the plot and characters that points out the salient literary features of the story.

History of Interpretation

Brenner, Athalya, ed. *A Feminist Companion to Esther, Judith and Susanna*. Sheffield: Sheffield Academic Press, 1995. A collection of essays written on sundry topics, such as honor and shame in Esther, a *haggadic* approach to reading Esther, and Queen Esther as interpreted in fine art (with illustrations).

Sabua, R. "The Hidden Hand of God." *Bible Review* 8 (February 1992): 31–33. A modern example of a mystical approach to Scripture used throughout history by some Jewish interpreters to find hidden messages encoded in the Hebrew text of Esther.

Walfish, Barry Dov. *Esther in Medieval Garb: Jewish Interpretation of the Book of Esther in the Middle Ages*. Albany: SUNY Press, 1993. A thorough study of the interpretation of Esther during medieval times, when the book enjoyed widespread popularity.

Theological Significance and Application

Fox, Michael V. "The Religion of the Book of Esther." *Judaism* 39/2 (1990): 135–47. A discussion of divine providence as evidenced in Esther written from the perspective of a modern Jewish scholar.

Pierce, Ronald W. "The Politics of Esther and Mordecai: Courage or Compromise?" *BBR* 2 (1992): 75–89. Explores the view that Esther, Mordecai, and their fellow Jews of Persia had become secularized and had compromised their spiritual identity. Explains the events of the story as God's wake-up call to his lethargic people, making them more fully aware of their calling.

On the Doctrine of Divine Providence

Berkouwer, G. C. *Studies in Dogmatics: The Providence of God*. Grand Rapids: Eerdmans, repr. 1983. This classic work on the Christian doctrine of divine providence fails to mention the book of Esther, but provides a comprehensive discussion of God's ordinary work in human history.

Carson, D. A. *Divine Sovereignty and Human Responsibility: Biblical Perspectives in Tension*. Grand Rapids: Baker, 1994. A fine discussion of the intriguing relationship between God's sovereignty and human will.

Sproul, R. C. *The Providence of God*. Video and audio series. Orlando: Ligonier Ministries, 1990. A cogent presentation of the doctrine of divine providence, including a discussion of God's involvement in human evil, the issue of human freedom, and the motivation for prayer in light of God's providence. Comes with *Study Guide*.

Esther 1:1–8

THIS IS WHAT happened during the time of Xerxes, the Xerxes who ruled over 127 provinces stretching from India to Cush. ²At that time King Xerxes reigned from his royal throne in the citadel of Susa, ³and in the third year of his reign he gave a banquet for all his nobles and officials. The military leaders of Persia and Media, the princes, and the nobles of the provinces were present.

⁴For a full 180 days he displayed the vast wealth of his kingdom and the splendor and glory of his majesty. ⁵When these days were over, the king gave a banquet, lasting seven days, in the enclosed garden of the king's palace, for all the people from the least to the greatest, who were in the citadel of Susa. ⁶The garden had hangings of white and blue linen, fastened with cords of white linen and purple material to silver rings on marble pillars. There were couches of gold and silver on a mosaic pavement of porphyry, marble, mother-of-pearl and other costly stones. ⁷Wine was served in goblets of gold, each one different from the other, and the royal wine was abundant, in keeping with the king's liberality. ⁸By the king's command each guest was allowed to drink in his own way, for the king instructed all the wine stewards to serve each man what he wished.

THE BOOK BEGINS "This is what happened . . ." (Heb., *wyhy*), which is the introductory formula found in other historical books, such as Joshua, Judges, and Samuel. Regardless of how we judge the historicity of the book, the author's introduction to the story suggests he intends for his readers to understand the ensuing story as events that actually happened.

These events occurred during the time of Xerxes, the Persian king who reigned from 486–465 B.C. *Xerxes* is probably the Greek transliteration of his Persian name *Khshayarshan*. In the Hebrew language his name takes the form *Ahasuerus* (pronounced *Ahashwerosh*). This name has no meaning in Hebrew, but when pronounced aloud sounds something like King Headache in English.[1]

Xerxes was the son and successor of Darius I Hystaspes, under whose benefaction the temple in Jerusalem had begun to be rebuilt (Hag. 2:1–9; Zech. 7:1; 8:9). Xerxes is also mentioned in Ezra 4:6 as the reigning king when those opposed to that rebuilding project brought accusations against it.

Xerxes was known for his consolidation of the Persian empire "from India to Cush," corresponding to the regions of modern Pakistan and northern Sudan, respectively. The reference to 127 provinces has been taken by some scholars as a historical inaccuracy. The standard administrative region within the Persian empire was known as a satrapy and was governed by an official called a satrap. The satrap was responsible for all administration of the region, including collecting tribute (i.e., taxes) and raising an army on the king's behalf. A vast administration was required to govern and collect tribute throughout an empire that encompassed many nations and peoples of various languages. According to Herodotus, Xerxes' father, Darius, created twenty satrapies comprised of sixty-seven tribes or nations.[2] There is no extant historical evidence that at any time were there as many as 127 satrapies, nor even 120 (as mentioned in Dan. 6:1).

In 1:1, however, the Hebrew word used does not mean "satrapy" but "province" and probably refers to a smaller metropolitan region that encompassed a city. In Daniel 2:49 the same Hebrew word refers to the "province of Babylon"; in Ezra 2:1 and Nehemiah 7:6 it refers to the province of Judea surrounding the city of Jerusalem. Jerusalem and Judea were a small part of the large satrapy of the Trans-Euphrates region. The relationship between the provinces and satrapies is unclear, but there were presumably a considerably larger number of provinces than satrapies. Furthermore, the number of provinces probably

---

1. See Yehuda T. Radday, "Esther With Humor," *On Humour and the Comic in the Hebrew Bible* (Sheffield: Almond, 1990), 296.

2. LCL: *Herodotus* 3.89.

changed as cities were gained and lost in war. Moreover, since a satrapy was an arbitrary administrative unit, their number also likely changed to meet changing administrative needs. It is not surprising that documents written at different times during the Persian period may disagree on the numbers.

Since the authors of both Esther and Daniel use approximately the same number, most likely they are referring to smaller administrative units.[3] Some commentators, especially in antiquity, have taken the number to be symbolic of Xerxes' reigning over all the whole earth (e.g., 12 [the number of the tribes of Israel] x 10 [the number of completeness] + 7 [the number of perfection]).[4] F. Bush points out that the concern for historicity in this instance obscures the purpose of the number in the narrative: "By the choice of the larger number, the pomp and glory of the empire is magnified, contributing to the sardonic picture presented in this whole chapter."[5] This use of the number is consistent with the grandiose picture painted of the Persian empire by the author in chapter 1. By choosing to refer to the smallest administrative units of the empire (hence the larger number), the author may also be implying that there was nowhere the Jews could go to hide from the decree of death that would be pronounced against them.

Susa was one of the four capital cities from which the Persian monarchs ruled (the others were Ecbatana [cf. Ezra 6:2], Babylon, and Persepolis). The royal court wintered at the palace in Susa, for the summer temperatures there were intolerable. Daniel previously had a vision at Susa (Dan. 8:2), and later Nehemiah served in Susa as cupbearer to Xerxes' son, Artaxerxes I (Neh. 1:1).

Xerxes ascended the throne in November 486 B.C. at the age of thirty-two. The events of the Esther story span a period of about ten years, beginning in the third year of his reign, 483 B.C. At the time Xerxes ascended the throne, Persia was in conflict with the Greeks on their western frontier. Xerxes' father Darius had been defeated in his attempt to take Athens. The empire was resting in preparation for its next campaign against the Greeks.

---

3. Note, however, that Dan. 6:1 does refer to the leaders of the 120 regions as "satraps."
4. L. B. Paton, *Esther*, 124.
5. F. Bush, *Ruth/Esther*, 345.

The banquet held "in the third year" of Xerxes' reign (1:3) corresponds well with the great war council of 483 B.C., held to plan for the Persian invasion of Greece. Xerxes was mustering the nobles, officials, military leaders, princes, and governors of the provinces in Susa to rally support for his military campaign against the Greeks. The vast expanse of the Persian empire, from modern Pakistan in the east to modern Turkey in the west, encompassed many people groups with different languages, ethnic origins, and religions. Maintaining their support and loyalty over such a diverse and far-flung empire was no small feat. During the 180 days of the council, Xerxes displayed his wealth and glory to consolidate the leaders of the many provinces of the empire under his authority and to gain their loyalty to his cause. Herodotus records Xerxes as saying to his assembled nobles, possibly during the very banquet described in Esther:

> For this cause I have now summoned you together, that I may impart to you my purpose. It is my intent to bridge the Hellespont and lead my army through Europe to Hellas [Greece], that I may punish the Athenians for what they have done to the Persians and to my father. You saw that Darius my father was minded to make an expedition against these men. But he is dead, and it was not granted him to punish them; and I, on his and all the Persians' behalf, will never rest till I have taken and burnt Athens. . . .
>
> As for you, this is how you shall best please me: when I declare the time for your coming, everyone of you must appear, and with a good will; and whosoever comes with his army best equipped shall receive from me such gifts as are reckoned most precious among us.[6]

Xerxes displayed his wealth to show that he could make good on his promise and reward those who would rally to support his campaign.

Persia and Media were two separate, but ethnically related, nations that had a long but uneasy history prior to this period. The Medes' greatest claim to fame came from joining forces with the Babylonians to overthrow the Assyrian empire. The prophet Jonah had predicted the eventual destruction of the Assyrian capital city, Nineveh, fulfill-

---

6. LCL: *Herodotus* 7.8.

ment of which, though deferred, was accomplished by the Medes in 612 B.C. Prior to the time of Cyrus, the Medes were the dominant nation of the two. Cyrus won the allegiance of both the Medes and Persians because his father was a Persian and his mother a Mede. In himself he united these two great nations and had the military power to enforce a union of both into one great empire. From the time of Cyrus onward the consolidated empire he founded was referred to as the Persian-Median empire, showing the hegemony of the Persians within the joint empire. The reference here to the military leaders of Persia first, and of Media second, is historically accurate for the time of Xerxes, who reigned after Cyrus.

A banquet of seven days was held for all the residents of the citadel of Susa, "from the least to the greatest," to culminate the six months of festivities (1:4–5). This event would have further consolidated support for the king and his campaign among all his subjects who lived and served him in Susa. These people had no doubt provided many of the services demanded by the lavish hospitality of the previous 180 days, and they were perhaps being feted for their efforts.

The description of the banquet focuses on the opulence of its setting in the king's garden and the abundance of wine "in keeping with king's liberality" served in goblets of gold (1:6–7). Both emphasize the wealth, and hence the power, of the king, who was expecting the men of his empire soon to march into battle on his command. Both Persia and Greece held wealth commensurate with their position as the two world superpowers of that time. Persia's wealth and magnificence dazzled even Alexander the Great when more than a century later he entered the palace at Susa and found 40,000 talents of gold and silver bullion (1,200 tons) and 9,000 talents of minted gold coins (270 tons), which had been accumulated by the Persian kings.[7]

The might and glory of the Persian empire were at Xerxes' disposal in order to reward those who would remain loyal to his cause and obedient to his command. This description of the lavish banquet shows that Xerxes was a force to be reckoned with.[8]

---

7. Ibid., 17.66.

8. Excavations of Susa by the French archaeologist M. A. Dieulafoy between 1884 and 1886 have produced many treasures from the palace built by Darius I and occupied by Xerxes. Sculptures, colorfully glazed bricks, jewelry, and other treasures from Susa can be viewed today in the Louvre in Paris.

IN THESE VERSES the author sets an elaborate stage for the opening act of the story. The king's power, wealth, majesty, and generosity are being highlighted by the description of the opulent banquets in the Persian court at Susa, where the king is gathering support and loyalty for his campaign against Greece. The irony of this description is lost on modern readers. The original readers would have known that Xerxes returned from Greece four years later after a surprising defeat that depleted his royal wealth. Since the author of Esther was writing long after Xerxes' defeat, he could have introduced Xerxes as the Persian king who lost a famous battle to the Greeks at Hellespont. Instead, he chose to introduce Xerxes in the splendor and optimism of his glory days. The unstated reversal of the king's fortune, which would have been known to the author and original readers, sets the stage and foreshadows another reversal of destiny within the book.

The elaborate description of the palace found in these verses is unusual for biblical narrative. Only the description of the tabernacle and Jerusalem temple receive similar treatment. The description of the colors and materials of the Persian palace are reminiscent of the description of the tabernacle in Exodus 25–28 and the descriptions of the temple in 1 Kings 7 and 2 Chron. 3–4. The magnificent temple in Jerusalem had been the throne of Yahweh's theocracy. At its dedication the Lord promised that if the king of Jerusalem walked before him in obedience, "You shall never fail to have a man on the throne of Israel" (1 Kings 9:5).

The Jews found themselves in Susa beholden to the glory of a pagan king because of the other side of that promise made at the dedication of the temple (1 Kings 9:6–9):

> But if you or your sons turn away from me and do not observe the commands and decrees I have given you and go off to serve other gods and worship them, then I will cut off Israel from the land I have given them and will reject this temple I have consecrated for my Name. Israel will then become a byword and an object of ridicule among all peoples. And though this temple is now imposing, all who pass by will be appalled and will scoff and say, "Why has the LORD done such a thing to this land and to this

temple?" People will answer, "Because they have forsaken the LORD their God, who brought their fathers out of Egypt, and have embraced other gods, worshiping and serving them—that is why the LORD brought all this disaster on them."

When Esther 1:1–8 is read in light of Xerxes' defeat, the description of the splendor of his palace in Susa while he planned for war foreshadows his reversal of fortune. The Jews had also previously experienced a humiliating reversal of fortune that had brought them to Susa. Nevertheless, because of the covenant Yahweh had made with them when he "brought their fathers out of Egypt," the ultimate destiny of God's people was secured. Despite the great power and wealth of the Persian empire, it could never frustrate the plan and promise of God.

Though God chastened his people in the affliction of the Exile, it was never his intent to destroy them completely. Because the Jewish nation was delivered from genocide, it survived to bear the Messiah, through whom all nations have been blessed (cf. Gen. 12:2–3). The Messiah fulfilled all of the demands and promises of the covenant God had made with his people at Sinai. He is the man promised in 1 Kings 9:5, seated on the throne of his father David and ruling over an eternal dynasty.

ALTHOUGH THE GREAT splendor of Xerxes' empire now lies in ruins beneath centuries of dust, the world continues to see opulent displays of military bravado. After the Persians, the Greek Ptolemies and Seleucids dominated the eastern Mediterranean, bringing conflict and tumult to the Jewish people. Then the Romans, perhaps the greatest military machine the world has ever seen, tried to destroy the infant Christian church. The book of Revelation, which contains a description of the opulent royal city of God and the Lamb, was written to assure the early Christians that the persecutions of even the mighty Romans could not thwart or frustrate God's sovereign plan to bring all of history to culmination in Jesus Christ.

In our own time, one thinks of Adolph Hitler and the massive display of power he brought against the Jews and others in his attempt to establish the Third Reich as a world government. The May Day celebrations in Moscow, where the military might of the former Soviet

Union was paraded through Red Square, are another example of military power that has at times been turned against both Jews and Christians. After almost a century of state-sponsored atheism, the mighty communist state, powerful both militarily and intellectually, was unable to extinguish the church, which is now experiencing a new renaissance in the former Soviet Union. In Beijing's Tiananmen Square, China's crushing military power was displayed against students protesting for democracy. Through the centuries and around the world political and military might has been glorified as the epitome of a nation's strength.

America, too, must take heed that, though perhaps founded for Christian liberty, its might and power are nonetheless worldly might and power. Name whichever empire, nation, or government you wish as the mightiest, the greatest, and the most powerful, the King of the universe sits high above on his throne, laughing at the impotence of even the greatest of nations. Psalm 2 reflects on the majesty of God above the din of the nations' worldly power:

> Why do the nations conspire
>> and the peoples plot in vain?
> The kings of the earth take their stand
>> and the rulers gather together
> against the LORD
>> and against his Anointed One.
> "Let us break their chains," they say,
>> "and throw off their fetters."
> The One enthroned in heaven laughs;
>> the Lord scoffs at them.
> Then he rebukes them in his anger
>> and terrifies them in his wrath, saying,
> "I have installed my King
>> on Zion, my holy hill."
> I will proclaim the decree of the LORD:
> He said to me, "You are my Son;
>> today I have become your Father.
> Ask of me,
>> and I will make the nations your inheritance,
>> the ends of the earth your possession.

You will rule them with an iron scepter;
    you will dash them to pieces like pottery."
Therefore, you kings, be wise;
    be warned, you rulers of the earth.
Serve the LORD with fear
    and rejoice with trembling.
Kiss the Son, lest he be angry
    and you be destroyed in your way,
for his wrath can flare up in a moment.
    Blessed are all who take refuge in him.

Through invisible and inscrutable means, God continues to move all of history to fulfill his covenant in Jesus Christ. He alone truly is the King of kings. The one who opposes Christ the King opposes God. To such a person, the Esther story stands as a warning that whatever ease and prosperity one might enjoy, whatever worldly power and position have been attained, ultimately there will be a reversal of fortune that will end in death and destruction.

For the Christian, the sovereign power of the Lord is of greatest comfort. Throughout every generation in every corner of the world, God rules supreme "to bring all things in heaven and on earth together under one head, even Christ" (Eph. 1:10). To be in Christ is to be on the winning side of history, to be victors even in the face of life's greatest threats.

Esther 1:9–12

QUEEN VASHTI ALSO gave a banquet for the women in the royal palace of King Xerxes. [10]On the seventh day, when King Xerxes was in high spirits from wine, he commanded the seven eunuchs who served him—Mehuman, Biztha, Harbona, Bigtha, Abagtha, Zethar and Carcas—[11]to bring before him Queen Vashti, wearing her royal crown, in order to display her beauty to the people and nobles, for she was lovely to look at. [12]But when the attendants delivered the king's command, Queen Vashti refused to come. Then the king became furious and burned with anger.

Original Meaning

AT THE TIME of the war council, according to the book of Esther, Xerxes was married to Queen Vashti. Scholars have used this point to argue against the historicity of the story, because the Greek historian Herodotus gives the name of Xerxes' wife as Amestris, not Vashti, and he mentions no other wives.[1] Furthermore, some understand Herodotus to say that Amestris accompanied Xerxes during his campaign in Greece, though this point is less clear. It is known that Amestris was the queen mother during the reign of her son, Artaxerxes I, who succeeded Xerxes.

Although Herodotus has been shown to be sometimes wrong, many biblical scholars nevertheless favor Herodotus where he disagrees with the author of Esther. To harmonize Herodotus with the Esther story, some have identified Amestris with Vashti by suggesting that Amestris was her Greek name and Vashti the transliteration of her Persian name into Hebrew. It is of course difficult for scholars to identify with certainty vocabulary words from Old Persian, then to know how they would have been pronounced, and furthermore, how that Persian pronunciation would have been represented by the Hebrew alphabet. Some have claimed the name Vashti sounds similar to the Old Persian

---

1. LCL: *Herodotus* 7.114; 9.110–13.

for beautiful woman.[2] If so, the name simply may be a literary device used to characterize the woman otherwise known to history as Amestris.

Perhaps Herodotus mentions only Amestris, whether or not she was Vashti, because he was interested only in the royal wives who bore the successors to the throne. All other royal wives and concubines, of which Persian kings typically had many, were presumably irrelevant to his purpose of tracing the succession of the Persian dynasty. This motivation seems probable because Herodotus mentions only two of the several wives of Xerxes' father, Darius. Both of these named women bore sons who contended for the throne of their father, which Xerxes eventually won. If Herodotus includes in his history only the royal wives who were directly relevant to the succession of the throne, then this historical problem in Esther disappears. Only Amestris would be expected to be named by Herodotus since she gave birth to Xerxes' successor, Artaxerxes. Whether or not Amestris and Vashti are one and the same woman, there is nothing in Herodotus that is inconsistent with Vashti's being Xerxes' wife or with her fall from his grace as recorded in Esther.

After seven days of drinking, when Xerxes was "in high spirits from wine," he sent for his queen to display her royal beauty before the men of Susa. In order to secure the loyalty and support of his empire as he went to war against the Greeks, King Xerxes was displaying "the vast wealth of his kingdom" and "the splendor and glory of his majesty" (1:4). The beautiful Vashti, wearing her royal diadem, was a living trophy of his power and glory. He sent seven eunuchs to fetch her, perhaps the number needed to carry her seated in the royal litter. This would create a dramatic and majestic entrance for her before the men being asked to go to war for the empire. Perhaps the sight of the queen in her royal glory was intended to inspire patriotism and loyalty, as public appearances of the British queen do today.

Within our modern culture we think of drinking as a social custom, often with negative connotations. However, the Greek historian Herodotus explains the interesting fact that the Persians drank as they deliberated matters of state (cf. Est. 3:15):

> Moreover it is their [the Persians] custom to deliberate about the gravest matters when they are drunk; and what they approve in their counsels is proposed to them the next day by the master

---

2. See Carey A. Moore, *Esther*, 8; L. B. Paton, *Esther*, 66.

of the house where they deliberate, when they are now sober and if being sober they still approve it, they act thereon, but if not, they cast it aside. And when they have taken counsel about a matter when sober, they decide upon it when they are drunk.[3]

This custom may seem bizarre to us, but the ancients believed intoxication put them in closer touch with the spiritual world. If Herodotus is right on this point, excessive drinking would have been an essential element of Xerxes' war council.

Because Xerxes was displaying his power and might in order to solidify his nobles as he went to war against Greece, the refusal of his own queen to obey his command must have been extremely embarrassing. No wonder Xerxes became furious and burned with anger! He needed his men to obey his commands as they went to war, but in his own palace he could not even get his own wife to obey!

THE EXEMPLARY APPROACH. Many interpreters, from the earliest Jewish rabbis to modern preachers, have taken an exemplary approach to this passage. They use the king to preach against the evils of alcohol and Vashti to preach against rebellious wives. An exemplary approach to interpreting these characters is inadequate and misleading. It forces the interpreter to make ethical and moral judgments that the author himself refrains from making. It is natural for a reader to decide whether he or she likes or dislikes a character in a story. However, merely expressing one's opinion about Xerxes or Vashti, Mordecai or Esther, and quoting biblical proof texts to back it up, is not exegesis of the text. An exemplary approach produces an inadequate interpretation of this story.[4]

The narrator of the story tells us that Xerxes was "in high spirits from wine" when he ordered Vashti to be brought before the men of the

---

3. LCL: *Herodotus* 1.133.

4. As a general principle of biblical hermeneutics, interpreters must be cautious about taking an exemplary approach to any biblical character. As Christians our ethical and moral standard is exemplified by Jesus, to whose likeness the Holy Spirit conforms us in the process of sanctification (Rom. 8:29). While we may learn much from reflecting on the examples of biblical characters, the biblical writers may have included episodes from their lives as events relevant to the unfolding of redemptive history, and not as ethical models for us to imitate directly.

empire, who also had been drinking as each wished. By linking the king's drinking with the command to Vashti, the narrator implies that the king was influenced by alcohol and perhaps would not have given this command had he not been drinking. But the author of Esther does not make the evils of alcohol the main point of this passage. The point is that the Persian court was not a safe place because Xerxes held great power, and he wielded it unpredictably, making decisions from dubious motives with impaired judgment.

Herodotus tells how, a few years later during his campaign against the Greeks, Xerxes beheaded the men building a bridge at the Hellespont for his army when a storm delayed its completion.[5] When such absolute power is combined with decadence and ruthlessness, no one is safe. This scene, which shows the dangers of living under Xerxes' power in the Persian empire, provides a backdrop for the major conflict of the story when the power of the Persian empire will be turned against the Jewish people.

Throughout centuries of interpretation, Vashti has been interpreted as an exemplary model (in either a negative or a positive sense). Traditionally she has been villainized by both Jewish and Christian interpreters as a wicked and rebellious woman. According to Jewish tradition she was the granddaughter of the Babylonian king, Nebuchadnezzar, and was not only deposed but executed. This was her just end for forcing good Jewish girls to work on the Sabbath.

Martin Luther also (mis-)used Vashti as a negative role model to illustrate one of his arguments for divorce:

> The third case for divorce is that in which one of the parties deprives and avoids the other, refusing to fulfil the conjugal duty or to live with the other person. . . . Here it is time for the husband to say, "If you will not, another will; the maid will come if the wife will not." Only first the husband should admonish and warn his wife two or three times, and let the situation be known to others so that her stubbornness becomes a matter of common knowledge and is rebuked before the congregation. If she still refuses, get rid of her; take an Esther and let Vashti go, as King Ahasuerus did.[6]

---

5. LCL: *Herodotus* 7.35.

6. Walther I. Brandt, ed., *Luther's Works: The Christian in Society*, vol. 45 (Philadelphia: Muhlenberg, 1962), 33—34.

On the other hand, some interpreters have seen Vashti's refusal to be put on display as evidence of noble character. The Reformed theologian Abraham Kuyper, for example, writes of her, "Vashti is one of the nobler women of humanity."[7] She has also recently been commended by feminist interpreters for standing up to the king and refusing to be treated as a sex object, something Esther is accused of failing to do. Regardless of whether one considers Vashti noble or rebellious, both interpretations share the mistake of taking an exemplary approach.

Is sexism a major theme of Esther? The feminist interpretation of Vashti and Esther mistakenly views sexism as a major theme of the book. In the nineteenth century, both Vashti and Esther were commended as upholding the dignity of women. In *The Women's Bible*, Elizabeth Cady Stanton describes Esther as "noble and self-sacrificing," Vashti as "self-respecting and brave."[8] In this century, Esther continues to be a heroine to some, but has fallen into disfavor with many feminist interpreters because she did not assert herself against what is viewed as male domination. In comparison to Esther, Vashti's refusal to obey the king is applauded as an admirable attack on patriarchy. Alice Laffey writes:

> . . . feminist interpreters have begun to see that buried in Esther's character is also full compliance with patriarchy. In contrast to Vashti, who refused to be men's sexual object and her husband's toy, Esther is the stereotypical woman in a man's world. She wins favor by the physical beauty of her appearance, and then by her ability to satisfy sexually. . . . Rather than defend Vashti's decision and protest the injustice of her banishment, Esther uses Vashti's rejection for her own benefit. When feminists compare the two women, they extol Vashti, though they are not at all surprised that the literature, produced as it was in a patriarchal culture, honors Esther and relegates Vashti to oblivion. Their concern, however, is to reclaim Vashti.[9]

By introducing Esther's story with Vashti's, the author does invite a comparison of the two women. However, he does not play the char-

---

7. Abraham Kuyper, *Women of the Old Testament* (Grand Rapids: Zondervan, 1936), 143.

8. Elizabeth Cady Stanton, *The Woman's Bible*, part II (1895; repr. Boston: Northeastern Univ. Press, 1993), 92.

9. Alice A. Laffey, *An Introduction to the Old Testament: A Feminist Perspective* (Philadelphia: Fortress, 1988), 216.

acter of the two against each other, as recent feminist interpreters do. Feminist interpreters seem to overlook the fact that, like Esther, Vashti was herself a beautiful woman, who no doubt had ability to satisfy sexually. Her "compliance with patriarchy" had no doubt been as extensive as Esther's, having won the bed (if not the heart) of the most powerful man in the empire. The feminist assumption is that Esther has an honored place in the canon only because she was viewed as nonthreatening to the patriarchal society that preserved and published her story.

One could argue, however, that Esther was an even more subversive presence in her "patriarchal" society than Vashti (if it's even legitimate to characterize the Persian culture by this modern label). This book of the Bible bears the name of a woman who outwitted powerful, evil men and lived to write a decree celebrating it (9:29, 32). This was such a remarkable feat for a woman in the ancient world (patriarchal or otherwise) that an author, who was almost certainly a man, dared to write a book about it that has survived well over two thousand years. Because of the part a woman played in the deliverance of her people, the author *is* interested in gender politics throughout the story. Especially in verses 1:13–22 (see comments), the dynamics between the women and men of Esther's world is a topic addressed at length.

This is not to say, however, that the author intended to write a feminist tract, holding up Vashti and Esther as feminist role models—in either a positive or negative light. Sexism is not the major theme of the book, and those who interpret the story through that lens have either missed or ignored the author's concerns in favor of an ideological reading. One such modern reading of Esther arises from the sociological struggle of black women in South Africa. Using self-consciously a "hermeneutics of liberation," Itumeleng Mosala indicts the book of Esther for sacrificing

> gender struggles to national struggles. In the name of the struggle for the national survival of the Jewish people it disprivileges the question of gender oppression and exploitation. The matter of the subsumption of some struggles under others is a serious issue of discourse imperialism.[10]

---

10. Itumeleng J. Mosala, "The Implications of the Text of Esther for African Women's Struggle for Liberation in South Africa," *Voices from the Margin: Interpreting the Bible in the Third World*, R. S. Sugirtharajah, ed. (Maryknoll, N.Y.: Orbis, 1995), 176.

Such readings of biblical texts arise from the personal, and usually painful, experiences of the interpreters. Their problems and pain are real, causing them to identify with the characters in the biblical stories they interpret differently from how those readers who have not similarly suffered interpret them. We can gain valuable insights from listening to readings of the biblical texts from others who have been shaped by experiences significantly different from our own. However, such readings must not be confused with the authoritative message of the biblical text as intended by its author, which must form the basis of normative application to our lives today.

The struggles of twentieth-century South Africa, for instance, are not the same struggles experienced by the Jewish people of ancient Persia, though both may be rooted in the universal depravity of human nature that has been unjustly structuring societies from Eden to Susa to Johannesburg. The threat of genocide faced by the Jewish people in Persia and the struggles of black women in South Africa may be two examples (out of countless many) of the horrific power of human evil, but their respective historical locations, and the issues specific to each, must be respected.

For the author of Esther the issue of the dignity and position of women in the Persian court paled in contrast to the pressing threat of death for an entire race of people, who were God's covenant people at that. The threat against the Jews of Persia was a threat against God's plan of redemption. This distinguishes it from other instances of genocide against other peoples, evils that are no less morally reprehensible. The major sociological distinction within the book is an adversarial relationship between Jew and Gentile, not between men and women. Feminist interpretations fail to note that although both Vashti and Esther are women, Vashti was a Gentile and Esther a Jew. That difference is of far greater significance to the story than their common gender.

Feminist interpreters who condemn Esther for not directly opposing blatant sexism are missing an important point. If there is any lesson to be learned from Vashti's experience, it would seem to be that women who directly oppose the male power structures will simply be banished, with no opportunity for further influence on those structures. Esther, who is accused by some feminists of playing into the hands of men, skillfully uses the power of a male-dominated world to accomplish something still celebrated annually twenty-five hundred years later. If we wish to use Vashti and Esther as focal points of a discussion on women's empowerment (even though that is not their significance to the ancient author), Esther is arguably the more empowered of the two.

It is not sound hermeneutics to interpret an ancient text through the lens of any modern ideology, regardless of the social value of that ideology. The interpreter must respect the concerns of the author of Esther, which were indigenous to his own times and culture, not ours. Therefore, we must not read Esther as if the author's intended purpose was to address the concerns of feminism as articulated in our own time.

Vashti and marital relationships. Some Christian interpreters have been quick to see Vashti as a negative example of the wifely submission commanded by Ephesians 5:22–23: "Wives, submit to your husbands as to the Lord. For the husband is the head of the wife as Christ is the head of the church, his body, of which he is the Savior." Such a reading is just as anachronistic as the feminist approach, because it, too, reads concerns of a later time, albeit biblical concerns, into a text that were not intended by the author.

Even if Vashti is taken as an example of a rebellious wife, Ephesians 5:22 would not necessarily condemn her. Christian interpreters of this verse by and large agree that if an ungodly husband makes unholy demands of his wife, the wife can justifiably disobey them. Given the state of mind of Xerxes and the implied purpose of his command, one might be inclined to give Vashti the benefit of the doubt in this case. Perhaps she was the more noble of the two, after all.

There is further reason why Vashti's refusal should not be viewed through the lens of the husband-wife relationship of Ephesians 5:22. Just as the author of Esther is not concerned with the interests of modern feminists, he is also not concerned with Xerxes and Vashti as a married couple. He repeatedly refers to *King* Xerxes and *Queen* Vashti, but not once does he mention them as the spouse of the other. Vashti's refusal to be displayed before drunken men was perhaps motivated by personal reasons, but it was a public political embarrassment to Xerxes, especially so because it caused Xerxes to lose face in front of his entire administration during an important war council. In the verses that follow, the king's advisors rather humorously turn this political embarrassment into an issue concerning the relationships between husbands and wives throughout the empire, but certainly not in a way that exemplifies Ephesians 5:22–25 (see comments on 1:12–22).

The author views Vashti specifically as the queen, not the wife, who refuses. The political ramifications of her decision foreshadow that of her successor, Esther. Both Vashti and Esther are portrayed in the story in their role as queens, not as wives. To color Vashti as the bad wife and Esther as the good one is to lose sight, as feminist interpreters do, of the major sociological division in the book between Jew and Gentile. Judging strictly from the letter of the law, we would have to condemn Esther as well, for she should not have accepted marriage to a Gentile according to the Torah (see comments on 2:1–11).

By introducing Vashti's refusal with the remark that the king was "in high spirits from wine," the author seems to subtly cast Vashti in a better light than Xerxes. The implication is that Xerxes' judgment was impaired. If Vashti and Amestris were in fact the same woman, she would have been in the late stage of her pregnancy with Xerxes' son, Artaxerxes, and perhaps unable to appear in public. The author does not label Vashti as a rebellious wife nor does he evaluate her refusal as good or bad, right or wrong. Interpreters should also resist the temptation to build an interpretation by imposing such judgments.

The ambiguity of Vashti's action and motives must be allowed to stand as the deliberate intention of the author, for he could have easily supplied an evaluation. Either a moral appraisal of Vashti's refusal is irrelevant to the author's point or the ambiguity is itself a part of what he is saying. If the former, then an exemplary approach is completely inappropriate because it violates the author's intention. If the later, then an exemplary approach blinds us from seeing the author's point. Though the exemplary approach has been most frequently used, it is almost certainly not how the author intended us to understand the characters in this story.

Queen Vashti as the context for Queen Esther. The author refrains from commenting not only on Vashti's behavior and motives, but also does not supply such an evaluation of any of the people in the story. This unusual silence creates such a conspicuous ambiguity that it cannot be ignored if an interpreter insists on taking an exemplary approach. It can be fixed only by filling in motives and evaluations that simply are not in the text. The present commentary takes the ambiguity not as a problem to be overcome in order to interpret the text, but as part of the literary fabric of the story.

Note that this passage is the first of many in which the author refrains from making any moral or ethical evaluation. He does not fault the king for drinking, nor does he commend or condemn Vashti for refusing to appear at the king's command. The ethical and moral ambiguity of the characters is an important element in the story and is particularly appropriate to its meaning and application, for divine providence works through human behavior that flows from even the most ambiguous and confused of motives.

This episode between Vashti and Xerxes paints a picture of life in the Persian court that provides a context in which the later events of the story are to be understood. (1) In the Persian court the king holds tremendous power and uses it ostentatiously to reinforce his own glory with little or no thought for the consequences to others. The reader begins to see a glimpse of what life under the Persian king was like. Mordecai, and especially Esther, are up against tremendous odds as they seek to survive in the Persian court. They not only survive; they gain power, which is even more remarkable.

(2) This portrayal of Queen Vashti provides the reader with a context in which to understand her successor, Queen Esther. Both women are locked in a relationship with Xerxes that is sexually and politically charged. By introducing Esther's story with Vashti's, the author invites the reader to make comparisons between the two that amplify the irony and power of its message.

 THE AUTHOR OF the book of Esther knew when he began to write that he was telling a story about how, against all odds, the fate of God's people was reversed and became the reason for the celebration called Purim. One seemingly insignificant event led to another, and in this mysterious chain of human actions the promise of the covenant made long before between God and his people was upheld and fulfilled. It is therefore worth noting with what event the author begins to tell this story.

The author does not begin with Mordecai or Esther. He does not retell the history of the Jews. He begins the story with the Persian king Xerxes, who neither knew nor worshiped the God of the Jews. Xerxes decides to give a banquet, apparently from the purely political need to solidify support for his impending military campaign. A completely pagan king decides for purely worldly reasons to give a banquet designed for self-aggrandizement. On the last day of the banquet, he decides to treat the men of his empire to a good look at his beautiful Queen Vashti. This decision is probably not made from the most admirable of motives, at least not as judged by Christian standards. With this, Xerxes sets in motion a chain of events that takes on a life of its own.

In reaction to Xerxes, Queen Vashti, who also is not a worshiper of Yahweh, decides, for whatever reason, to refuse the king's command. She probably does not realize at the moment that her decision will change her life forever and bring another woman to the throne of Persia. With his one decision to display Vashti at his war council, Xerxes sets in motion a chain of events that culminates in the deliverance of God's people, fulfilling the promise of the ancient covenant made ages before in a faraway place.

When we think of redemptive history, we think of the great miracles that display God's power. But these mighty acts of God are linked together through long years of human history by a chain of seemingly insignificant, ordinary events. We are now living in one of those long stretches of history between the ascension and return of Jesus Christ. Like Xerxes of long ago, modern kings, presidents, and rulers make decisions from purely political motives. Like Vashti, people today unwittingly make decisions that have long-reaching consequences far beyond what they could have foreseen. These events may be completely secular and perhaps made by people who give Christ no thought. Nonetheless, through them God is moving all of history forward to accomplish all that must happen before the return of his Son, Jesus Christ, the true King of kings.

Esther 1:13-22

❦

SINCE IT WAS customary for the king to consult experts in matters of law and justice, he spoke with the wise men who understood the times ¹⁴and were closest to the king—Carshena, Shethar, Admatha, Tarshish, Meres, Marsena and Memucan, the seven nobles of Persia and Media who had special access to the king and were highest in the kingdom.

¹⁵"According to law, what must be done to Queen Vashti?" he asked. "She has not obeyed the command of King Xerxes that the eunuchs have taken to her."

¹⁶Then Memucan replied in the presence of the king and the nobles, "Queen Vashti has done wrong, not only against the king but also against all the nobles and the peoples of all the provinces of King Xerxes. ¹⁷For the queen's conduct will become known to all the women, and so they will despise their husbands and say, 'King Xerxes commanded Queen Vashti to be brought before him, but she would not come.' ¹⁸This very day the Persian and Median women of the nobility who have heard about the queen's conduct will respond to all the king's nobles in the same way. There will be no end of disrespect and discord.

¹⁹"Therefore, if it pleases the king, let him issue a royal decree and let it be written in the laws of Persia and Media, which cannot be repealed, that Vashti is never again to enter the presence of King Xerxes. Also let the king give her royal position to someone else who is better than she. ²⁰Then when the king's edict is proclaimed throughout all his vast realm, all the women will respect their husbands, from the least to the greatest."

²¹The king and his nobles were pleased with this advice, so the king did as Memucan proposed. ²²He sent dispatches to all parts of the kingdom, to each province in its own script and to each people in its own language, proclaiming in each people's tongue that every man should be ruler over his own household.

KING XERXES CANNOT afford to overlook
Queen Vashti's public defiance and thus
turns to his political advisors to see what,
according to Persian law, must be done to
Vashti. Only seven closest advisors (lit. in Heb. idiom, "the seven
who see the face of the king") were permitted to enter the king's
presence uninvited and unannounced.[1] These wise men understood
"the times"; that is, they used astrology and other forms of divination
to discern the propitious course of action. It "was customary" for
Xerxes to consult these "experts in matters of law and justice," though
one might have thought that in reference to a conflict with his own
wife he might have taken a more personal approach. Xerxes' reaction
highlights the political ramifications of Vashti's defiance. It is unlikely
that there was a legal precedent on the books stating what must be
done in this specific situation. More likely, "according to law" (v. 15)
refers to the expedient counsel of the advisors, from which Persian
"law" was derived.

Irrevocable royal decree rather than personal reconciliation will
determine Vashti's fate. The decree will formalize permanently what
Vashti had chosen in one moment. Because she refused to come to
the king, she will be demoted to the status of those who may not enter
the king's presence. In the decree (v. 19) she is stripped of her position,
and for the first time in the story is referred to simply as "Vashti" instead
of "Queen Vashti." Memucan suggests that her position as queen be
given to another woman who is "better" than she. Presumably "better"
means more obedient, though Memucan leaves it to the king to interpret what "better" may mean. This royal decree is to be written into the
irrevocable laws of Persia and Media. The finality of Vashti's fate as
determined by the seven is being sealed.

The irrevocability of the king's decree is also mentioned in a similar situation in Dan. 6:8, 12, 15. There, Xerxes' father, Darius, is manipulated by his administrators to issue an irrevocable decree forbidding
prayer—a ploy intended to trap the godly Daniel. There is, however,
no extrabiblical evidence that the Persian laws were actually irrevocable, and as M. Fox points out, it is hard to imagine running an empire

---

1. LCL: *Herodotus* 1.99; 3.77, 84.

on this basis.[2] Others comment that this detail, though not historically true, functions to heighten the dramatic tension of the story.[3]

In the two biblical contexts in which reference to this legal policy occurs, however, it not only heightens the dramatic tension of the story, it also reveals the pretentious arrogance of the Persian king and his counsel, who are thereby portrayed as thinking that they can control circumstances by merely decreeing their wishes to be irrevocably so. In both Daniel and Esther the ultimate impotence of such human reasoning is revealed. The statement that the laws of Persia and Media cannot be repealed satirizes the way the authority of the Persian monarchy was perceived, not necessarily the way Persian law formally operated.

Although Xerxes invites the counsel of his seven advisors concerning what is to be done to Vashti in this one instance, the advice he gets goes beyond this instance. Memucan, for whatever reason, takes Queen Vashti's disobedience personally. He perceives it to be not only an affront to Xerxes' authority, but to all the seven nobles and "the peoples of all the provinces" as well (v. 16).[4] What began as an issue between two people suddenly is escalated into a crisis of empire-wide proportions. By universalizing the incident Memucan can express his personal anxiety and fears in terms of the good of the empire and thereby manipulate the king to his own ends. Haman later uses the same tactic against the Jews in 3:8.

Vashti is assumed to have such influence on the women of the empire that when they hear of her disobedience, they will similarly respond to their husbands, starting with the wives of the king's seven advisors. Therefore, the king must make sure that these women also hear that Vashti has been deposed as a result of her insolence. When the women see what harsh consequences follow disobedience, they will be intimidated into "respect[ing] their husbands, from the least to the greatest" (v. 20). Xerxes and the seven nobles find this reasoning to be sound, and so the king issues a decree throughout his empire "to each province in its own script and to each people in its own language."

Adele Berlin sees the reaction of the seven advisors as out of proportion to the incident itself and suggests the advisors at this point are

---

2. Michael V. Fox, *Character and Ideology in the Book of Esther*, 22.

3. See, e.g., Jon D. Levenson, *Esther*, 52.

4. As in 1:5, the phrase "the peoples of all provinces" refers to all the men, because the women are referred to separately in both 1:9 and 1:17.

expressing their own sexual anxiety.[5] Noting the sexual innuendo of Vashti's refusal to be displayed before Xerxes' men, she speculates that the seven are fearful that the incident between Vashti and Xerxes might trigger a sexual strike by the women of Persia similar to that which was performed several decades later in Aristophanes' Greek comedy *Lysistrata* (ca. 450–ca. 388 B.C.). It is possible that such a theme was circulating at the time Esther was written, or even that the author of Esther may have been familiar with *Lysistrata*, though this is pure speculation. If Berlin is right, then the author of Esther is being extremely subtle here because the decree issued has a much broader concern with power and submission. Conjugal submission may be viewed as a part of the "respect" being demanded by the men, but does not exhaust their concern.

Ironically, by accepting Memucan's advice, the king ends up publicizing his embarrassing plight by ordering throughout the empire what he himself could not accomplish in his own palace, that every man "should be ruler over his own household" (v. 22). Afraid that all the women of the empire will hear about Vashti, he ends up assuring what he fears by sending a dispatch to every province of the empire! The blindness in Memucan's advice as this scene unfolds gives it a depth of irony and even humor. However, because the Bible is sacred Scripture, many readers assume that it speaks only in hushed and reverent tones, and they cannot see or appreciate the ironic humor found in biblical stories.

Perhaps it does seem odd and even inappropriate to modern readers that the author of Esther would use parody and even humor to introduce the Persian powers that came treacherously close to extinguishing his own people. It seems improper to tell a funny story about genocide and, therefore, many readers may deny that there is any humor intended in this book. M. Fox is one of several commentators who recognize humor in the Esther story and offers helpful insight into its significance:

> The book's incongruous humor is one of its strange hallmarks. It mixes laughter with fear in telling about a near-tragedy that is

---

5. Adele Berlin, "The Place of the Book of Esther in the Religion of Israel," in a lecture delivered at the Center for Judaic Studies, University of Pennsylvania, November 19, 1997, communicated this to this author by personal correspondence. See her forthcoming commentary on Esther from the Jewish Publication Society.

tellingly reminiscent of actual tragedies. We laugh at the confused sexual politicians, the quirky emperor, and, above all, the ludicrous, self-glorifying, self-destructive villain....

Humor, especially the humor of ridicule, is a device for defusing fear. The author teaches us to make fun of the very forces that once threatened—and will again threaten—our existence, and thereby makes us recognize their triviality as well as their power. "If I laugh at any mortal thing," said Byron, "'tis that I may not weep." Jews have learned that kind of laughter. The book of Esther begins a tradition of Jewish humor.[6]

Adele Berlin goes so far as to call this story "burlesque," defined as "an artistic composition ... that for the sake of laughter, vulgarizes lofty material or treats ordinary material with mock dignity." She continues: "Understanding the Book of Esther as a burlesque or a farce allows us to understand that while the threat to the Jews is serious, it is not real."[7] If she means that the threat is not real because at the time the author writes the book of Esther he knows that the threat is past and the Jews have been delivered, I would probably agree with her. The fact that the author of Esther can write this story with humor, expecting his readers to appreciate it, suggests that the book was probably written at least a generation or two after the events occurred. By that time, the festivities celebrating Purim may have allowed the author to introduce humorous elements in keeping with the joyful nature of the feast. Time must pass before one can look back on a bad situation and appropriately laugh about it.

One of the repeated elements throughout the story is the emphasis on the multilingual character of Persian society. A threefold repetition in verse 22 emphasizes that the king's decree was sent "to each province in its own script," "to each people in its own language," making its declaration "in each people's tongue." The universal dissemination of the decree contrasts with the original fear that women throughout the empire would hear of this episode. It also raises the serious issue of preserving ethnic identity in a multicultural conglomerate society.

---

6. Fox, *Character and Ideology in the Book of Esther*, 253.

7. Berlin quoted this definition from the *Random House Dictionary of the English Language*, 2d ed. (1987) in "The Place of Esther in the Religion of Israel."

Because the Persian empire encompassed such a vast geographical area and had conquered so many different peoples, many languages were spoken within the realm of Xerxes. Most inscriptions from that period are trilingual, written in Old Persian, Elamite, and Babylonian or Aramaic. The Persian court employed large numbers of scribes who could write in every language of the empire. Written memos, such as those preserved in Daniel, Nehemiah, and Ezra, were prepared and filed for every point of business, making the Persian empire a large bureaucracy. In order to make written communication timely, a system similar to the Pony Express of the American West was used. Dispatches sent from the royal cities were relayed from point to point by messengers on horseback, reaching the farthest points of the empire with surprising speed. Thus, the news that Vashti has been deposed goes out, and with it the irrevocable decree that every man should be ruler in his own home—like the king was in his!

The Hebrew in verse 22 may also be construed to read that every man should be ruler in his own home *and* speak according to the language of his people (cf. NASB, NKJV, NRSV footnote). Because many languages were spoken by the various people groups that comprised the vast Persian empire, the language one chose to speak had political and sociological implications. Note how the choice of language used in the home of ethnically mixed marriages of this period was a special problem for the Jewish remnant who returned to rebuild Jerusalem (Neh. 13:23–24):

> Moreover, in those days I [Nehemiah] saw men of Judah who had married women from Ashdod, Ammon and Moab. Half of their children spoke the language of Ashdod or the language of one of the other peoples, and did not know how to speak the language of Judah.

While this passage has no direct relevance on Xerxes' decree in Esther 1:22, it does provide insight into the political and sociological implications of the linguistically mixed society of the Persian empire. Nehemiah was deeply concerned that the next generation who would populate the restored Jerusalem and Judah would not know the language of their ancestors. This situation was the result of Jewish marriages to foreign women, those who were not members of the covenant community. By adopting the woman's language in their homes, the foreign culture of the mother was extended into Judah, instead of incorporating the foreign woman into the culture and religion of Yahweh's covenant people (cf. Ruth, the Moabitess).

Thus, in the historical context of restoring God's people to their land, this situation had to be corrected if their national and covenantal identity was to survive. The use of the man's language in his home was a sign of his leadership, and in the sociological context of postexilic Judah implied that his wife and children were to join the restored covenant community of Yahweh. This emphasis on the husband's language (word) as an instrument of rule in the home mirrors its correlate that the king's language (word) in the form of decree was the instrument of rule throughout the empire.

 WHAT HAPPENED TO Vashti after her deposition is not developed within the story, and there is no further discussion of whether the king's decree demanding respect from the wives of the empire was effective or not. Therefore, this scene functions to provide general background for the story of Esther and Mordecai that follows and cannot be construed as a main point of the story. This episode exposes the inner workings of the Persian monarchy and indicates precedents and patterns for the events that will follow.

Why does the author of Esther include this episode about men and women as he sets the stage for his story? Why bring up the "battle of the sexes" in a story that tells about the salvation of the Jewish people from genocide? Surely the author could have chosen some other event to paint life at the Persian court, but he chooses one that involves the relationship between women and men.

The author of Esther is revealing the workings of worldly power and mocking its ultimate inability to determine the destiny of God's people. At that time and place, worldly power was held by Persian men. The author chooses to include and highlight an incident involving the interaction between men and women because in this story powerful *Persian men* are outwitted by a *Jewish woman.*[8] Esther has to overcome two

---

8. Perhaps this is an example of God's using the "foolish" to shame the "wise" and the "weak" to shame the "strong," as recorded by the apostle Paul in 1 Cor. 1:27.

levels of conflict, both as a woman and as a Jew, to come into her own as Queen of Persia. We modern readers probably cannot fully appreciate how truly remarkable a feat that was.

It is therefore a bit surprising that instead of applauding Esther, many feminist interpreters are so critical of her and her role in the deliverance of the Jewish people. The South African interpreter Itumeleng J. Mosala finds that

> the text's choice of a female character to achieve what are basically patriarchal ends is objectionable. The fact that the story is woven around Esther does not make her the heroine. The hero of the story is Mordecai who needless to say gives nothing of himself for what he gets. Esther struggles, but Mordecai reaps the fruit of the struggle. African women who work within liberation movements and other groups will be very familiar with these kinds of dynamics. A truly liberative biblical hermeneutics will struggle against this tendency.[9]

Alice Laffey notes that feminist interpreters see "full compliance with patriarchy" in Esther's character and describe her as "the stereotypical woman in a man's world," who uses her beauty to please men in power.[10] Fox critiques such feminist interpretations by pointing out that the book does not teach compliance with patriarchy; rather, "it teaches that *even* a stereotypical woman in a world of laughably stereotypical males is capable of facing the ultimate national crisis and diverting the royal power to her own ends" (emphasis original).[11] Although Esther may start out as a sexual stereotype, she develops into a leader within her religious community, upon whose authority Purim still stands.

This episode between Vashti and Xerxes suggests that by all human reasoning, Esther should have ended up like her predecessor—banished from the center of power and unable to exert significant influence. That she actually succeeds in outwitting Haman and reversing his decree is almost a miracle. Other women in the Bible are renown

---

9. Itumeleng J. Mosala, "Implications of the Text of Esther for African Women's Struggle for Liberation in South Africa," in *Voices from the Margin: Interpreting the Bible in the Third World*, R. S. Sugirtharajah, ed. (Maryknoll, N.Y.: Orbis, 1995), 176.

10. Alice A. Laffey, *An Introduction to the Old Testament: A Feminist Perspective* (Philadelphia: Fortress, 1988), 216.

11. Fox, *Character and Ideology in the Book of Esther*, 207.

---

because they were the mothers of sons who became great in Israel (e.g., Sarah, Rebecca, Hannah). The only other book of the Bible named for a woman is Ruth, a Gentile, whose role in biblical history was to give birth to an ancestor of King David. In contrast, Esther is renown because her political acumen saved her people and on her authority a religious holiday was proclaimed, which has been celebrated for more than two thousand years. The opportunity for Esther to use royal power to her own ends was possible because of the manipulating way power was wielded in the Persian court. This is precisely what the author is revealing in this episode of the king with his seven advisors making Persian "law" to deal with Vashti's disobedience.

Rather than affirming patriarchy, Fox sees the author of Esther himself as "something of a protofeminist" because of the book's sustained interest in the sexual politics of the Persian court.[12] He observes that as the author tells it, the story is not aligned to the men's side in this conflict. The king's decree that every man should be the ruler in his own home is not an affirmation of patriarchy, but a cynical commentary on the character of leadership in the Persian court. Indeed, the author portrays the demand of the men in power for the respect of the women as self-defeating. Memucan's view of respect and how to get it reveals the inner workings of Persian power as brute force, fueled by the need to control. He fears female "disrespect" (v. 18) and apparently believes respect can be acquired through the brute force of a royal decree.

However, such a tactic is hollow and self-defeating, for if a man has to command a woman to respect him, then whatever "respect" is so rendered loses its meaning. Those who can gain respect and obedience only by holding enough power to command it live with the constant anxiety of losing it. Far from affirming a brutish patriarchy, the author is cynical about the Persian masculine ego that will use the full power of the empire to alleviate its own personal anxieties. The author is cynical about the powers of this world. Although the Persian king and his officials hold such power, with this episode the author questions if they are really ever in control. Is their word truly irrevocable? In his description of how Vashti's defiance was handled, the author is mocking the inner weakness of the outwardly most powerful empire of that time.

---

12. Ibid., 209.

Moreover, as Fox points out in his critique of feminist interpretations, the parody of male dominance is told from "a Jewish—not a feminist or even specifically female—perspective."[13] This episode should be understood not as an attack on the male gender in general, but as an exposé of the political motivations that characterize the ungodly powers of the Gentile world—in other words, the world in which God's chosen people must somehow survive. The worldly power of Persia was wielded at the personal whim of the king's closest advisors, who manipulated him with great skill. The well-ordered machine of the Persian empire, structured ostensibly on "law and justice," is shown here to be actually driven by the megalomaniac needs of the king for glory and the insecurity of the most powerful men in the empire. In this scene, Persian "law" is made up on the spot and in accordance with the personal interests of the king and his seven close advisors. The irrevocable law of the king that went out to the ends of the empire originated in Memucan's personal anxiety over Vashti's disobedience. Is this any way to run an empire?

 THE DANGER OF **absolute power.** This scene in 1:13–22 is an inside look at just what makes the world go round. Law and justice may be the public ideal of every great government, but people in power, compelled by their own fears and anxieties, all too often abuse the power with which they have been entrusted. Absolute power held by flawed leaders is a terrifying scenario.

The stewardship of power is a major theme running throughout the Bible. Esther 1:13–22 exposes what went on under the pretense of law and justice in the inner councils of one of the most powerful of the Persian kings. The tendency to abuse power under the rationale of the good of those governed is certainly not a problem limited to ancient society. Every period of human history has been marked by those who have risen to positions of power and who have exposed their personal flaws, which in turn led to reigns of terror.

One has only to mention names from recent world history, such as Stalin, Mussolini, and Hitler, to bring to mind the terrors wrought by

---

13. Ibid., 210.

unchecked worldly power. Mass graves throughout Siberia filled with skulls riddled with bullet holes attest to Stalin's Great Purge of the 1930s. The horrific memories of tens of thousands of survivors of the gulags and concentration camps of Europe during Hitler's regime are evidence that the chilling biblical tale of threatened genocide under Xerxes is all too historically probable. The failure of Stalin's ideology evidenced by the collapse of the communist government in the Soviet Union has left a new criminal class to oversee this tumultuous time of transition and to determine who will now benefit from the nation's limited resources.

A quick scan of newspaper headlines in recent years shows political leaders around the globe who have fallen to the depraved temptations of dictatorial power. Marcos in the Philippines, Noriega in Panama, Khomeini in Iran, Hussein in Iraq, Deng Xiaoping in China, Pol Pot in Cambodia, and Idi Amin in Uganda are but a few of the many names of powerful leaders in our times involved in varying degrees of graft and violence to satisfy a personal lust for power.

Because of the checks and balances structure of our government, the United States has been spared dictatorship, but it has nevertheless seen its share of the corruption of leadership with the resignation of Richard Nixon, discussions of the moral failures of John F. Kennedy, and the continuing blight of ethical and moral allegations against the Clinton White House. American agencies such as the F.B.I. and the I.R.S. have come under suspicion of abusing the power and prerogatives that were put in place to serve the American people.

Big business in corporate America often lacks the checks and balances of government structure that, at least in principle, is intended to limit the power of any one individual. A lack of accountability permits corporations to exploit its employees, to cover up sexual harassment in the workplace, to manipulate stockholders, to engage in price gouging, and to buy political influence in Washington.

Even the Christian church is sadly not immune to the misuse of power by spiritual leaders. The Roman Catholic Church has been plagued by accusations and confessions of the sexual improprieties of priests who misuse their power over parishioners, especially children. Protestant leadership has similar problems with the corrosive effect of power, as the fall of televangelists Jim Bakker and Jimmy Swaggert and as the rise of "Christian" cults such as the Branch Davidians have so sadly demonstrated.

The Bible itself is full of examples of leaders who were not worthy of the power they held. The Lord made Solomon king of Israel to "maintain justice and righteousness" (1 Kings 10:9), but even Solomon had personal flaws that compromised his reign. The authors of Kings and Chronicles wrote to show the Jewish nation that the reason they went into Exile was because even Israel's kings, starting with Saul, had done the same things as pagan kings, disobeying the covenant with God and bringing its curses on the nation. Even Israel's greatest king, King David, on whose throne a perfect king would one day reign, used his power for adultery and murder (2 Sam. 11–12). Both Scripture and the newspaper concur that power has always and everywhere had a corrupting effect on those who yield to the temptation to use it for their own ends, no matter how just and reasonable those ends may at first appear. History has shown that absolute power corrupts absolutely.

The use of power by Jesus Christ. Only a king with perfect character is worthy of absolute power. Only a perfect king can wield power with true law and justice. God, the eternal king, both omnipotent and holy, is the ultimate author of the book of Esther, who alone can justly expose the fatal flaws of the world's greatest leaders because only he wields absolute power with moral perfection. The New Testament teaches that Jesus, the Son of God incarnate as the Son of Man, has been crowned King of kings and given dominion over all worldly powers. In the Gospels we read that it is Satan who empowers the kingdoms of the world with their splendor and that he tempted even Jesus to use his power for personal ends (Matt. 4:8–10):

> Again, the devil took him to a very high mountain and showed him all the kingdoms of the world and their splendor. "All this I will give you," he said, "if you will bow down and worship me."
>
> Jesus said to him, "Away from me, Satan! For it is written: 'Worship the Lord your God, and serve him only.'"

The nature of Jesus' omnipotent rule in submission to God contrasts sharply with the way the world yields its power for the satisfaction of personal lust.

Jesus' disciples carried within themselves the human flaw of a lust for personal power. They argued which of them was the greatest as they jockeyed for power in what they misunderstood would be a worldly kingdom. Jesus critiqued and corrected their understanding of leadership in Matthew 20:25–28 (cf. Mark 10:35–45; Luke 22:24–30):

> Jesus called them together and said, "You know that the rulers of the Gentiles lord it over them, and their high officials exercise authority over them. Not so with you. Instead, whoever wants to become great among you must be your servant, and whoever wants to be first must be your slave—just as the Son of Man did not come to be served, but to serve, and to give his life as a ransom for many.

The King of kings condemns the type of leadership exemplified in Xerxes' court and by the countless kings, presidents, and world leaders since. As a backdrop for the story of the salvation of God's people in the Persian period, the author of the book of Esther provides an example of the type of worldly leadership Jesus condemned: The rulers of the Gentiles were indeed lording it over the people of their empire and exercising their authority to demand a respect that they feared would not otherwise be forthcoming. In stark contrast, the leadership of Jesus was motivated not by his own personal fears and anxieties, but by the needs of those he governs as King of the universe.

The Gospel of John replaces the instruction on servant leadership found in the Synoptic Gospels with the example of Jesus' washing the feet of his disciples (John 13). The recollection of that moment served to explain by example the character of Jesus' kingship. His servant kingship extended all the way to death on the cross (cf. Phil. 2:5–8)—the lowliest form of execution at that time—in order to set his people free from the tyranny of Satan, who empowers the principalities of this world.

Power and leadership in marital relationships. The author of Esther uses the confrontation between Vashti and Xerxes to illustrate the tyrannical leadership of the Persian king and his closest advisors. Because the author chose an illustration that involved husbands and wives in the Persian empire, it is appropriate to consider the issue of power and leadership in that same social setting today. Both Esther 1:13–22 and Ephesians 5:21–33 discuss wives' respect for their husbands, but the difference between these passages in how wifely respect is attained is the difference between darkness and light. Ephesians 5 instructs Christians:

Submit to one another out of reverence for Christ.

Wives, submit to your husbands as to the Lord. For the husband is the head of the wife as Christ is the head of the church, his body, of which he is the Savior. Now as the church submits to Christ, so also wives should submit to their husbands in everything.

Husbands, love your wives, just as Christ loved the church and gave himself up for her to make her holy, cleansing her by the washing with water through the word, and to present her to himself as a radiant church, without stain or wrinkle or any other blemish, but holy and blameless. In this same way, husbands ought to love their wives as their own bodies. He who loves his wife loves himself. After all, no one ever hated his own body, but he feeds and cares for it, just as Christ does the church—for we are members of his body. "For this reason a man will leave his father and mother and be united to his wife, and the two will become one flesh." This is a profound mystery—but I am talking about Christ and the church. However, each one of you also must love his wife as he loves himself, and *the wife must respect her husband* (emphasis added).

In Esther 1:13–22, respect is demanded from the Persian wives by order of royal decree; in Ephesians 5, respect is to be the response of a woman toward a man who loves her as Christ loved the church and gave himself up for her. The placement of the NIV section break in Ephesians 5 between verses 21 and 22 is unfortunate because it divides what is one sentence in the Greek and obscures that the instructions for wives and husbands are given within the context of submitting to one another out of reverence to Christ. What is portrayed in worldly idiom as a battle between the sexes in Esther is recast in this New Testament principle of reciprocity to be a mutual submission of the wife and the husband to each other out of reverence for Christ. The wife and the husband are to serve each other, perhaps in gender-differentiated ways, but with both emulating the self-denying servanthood of their Lord Jesus Christ.

This same principle of reciprocity in marriage for the sake of Christ is found in 1 Peter 2:13–14; 3:1–2, 7:

Submit yourselves for the Lord's sake to every authority instituted among men: whether to the king, as the supreme authority, or to governors, who are sent by him to punish those who do wrong and to commend those who do right. . . .

Wives, in the same way [i.e., for the Lord's sake] be submissive to your husbands so that, if any of them do not believe the word, they may be won over without words by the behavior of their wives, when they see the purity and reverence of your lives. . . .

Husbands, in the same way [i.e., for the Lord's sake] be considerate as you live with your wives, and treat them with respect as the weaker partner and as heirs with you of the gracious gift of life, so that nothing will hinder your prayers.

In his NIV Application Commentary on this passage Scot McKnight includes an anecdote that well illustrates the contemporary significance of Esther 1:13—22 as viewed in light of the New Testament. In a private conversation on wifely submission, McKnight recounts what a well-known evangelical scholar said:

I believe in a wife submitting to her husband, *but I don't believe the husband ever has the right to demand it*. In fact, I know that when I am worthy of submission, my wife submits; and when I am unworthy of it, she does not. My responsibility as a husband is to be worthy. (emphasis added)[14]

How different is to be the attitude of the Christian man toward his wife compared to that of the men of the Persian court!

According to statements entered in the *Congressional Record* documenting the need for legislation against domestic violence, every fifteen seconds in the United States a woman is beaten by her husband or boyfriend. Four women die every day from the attack.[15] This form of violence costs employers between three and five billion dollars per year, because the abused woman typically is late for work at least five times a month, leaves work early at least as often, and misses at least three full days of work per month.[16]

In a society where such domestic violence pervades even Christian homes, the church must not allow its biblical teaching on marriage to

---

14. Scot McKnight, *1 Peter*, NIVAC (Grand Rapids: Zondervan, 1996), 191—92.

15. *Congressional Record*, v. 142, no. 141 (October 3, 1996), p. S12341.

16. *Congressional Record*, v. 143, no. 22 (February 26, 1997), p. S1659—81.

be misunderstood as a doctrine of male dominance that justifies the abuse of domestic power or that tones down the husband's responsibility for self-sacrifice for the good of his wife. In teaching wifely submission to counteract what has been perceived as an unbiblical feminist agenda in our society, the church has inadvertently encouraged the dangerous belief in the absolute headship of the husband in the home. For some men with a domineering temperament, this becomes a license to assert themselves and demand obedience, including conjugal submission, even if it means resorting to violence.

The author of Esther suggests that by using a royal decree to demand respect and obedience from their wives, Xerxes and his closest advisors were not worthy of it and that they were not above misusing the tremendous power they held. If they used their power to demand the respect and submission of their own wives, to what further misuse of power would they stoop?

The scene in Esther 1 forms a context in which the salvation of God's people from the threats of worldly power is to be understood. The contemporary significance of this passage calls Christians to be worthy of the personal power that each of us holds by wielding that power as Jesus wielded his. Whether as a husband or wife in the privacy of our homes, as a spiritual leader in the church, as CEO of a large corporation, or as the head of state of a great nation, we are responsible to resist the temptation of misusing our power for the satisfaction of ungodly lust in any of its forms.

Esther 2:1–11

L
ATER WHEN THE anger of King Xerxes had subsided, he remembered Vashti and what she had
done and what he had decreed about her. ²Then
the king's personal attendants proposed, "Let a search be
made for beautiful young virgins for the king. ³Let the
king appoint commissioners in every province of his
realm to bring all these beautiful girls into the harem at
the citadel of Susa. Let them be placed under the care of
Hegai, the king's eunuch, who is in charge of the
women; and let beauty treatments be given to them.
⁴Then let the girl who pleases the king be queen instead
of Vashti." This advice appealed to the king, and he followed it.

⁵Now there was in the citadel of Susa a Jew of the
tribe of Benjamin, named Mordecai son of Jair, the son
of Shimei, the son of Kish, ⁶who had been carried into
exile from Jerusalem by Nebuchadnezzar king of Babylon, among those taken captive with Jehoiachin king of
Judah. ⁷Mordecai had a cousin named Hadassah, whom
he had brought up because she had neither father nor
mother. This girl, who was also known as Esther, was
lovely in form and features, and Mordecai had taken her
as his own daughter when her father and mother died.

⁸When the king's order and edict had been proclaimed, many girls were brought to the citadel of Susa
and put under the care of Hegai. Esther also was taken
to the king's palace and entrusted to Hegai, who had
charge of the harem. ⁹The girl pleased him and won his
favor. Immediately he provided her with her beauty
treatments and special food. He assigned to her seven
maids selected from the king's palace and moved her and
her maids into the best place in the harem.

¹⁰Esther had not revealed her nationality and family
background, because Mordecai had forbidden her to do

so. ¹¹Every day he walked back and forth near the courtyard of the harem to find out how Esther was and what was happening to her.

VASHTI REFUSED TO come to King Xerxes in the third year of his reign, 483 B.C. Esther was made queen in the seventh year of his reign, 479 B.C. (2:16–17). During the intervening years Xerxes was off fighting a disastrous war with Greece. His humiliating defeat depleted the treasuries of the Persian empire and discredited him in the eyes of his subjects. Shortly after his return from Greece, Esther was chosen as his new consort. Herodotus describes the king's life after his military defeat as one of sensual overindulgence.[1] He dallied with the wives of some of his officers, sowing an anger that led to his assassination in his bedroom in 465 B.C.

The gathering of all the beautiful young virgins from throughout the empire seems outrageously unlikely to our modern thinking. Even by Persian standards, this was not the way a queen was normally chosen. According to Herodotus, Xerxes' father, Darius, took his wives from the noble families of Persia.[2] Often they came from the families of the king's seven closest advisors (1:14). (Perhaps one of Memucan's ulterior motives in having Vashti banished was the hope that her replacement would be chosen from his family, thereby increasing his influence on the king.) Some have concluded that the royal wives were chosen only from among high-ranking families, so that the story of Esther is a fairy-tale. Plutarch, however, reports that other Persian kings did sometimes marry, contrary to law, women with whom they had fallen passionately in love.[3] Surely a king who held absolute power could have married any woman he wanted.

In addition to one or more wives, Persian kings typically had many concubines, women who came as virgins to the king's bed and then lived in luxurious desolation in his harem. Artaxerxes II is said to have had 360 concubines of surpassing beauty in his harem, who were replenished by gathering virgins from the land.

---

1. LCL: *Herodotus* 9.109–13.
2. Ibid., 3.8.
3. LCL: *Plutarch's Lives: Artaxerxes* 23.3.

In 2:1–11 the word of the king went forth, and "many" young girls were brought into the harem of Xerxes' court. This herding of virgins offends our modern sensibilities, and feminist critics especially see it as a demeaning and sexist affront to women that the biblical author should have denounced. However, Herodotus also reports that five hundred young boys were gathered each year and castrated to serve as eunuchs in the Persian court.[4] One might argue that the young women actually got the better deal. The gathering of the virgins, whether consensual or not, is not sexism. It is a brutal act typical of how power was used in the Persian court. Everyone, whether male or female, was at the disposal of the king's personal whims.

Mordecai is introduced as "a Jew of the tribe of Benjamin," a descendant of a man named Kish (2:5). These verses suggest that Mordecai was taken into exile with Jehoiachin, king of Judah, in 597 B.C. If so, Mordecai would have been more than one hundred years old at the time he served Xerxes! One way of resolving this problem is to read the relative clause in the Hebrew text as saying that Mordecai's great-grandfather, Kish, was the one taken into exile with Jehoiachin (though such a reading is not the most natural way of taking the Hebrew).

This reference need not be taken to mean that Mordecai and Jehoiachin were contemporaries, but rather to indicate the solidarity of God's covenant people. The author's point in mentioning the exile of the king of Judah is to associate Mordecai with the exile out of the Promised Land and all that it connotes, thereby providing a historical context within which to understand the events that are about to transpire. When the king of Judah went into exile, all of the covenant people of God went into exile, including those who would subsequently be born in Babylon. Such an association between Mordecai and his ancestors is congenial to the theme of divine providence: How is it that we have been positioned where we find ourselves historically and geographically?

Furthermore, the author is associating Mordecai with another Benjamite, King Saul, whose father's name was Kish (1 Sam. 9:1–2). Perhaps he wishes his readers to understand that Saul's father was an ancient ancestor of Mordecai's. This reading takes the phrase "son of" in the way it occurs in other biblical genealogies, where it means

---

4. LCL: *Herodotus* 3.92.

"descendent of." If, however, we interpret the Hebrew to mean that Kish was the one taken into exile, then of course Saul's father and Mordecai's ancestor could not be the same person. In any case, the author is introducing Mordecai in a way that identifies him with the Exile and which allows the reader to draw an analogy between Mordecai and Saul that will be amplified later (see comments on 3:1).

Although neither the names of Vashti or Esther are mentioned outside of this book, there is extrabiblical evidence for the existence of Mordecai. A tablet discovered in 1904 at Persepolis, another Persian royal city, contains the name *Marduka* as a Persian official during the early years of Xerxes' reign, which corresponds in time to the setting of the Esther story.[5] The name *Marduka* means "man" or "worshiper" of Marduk, the male deity of the Babylonians. Although it may have been too common a name to identify conclusively the Marduka of the Persepolis tablets as the Mordecai in Esther, the correspondence is striking.

Esther is introduced as Mordecai's "cousin . . . whom he had brought up because she" was an orphan. Nothing is said of her except her beauty. According to the rabbis, she was one of the four most beautiful women in the world, the other three being Sarah, Rahab, and Abigail (*Megillah* 15a). In Hebrew narrative the physical attributes described when a character is first introduced is of special relevance to his or her role in the story. By describing Esther's beauty, the author is aligning her with the women already mentioned in the story, beautiful queen Vashti and the beautiful young virgins, thus creating a certain expectation of how Esther will fare in the Persian court.

Esther is also known by her Hebrew name, Hadassah. The name *Esther* may be the Persian word for star, or it may be a Hebrew transliteration of *Ishtar*, the name of the Babylonian goddess of love and war. The Targums of Esther suggest that *Esther* was a nickname given to the queen by the Gentiles of the empire.[6] Some interpreters believe that the biblical Esther story was adapted from a Babylonian myth and that the names Mordecai and Esther are theonymic derivations from the god Marduk and the goddess Ishtar, respectively.

---

5. Edwin M. Yamauchi, *Persia and the Bible*, 235.

6. A targum is an ancient translation of a book of the Hebrew Bible into Aramaic, a Semitic language spoken by the Jewish people from the time of the Exile on. See the English translation of the targums in *The Two Targums of Esther*, trans. Bernard Grossfeld (Collegeville, Minn.: Liturgical Press, 1991), 42–43.

Without accepting this theory about the book's origin, an allusion to love and war does fit well Esther's role in the story. (1) She is beautiful, and in just one night, she pleases the king more than all the other virgins. He falls deeply in love with her and makes her his queen—a "goddess" of love. (2) It is Esther who asks for a second day for the Jews to make war in Susa and for the bodies of Haman's sons to be hanged on display—a "goddess" of war (9:13). It is thus easy to see how she may have been given this nickname by her subjects after the Babylonian goddess of love and war, or alternatively, why the author may have assigned this literary nickname to her. This suggests that the name Esther probably is not her historical name. This Jewish heroine is memorialized not by her Hebrew name but by the Babylonian name that so aptly fits her role in the events.

The choice of the presumably Jewish author to memorialize Mordecai and Esther using Babylonian theonyms affords interesting reflection on his intention. Is he subtly condemning those Jews who had become too comfortable in exile while still acknowledging the great role they played in the survival of his race? Ronald Pierce takes this view, understanding the absence of Yahweh in the book "to highlight the secular nature of the people of God in the ancient diaspora."[7] He sees in the events of the story a failure on the part of Esther and Mordecai, who represent the secular direction in which the Jewish people were heading until they were shaken from their lethargy by the threat of genocide. Yet even if the names of Esther and Mordecai are theonymic and allude to their assimilation into Babylonian culture, the outcome of the story suggests to the Babylonian pagans that Marduk and Ishtar are subservient to the purposes of the unnamed God of the Jews. The victory of the Jews in this story would then function as a polemic against the pagan deities.

Esther is the only person in the story with two names. Leland Ryken interprets this as the author's way of depicting Esther as a young women trying to live in two worlds—the Jewish world in which she was raised and the opulent world of the Persian court into which she was thrust.[8]

---

7. Ronald W. Pierce, "The Politics of Esther and Mordecai: Courage or Compromise?" *BBR* 2 (1992): 77.

8. Leland Ryken, *Words of Delight: A Literary Introduction to the Bible* (Grand Rapids: Baker, 1987), 118.

It was not uncommon for Hebrew peoples to have both a Hebrew name and a second name taken from the culture in which they lived. Daniel and his three friends were given Babylonian names when they were taken into exile (Dan. 1:6–7). The great apostle to the Gentiles was known as both Saul and later Paul. Even immigrants into the United States will sometimes take an anglicized form of their given name. The fact of having two names, each derived from a different language and culture, implies a person's moving between two worlds, with two different cultural contexts. Therefore, Ryken's view does not necessarily imply that the author was simply making up two names to achieve a literary purpose. Nonetheless, by mentioning both her Hebrew and Babylonian name, the author is highlighting Esther as a woman with two identities, an issue that will be brought into sharp conflict later in the story.

Ryken sees Esther transformed in the story from a passive and compliant young woman who relies on her beauty to get ahead to a powerful leader of the Jews, on whose authority the customs of Purim still stand (9:32). She moves from being a person of "weak character" to one with "heroic moral stature and political skill." At the beginning of the story, Esther's identity as a Jewess and her identity as the Persian king's consort are not integrated. She cannot be both at the same time. At the end of the story, both of her identities have merged through the events of the story, and she is referred to as the Persian Queen Esther, the Jewish daughter of Abihail, writing with full authority to confirm the letter concerning Purim (9:29; cf. 2:15).

This daughter of Abihail is referred to only once by her Hebrew name, Hadassah, at the beginning of the story (2:7). In the only other time she is referred to as "daughter of Abihail," at the end of the story, the author calls her "Queen Esther" (9:29). Perhaps her transformation from "Hadassah" to "Queen Esther" implies not only the integration of her two identities personally, but the power of Persian royalty being transformed to serve the purposes of the God of the Jews. The personal story of Esther and the national story of God's people are eloquently intertwined.

Esther "was taken" (2:8) into the harem where the virgins were gathered. Some commentators have understood this to mean that the women, and particularly Esther, were taken against their will. This is probably overinterpreting the passive voice, which may have been used only to express that it was at Xerxes' initiative, not the women's, that this occurred. Some may have loathed the situation in which they found themselves, others may have reveled in it. What about Esther? Her thoughts about being "taken" are not revealed. The passive voice is used frequently throughout the story, suggesting that the characters are caught up in events by some unseen force that has ultimate control. Moreover, their own personal opinion about their circumstances seems irrelevant as the events of the story move inexorably to their climax.

The author also uses the passive voice to explain why Mordecai and Esther were living in Susa. The Jews had been "carried" into exile (2:6). Esther had been "taken" into Xerxes' harem, just as the Jews had been taken into exile. Regardless of how she felt about it or whether she cooperated, Esther was at the mercy of a ruthless pagan king, just as her people were. The use of the passive voice is appropriate in this story, for it expresses life from the perspective of being caught up in and swept along by circumstances beyond one's control.

Mordecai commands Esther to conceal her "nationality and family background" (2:10), even though it would certainly mean compromising whatever fidelity to the Torah she had. The author does not reveal Mordecai's motives for this. Perhaps he was concerned that Esther's chances of success with the king would be diminished were it known she was a Jew, although the author gives no hint that the king would have discriminated against a Jewish woman. It appears that Xerxes' only criteria were a woman's performance in his bedroom and her obedience before his court, not her ethnicity or religious convictions.

Mordecai had achieved a position in the Persian court, although perhaps he, too, had not revealed his identify as a Jew until Haman's demand for homage forced his hand (see comments on 3:1–4). As soon as Mordecai does explicitly identify himself as a Jew, Haman's immediate reaction is not just against Mordecai, but against all the Jews of the empire. This suggests that Mordecai counseled Esther to conceal her Jewish identity because he had good reason to fear that anti-Semitism was lurking close at hand. The fact that Mordecai checked daily on Esther shows that he was concerned for her welfare and about how she would fare in the harem.

The ambiguity of Esther's thoughts about her situation raises questions about her observance of God's law and her practices as a Jew. She was taken into the harem, gained favor with Hegai, the eunuch in charge, and received beauty treatments, special food, and seven servants. Unlike Daniel and his friends, Esther does not protest. Because she could so successfully hide her identity as a Jew, she apparently had adopted Persian dress and customs at least to the extent that she was indistinguishable as a Jewish woman.

LIFE IN THE **Persian court**. The author has used the first chapter to introduce the reader to Xerxes, showing what life in the court was like for those closest to him. Of the sixteen people mentioned by name in the first chapter (Xerxes, Vashti, the seven eunuchs, and the seven advisors), only Xerxes remains in chapter 2. Vashti is now only a memory.

In chapter 2 the author continues to show what Mordecai and Esther will be up against. He continues to mock the king, whose word is irrevocable law. In chapter 1, Memucan uses the king's need for glory and honor to manipulate him, and a decree goes out that becomes the law of the land. Now the king's attendants pander to his desire for women, and once again the machinery of the empire is put in motion. In other words, twice the king, who holds absolute power, has allowed others who have their own agendas to decide what he will decree. The modus operandi of the king is being illustrated by these two events. What becomes the irrevocable law of the Persians and Medes is the will of those closest to the king, who know how to skillfully manipulate his needs.

The author chooses to tell of these two cases where the fate of women is being decided, first for Vashti, then for all the beautiful young virgins of the empire. This reflects the same outwardly expanding pattern of 1:16–22, where the offense to Xerxes is extended universally to all the men of the empire. Vashti had been used sexually by the king and then banished from his presence. All the young virgins will be used by the king, probably only once, and then banished from his presence to spend the rest of their lives secluded in the harem. This makes Esther's rise to power within the court all the more remarkable.

The author is carefully stacking the odds against the success of Esther and Mordecai. He is showing that in this world the fate of people is decided not by law and justice, but by the personal agendas of those who can manipulate the self-aggrandizing needs of the powerful. It is terrifying to become the target of such impulsive and unstable power. Those who hold the reigns know this and are compelled to tighten their grip lest the beast turn and devour them.

Rooted in Jewish history. By introducing Mordecai as a Jew of the tribe of Benjamin, the story is firmly rooted in Jewish history. This fact may seem too obvious to mention, but it is important for rightly understanding the message of the story, especially with its lack of references to God. Esther and Mordecai's first actions distinguish them significantly from other biblical heroes and heroines, who would rather risk death than compromise their obedience of the Torah. Rather than stand up for their faith in the one, true God, Mordecai instructs Esther to conceal her faith, and she complies. This compliance is viewed by some as a godly example of female submission to male headship. But the author does not commend Esther, and it is certainly questionable that a woman should obey male authority if and when that means violating the Word of the Lord.

Moreover, some interpreters have faulted Mordecai for his failure to protect Esther from being put in such a situation. The fifteenth-century Jewish commentator Abraham Saba writes:

> Now when Mordecai heard the king's herald announcing that whoever had a daughter or a sister should bring her to the king to have intercourse with an uncircumcised heathen, why did he not risk his life to take her to some deserted place to hide until the danger would pass? ... He should have been killed rather than submit to such an act.... Why did Mordecai not keep righteous Esther from idol worship? Why was he not more careful? Where was his righteousness, his piety, and his valor? ... She [Esther] too should by right have tried to commit suicide before allowing herself to have intercourse with him [Xerxes].[9]

The biblical author makes no attempt to vindicate Esther and Mordecai by explaining extenuating circumstances or reporting that they had divine counsel to behave as they did.

---

9. Quoted in Barry D. Walfish, *Esther in Medieval Garb: Jewish Interpretation of the Book of Esther in the Middle Ages* (Albany, N.Y.: SUNY Press, 1993), 122–23.

Motives for compliance. Modern interpreters also question Esther and Mordecai's compliance. As Ronald Pierce points out, Xerxes seems to be a gracious and benevolent king, who entertains his guests according to the desires of each. Even his angry reaction to Vashti's defiance was relatively irenic. He sees no reason to believe that Esther would have been killed for identifying herself as a Jewess, nor even for refusing to participate in the new-queen contest. "Instead, one finds here a diaspora Jewess who desires a chance at the throne so greatly that she is willing to betray her heritage at the advice of her cousin without a hint of resistance."[10] Certainly the temptation to compromise Jewish religious and ethical principles would have been an important issue for the Jews of the Diaspora. It is no less a temptation for Christians today, living in a society that is becoming increasingly hostile to biblical principles.

The questionable character and spiritual fidelity of Esther and Mordecai were noticed even by the first translators of the book, who attempted to exonerate them by adding explanation. A translation of the Esther story was made into the Greek language in the second or first century B.C.[11] In the Greek version of the story, Esther announces that she in fact had not violated the food laws and that she abhorred "the bed of the uncircumcised."

Viewing Esther and Mordecai in a positive light, Jon Levenson suggests that their story "can be read as the story of the transformation of the *exile* into the *Diaspora*."[12] According to him, the author portrays Esther and Mordecai as representing the Jewish people of the Diaspora collectively, whose hope for the advent of the Messiah or the apocalyptic overthrow of Gentile power and a restoration to the theocratic Promised Land were diminished by the realities in which they found themselves. The transformation "from refugee to prime minister and from orphan to queen recall prophetic visions of restoration after exile (e.g., Isaiah 54) and suggest that Mordecai and Esther, for all their particular character, are also allegorizations of Israel's national destiny."[13]

---

10. Pierce, "The Politics of Esther and Mordeci," 84.

11. This is the translation known as the Septuagint (LXX). A modern English translation of this ancient Greek version of Esther, including the six additional chapters, is found in the NRSV; see *The New Oxford Annotated Bible with the Apocrypha* (New York: Oxford Univ. Press, 1994), AP 41–56.

12. Jon D. Levenson, *Esther: A Commentary*, 15 (italics in original).

13. Ibid., 16.

While the attempts made by interpreters throughout history to exonerate Esther and Mordecai are understandable, they dilute the message of the original Hebrew and its power. The divinely inspired author chose not to reveal Esther's reaction to being taken into the harem or Mordecai's motives for commanding Esther to conceal her identity. It is natural to pass judgment on these two, whether positive or negative, but in doing so we may miss an important point. This deliberate silence is part of the message. Regardless of their character, their motives, or their fidelity to God's law, the decisions Esther and Mordecai make move events in some inscrutable way to fulfill the covenant promises God made to his people long ago.

DELIVERANCE FOR GOD'S **covenant people.** These verses that identify Mordecai and Esther as Jews are essential for understanding the contemporary significance of the book. The book shows how against all odds, the fate of a marginalized people within a hostile world is reversed. These marginalized people not only survive, they rise to power within that world. There are clearly two sides pitted in conflict in the story, Mordecai and Esther versus Haman. One side will be victorious; the other will be destroyed. The author shows that powerful worldly forces are working against Mordecai and Esther.

However, these people do not represent just any two groups in conflict. The story is not about how, coincidentally, one group happens to win against the other through an extraordinary chain of events. Rather, these verses identify Mordecai and Esther as *Jews*. Haman is the *enemy* of the Jews. The story is not about conflict between any two hostile peoples, it is about the hostility of the world against God's people. Against all odds, in some inscrutable and mysterious way, the events of human history work to fulfill the promises of the covenant the Lord made with his people at Sinai (see the comments on 3:1). While God may be good to all his creatures in general, he is in a special relationship of protection and preservation with his covenant people.

Esther 2:5–7 shows that it was the Jewish nation who, against all odds, were delivered from the enemies who would destroy them. The New Testament teaches that the Christian church has inherited the promises of the covenant because the demands of the covenant were fulfilled by Jesus Christ.[14] The story of Esther and Mordecai is, therefore, a part of the Christian's heritage, even though the church does not commemorate the deliverance by celebrating Purim. The relevance of this story for Christians today goes far beyond the historical necessity that the Jewish people had to be preserved during the Persian period in order for Jesus to have been born from them centuries later. The deliverance of the Jewish people was rooted in the promise of the covenant God had made to them, to which Christians today are heirs.

The story of Esther and Mordecai shows the wonderful chain of events God used to fulfill his covenant promise to his people. Therefore, the book of Esther has theological implications for the church today. God continues to work through providence to fulfill the promises of his covenant with us in Jesus Christ. Through providential circumstances people have the opportunity to hear and respond to the gospel of Jesus. Through providential circumstances Christians are "conformed to the likeness of his Son" (Rom. 8:29), and through providence God is directing all of history toward its close in the return of Christ.

In but not of the world. Within the broad theological sweep of the book of Esther, the circumstance in which Mordecai and Esther find themselves also provides an opportunity for Christians today to reflect on the implications of being in the world but not of it (John 17:14–19). Some interpreters believe this story was written to instruct the Jews living in the Diaspora of the postexilic period how to survive and even thrive in a pagan culture in which anti-Semitism was an omnipresent threat. The old order of living under a theocratic king within the borders of their own land had passed. The Jews of the Diaspora struggled with issues of how to maintain their relationship to the one, true God in a polytheistic, pagan society. Should they maintain their distinctives in clothing, language, and custom, thereby identifying themselves as Jews? If they assimilated the culture in which they were living, would it compromise their faith? The experience of Esther and Mordecai in the Persian court suggest the complexity of such questions.

Even today, Jewish people are divided about how to live in non-Jewish society. There are some sects of Judaism, such as the Hassidic

---

14. The hermeneutical and theological debate continues over how Jewish people in general, and the modern nation of Israel in particular, are related to the ancient promises of God after the coming of Christ.

Jews of Brooklyn, New York, who believe that faithfulness to the Torah requires being distinctively separate in dress, manner, and customs from the culture in which they live. Other Jews find it proper to assimilate the culture in which they live, at least to some extent, while still maintaining certain distinctives of their Jewish faith.

The same issues pertain to Christians throughout the world today. The Christian is clearly instructed to be distinct from the world. For instance, Paul writes, "So I tell you this, and insist on it in the Lord, that you must no longer live as the Gentiles do, in the futility of their thinking" (Eph. 4:17). In Romans 12:2 we read, "Do not conform any longer to the pattern of this world, but be transformed by the renewing of your mind."

How Christians understand and apply this admonition varies greatly. The Amish of Lancaster County, Pennsylvania, have enshrined the nineteenth-century lifestyle as holy, believing that the modern world and its conveniences are an evil to be avoided. Many of them still ride in horse and buggy and live without telephones or electricity. At the other extreme are Christians who eagerly participate in worldly culture without giving a thought to whether it is compatible with a biblical worldview.

The extent to which a Christian adopts the culture and society in which she or he lives is a major issue, not only for the individual, but also for the apologist and theologian. Sincere Christians wishing to obey the Bible often disagree on how to dress, whether to drink alcohol, what music, movies, and other entertainment is appropriate, whether to run for public office, and so forth. Missionaries must think long and hard when taking the gospel to another culture, to decide what are the nonnegotiables of the Christian life and what are cultural options. The issue of relating one's faith to one's culture is ever-present, yet most Christians live without thinking deeply and seriously about its implications.

Christians living in Western countries today are generally not at risk by identifying themselves as Christians. However, untold numbers of our spiritual brothers and sisters have had to struggle with that very issue, living under communist regimes or in regions controlled by Muslim fundamentalists. Martyrdom has not been confined to the first-century church in Graeco-Roman culture. The issues raised by Esther and Mordecai living in Persia are analogous to the issue of how far to conceal one's Christian identity when living in a society that is hostile, at least potentially so, to those convictions.

The relationship of Christians in Germany to the Third Reich is one excruciating example from our own century. While the Jews suffered the most under Nazi Germany, it should not be forgotten that many devout Christians also found themselves the targets of the Gestapo, not infrequently for protecting their Jewish neighbors. The charge against them was the same as the charge the Romans brought against the first-century Christians: political treason. Dietrich Bonhoeffer (1906–1945) is perhaps the best-known Christian who resisted on Christian principle the Nazification of the German church and the oppression of the Jewish people. He, along with many other Christians, struggled intensely to know how to express their Christian identity in a society that was increasingly becoming hostile to their most fundamental convictions.[15]

Of course, each of us must decide how to live without knowing the end of a situation from the beginning. Many Christian pastors swore allegiance to Hitler, not knowing where his leadership would take Germany in the final analysis. Bonhoeffer himself was finally arrested by the Gestapo in April 1943, and he was executed on the charge of treason in April 1945. American Christians may live with the blissful illusion that our constitutional principle of the separation of church and state assures that a similar situation could not develop here. That may or may not be true. Nevertheless, Jesus Christ calls for the transformation of every area of our lives, and consequently, we must relate our Christian faith to the practices, morals, and ideologies of the society and culture in which we find ourselves, whether or not that culture is congenial or hostile to our faith.

Relating faith to culture. Esther and Mordecai were faced with the issue of relating faith in Yahweh to their lives in the Persian culture. All the Jews of the Diaspora had to grapple with that issue. Their theology and previous religious practices had assumed the political-sociological situation of life in their own land under a theocratic king and worship centered on the temple in Jerusalem. After the Exile, that was no longer an option for the majority of Jewish people. Even the remnant who returned to Jerusalem continued to be ruled by Persia, then

---

15. Dietrich Bonhoeffer, *Memories and Perspectives*, videocassette produced by Trinity Films, 1983.

by the Hellenistic kings, and finally, after a brief but corrupt independence, by Rome. In such a situation, one way to relate faith to culture is to give up on faith, at least in its practical, outward expressions, especially where there is reason to fear a lurking anti-Semitism in the dominant culture.

The complete absence of religious language in the book of Esther at least raises the possibility that Esther and Mordecai had done just that, and possibly for good reason. When Haman does convince Xerxes to annihilate the Jewish nation, it is on the convenient excuse of political disloyalty, a form of treason, "There is a certain people . . . who do not obey the king's laws; it is not in the king's best interest to tolerate them" (3:8). However, the Jews of Persia as a whole must have retained enough of their outward, visible distinctives to allow Haman to identify them as a socioreligious group, whose customs were, in his opinion, "different from those of all other people" (3:8).

Esther and Mordecai apparently had chosen to adopt the dress, customs, and practices of their Gentile neighbors, at least to the extent that they could successfully conceal their identity as Jews. (Mordecai did become known to the royal officials at the king's gate as a Jew, but according to 3:4, it was only because he had told them so.) Esther's decision to risk her life by finally identifying with the covenant people of God is, therefore, all the more poignant. Before Mordecai's conflict with Haman and the threat of genocide, had Esther and Mordecai compromised, or even abandoned, faith in Yahweh? Possibly, but not necessarily. The Bible does not tell us.

At what point does the assimilation of culture compromise our Christian faith and witness? Most American Christians today are indistinguishable from their unbelieving neighbors in dress, housing, professional vocations, entertainment choices, and so forth. Does this mean we are compromising our faith? Possibly, but not necessarily. And if a Christian living in a hostile land conceals his or her faith in Christ to avoid the threat of death, is that person being unfaithful to the Lord or simply prudent? These types of decisions are ones over which equally committed Christians can, and often do, disagree. Yet we make such decisions every day because there is no way to avoid making them. We should each strive to live in obedience to our Lord, but it is not always clear what that means in the nitty-gritty details of daily life in the twentieth century. Moreover, regardless of our good intentions, none of us has pure motives all of the time. Even when we know the right decision, our hearts are not always committed to it.

This is where the silence about Esther and Mordecai's character and spiritual fidelity becomes a powerful encouragement. Regardless of whether they always knew what the right choice was or whether they had the best of motives, God was working through even their imperfect decisions and actions to fulfill his perfect purposes. Other than Jesus, even the godliest people of the Bible were flawed, often confused, and sometimes outright disobedient. We are no different from them. Yet our gracious God omnipotently works his perfect plan through them, through us, and most surprisingly, even through powerful political structures that sometimes operate in evil ways.

The author of Esther knows the end of his story when he begins to tell it. He knows that God did not come down *deus ex machina* to save his people from the crushing power of the Persian empire. Yet, God's people were saved. Even though the decision that decreed the destruction of God's people was made by a pagan king who mindlessly allowed himself to be manipulated by the ulterior motives of others, God did not directly intervene, as he had, for instance, when Pharaoh's army was drowned in the Red Sea at the Exodus. In fact, in the Esther story, the same abuse of power that led to the threatened destruction of God's people also led further on to their deliverance! The same events that led to destruction also opened the way for salvation. It has often been said that "God works in mysterious ways." The author of the book of Esther is beginning to show us just how mysterious those ways can be.

Esther 2:12–18

BEFORE A GIRL'S turn came to go in to King Xerxes, she had to complete twelve months of beauty treatments prescribed for the women, six months with oil of myrrh and six with perfumes and cosmetics. ¹³And this is how she would go to the king: Anything she wanted was given her to take with her from the harem to the king's palace. ¹⁴In the evening she would go there and in the morning return to another part of the harem to the care of Shaashgaz, the king's eunuch who was in charge of the concubines. She would not return to the king unless he was pleased with her and summoned her by name.

¹⁵When the turn came for Esther (the girl Mordecai had adopted, the daughter of his uncle Abihail) to go to the king, she asked for nothing other than what Hegai, the king's eunuch who was in charge of the harem, suggested. And Esther won the favor of everyone who saw her. ¹⁶She was taken to King Xerxes in the royal residence in the tenth month, the month of Tebeth, in the seventh year of his reign.

¹⁷Now the king was attracted to Esther more than to any of the other women, and she won his favor and approval more than any of the other virgins. So he set a royal crown on her head and made her queen instead of Vashti. ¹⁸And the king gave a great banquet, Esther's banquet, for all his nobles and officials. He proclaimed a holiday throughout the provinces and distributed gifts with royal liberality.

Original Meaning

XERXES SPARED NO expense to prepare his women for one night in his bed. For twelve months they were lotioned and perfumed. Spices and fragrant oils were a major export of Persia, India, and Arabia, used liberally by the wealthy and powerful throughout the ancient Near Eastern world.

The famous archaeologist W. F. Albright has argued that cube-shaped spice burners excavated at the ancient site of Lachish in Israel were not for burning incense in religious rituals, as originally thought, but were cosmetic burners used by women to perfume their skin and clothing with the scent of oil of roses, oil of cloves, and essence of musk (scents still popular among perfumers today).[1] Albright proposes that such cosmetic devices were used by women widely throughout the ancient world for both hygienic and therapeutic value. The fragrant oil would be placed in the cosmetic burner and heated in a fire. The woman would perfume her skin and clothing by crouching naked over the burner with her robe draped over her body like a tent. Albright cites this passage from Esther as a biblical example of this process. Aromatic oils and spices were Persia's major export, so such a use in the Persian court would be expected.

After twelve months of preparation, the woman was given "anything she wanted" to take with her to the king. The phrase is vague and its meaning uncertain. It may refer to jewelry and clothing, but also to aphrodisiac potions or other such items to enhance pleasure. Some interpreters suggest that each young woman was allowed to keep the jewelry and clothing she wore on that night as a "wedding" gift from the king. In a less kindly light, it could be construed as payment for services rendered. After spending one night in the king's bed, the woman was returned to the harem of concubines, where she would spend the rest of her life in luxurious but desolate seclusion. Her life had been preempted by the king's pleasure. She could not leave the harem to marry or return to her family. The woman would not even see the king again, unless he asked for her by name. Children conceived by the king in these unions were raised to serve their father in high positions, but they were not legitimate heirs to the throne.

After her twelve months of beauty treatments, Esther's turn with the king came. She "was taken" to Xerxes in the tenth month in the seventh year of his reign (December 479/January 478 B.C.), four years after Vashti had been deposed. The passive voice used here suggests

---

1. W. F. Albright, "The Lachish Cosmetic Burner and Esther 2:12," reprinted in *Studies in the Book of Esther*, ed. Carey A. Moore (New York: Ktav, 1982), 361–68.

not so much that she was unwilling to go to the king, but that in any case it was beyond her control. The text says nothing of how she felt about her situation.

Esther asked for nothing except what Hegai, the keeper of the harem, suggested she take with her. Perhaps she disdained her circumstances and was unwilling to use them for personal gain, or possibly she was simply indifferent to the outcome of the night. Levenson suggests that because Esther knew she had won Hegai's favor, she wisely trusted in his expert knowledge of the king's desires rather than in her own instincts. He infers from this that Esther was "wise and forbearing rather than inpulsive, prideful, and self-destructively independent."[2] Esther's deference contrasts with Vashti's defiance and implies a different outcome.

Given the sensual atmosphere created by the author's description of the period of preparation and the competition Esther faced, the reader can hardly avoid wondering just how she won Xerxes in just one night with him. Did God give her favor with Xerxes? The text does not explain it that way. However, it is certain that because this young Jewish virgin apparently did whatever it took to please a lascivious pagan king, she won the position of queen, through which she later saved the whole of her nation, the nation from which the Messiah later came.

THE AUTHOR USES sexual innuendo in this passage to weave a complex of events full of ambiguity and tension. Through circumstances beyond her control, Esther finds herself in the sensual luxury of the Persian harem. "What's a nice Jewish girl like you doing in a place like this, Esther?" She is being lavishly prepared for a sensual night with a Gentile to whom she is not married. Because of her success, the king "set a royal crown on her head and made her queen" (2:17). Carefully, the author avoids the word "marriage," although it is implied. Jewish Esther marries Gentile Xerxes just around the time when marriage with Gentiles was an issue among the Jews who had returned to Jerusalem and were concerned with reestablishing a right relationship with God. Ezra strongly condemns the Jews

---

2. Jon D. Levenson, *Esther: A Commentary*, 62.

who returned to the Promised Land for marrying Gentiles and insists on their divorce (cf. Ezra 9:12; 10:10ff.). Although the author does not tell us what Esther thought of her marriage to Xerxes, she apparently did not protest. Should she have (see comments on 2:1–11)?

Perhaps Esther hated her circumstances with all her heart. Perhaps she felt that life in the harem violated every conviction and moral principle Mordecai had instilled in her. Maybe she wondered how God could have let such a horrible thing happen to her. On the other hand, perhaps Esther loved life in the harem. Perhaps the sensuality of harem life appealed to a part of her nature. Perhaps she was swept off her feet by the attention of the most powerful man in the empire. Maybe she knew that her lifestyle violated the Torah, but didn't really care. Maybe she thought this was the best thing that ever happened to her. Would such an attitude have pleased God? Was Esther in God's will or out of it?

Interpreters who insist on taking an exemplary approach to this story must guess the answers to such questions. If we want to make Esther a role model of some sort, then we must be able to pass judgment on both her situation and her behavior in that situation. If we insist on judging Esther, then the rest of the Old Testament provides the only standard. At first blush, it would seem that to conceal her identity Esther must have violated at least the dietary and Sabbath laws. While this would be a reasonable inference, the text does not actually say that she either kept the law or violated it. Interpreters have found ways of exonerating Esther by proposing that she ate only vegetables and that she kept track of when to observe the Sabbath by the daily rotation of the seven maids who attended her. If the text explicitly said that Esther managed to keep the law while concealing her identify, these suggestions might provide a reasonable explanation as to how she did it. But the text's silence does not allow us to assume she did.

A more egregious violation of the Old Testament standard is her night in the bed of a pagan man to whom she is not married, and her subsequent marriage to this Gentile.[3] But even here Esther's culpabil-

---

3. For a discussion of Esther's moral culpability as understood by medieval Jewish interpreters see Barry Dov Walfish, *Esther in Medieval Garb* (Albany, N.Y.: SUNY Press, 1993), 122–26.

ity is ambiguous. Some medieval Jewish interpreters believed that Esther's night with the king was tantamount to forcible rape and that she could not have reasonably resisted. Others believe she should have resisted even if it cost her life. Clearly her situation was not a simple case of fornication and permits no simple judgment.

Esther's marriage to the Gentile king has been the most troublesome moral problem for Jewish interpreters because it so clearly violates the Torah's prohibition of intermarriage (e.g., Deut. 7:3). Furthermore, note the comments above about the issue of intermarriage between Jews and foreigners, which Ezra insisted be dissolved by divorce (Ezra 10). How would he have judged this Jewish queen?

Some interpreters exonerate Esther on this point, deeming her marriage to the king beyond her control and therefore not a true marriage. Moreover, after spending the night with him, some interpreters say that marrying him was the only virtuous thing to do (an argument that apparently would have been lost on Ezra). Esther's marriage to Xerxes was the lesser of two evils, and in spite of the sin involved, led to the greater good for God's people. This approach comes dangerously close to saying that the end justifies the means.

The only way we can use Esther as a positive example of a virtuous woman today is by assuming, as most interpreters have done through the centuries, that her life in the harem was not a violation of God's dietary and moral laws. Unfortunately, the text does not commend Esther's obedience to those laws. She does not rise to her high position by consistent obedience to the law of God, the way, for instance, Joseph did in Egypt when he refused the sexual advances of Potiphar's wife and spent harsh years in an Egyptian prison as a result.

The author's silence makes it virtually impossible to use Esther's behavior as a moral role model. How would you use this episode from Esther's life to teach virtue to your teenage daughter as she stands on the threshold of womanhood? What message would she get? Make yourself as attractive as possible to powerful men? Use your body to advance God's kingdom? The ends justifies the means? The exemplary approach fails here because the author does not intend to hold up Esther as a moral example to be followed. Esther may well have been a virtuous woman obedient to God's law, but even if she was, the author chooses to veil her virtue in a morally ambiguous and complex situation. He does not allow us to come to simple answers when we consider

Esther's life in light of Scripture. The author is skillfully describing a morally ambiguous and complex situation because that is the way real life often is in this fallen world.

IF WE CANNOT use an exemplary approach to understand and apply this episode from Esther's life, how *do* we understand its contemporary significance? Perhaps the reader is thinking, "Well, clearly Esther should have done this," or, "She should not have done that." Or perhaps because we know that in the end Queen Esther saved her people from destruction, we feel no need to reflect too hard on the moral and spiritual implications of the means to that end.

It is easy to look at other people's decisions and size them up, thinking that we know clearly what is right from what is wrong, and that if we were in their shoes, we would have both known and done the right thing. We believe God will give us the wisdom to know what to do and the moral strength to do it. It is easy to talk about ethical and moral issues in the abstract, because in any theoretical situation we can define the situation simply enough to make the choices clear.

But life isn't always that neat and tidy. There comes a day when we find ourselves in a situation where right and wrong are not so clearly defined and every choice we have seems to be a troubling mixture of good and bad. We pray, believing that God indeed will give us wisdom and the strength to do the "right" thing. We search the Bible with open hearts, looking for "God's will" in a situation that perhaps the Bible does not directly address. While we are doing this, the situation continues to develop and either by deliberate action or by default we have to make decisions, ready or not. And in those times of great struggle, the last thing we want is for others to make simplistic moral judgments about us. Has God failed to provide the guidance and wisdom we need? In life's most difficult and complex situations, it may sometimes feel that way.

This episode from Esther's life offers great encouragement and comfort when we find ourselves in situations where every choice is an odd mix of right and wrong. Only God knows the end of our story from its beginning. We are responsible to him for living faithfully in obedience to his word in every situation as we best know how. Even if we make the "wrong" decision, whether through innocent blunder or deliberate disobedience, our God is so gracious and omnipotent that he is able to use that weak link in a chain of events that will perfect his purposes in us and through us. Esther may have looked back on this episode of her life with shame and regret, or she may have looked back on it with a clear conscience, knowing that she acted as wisely as she knew how at the time. In either case, every one of us also has both kinds of episodes in our own lives. Esther's story shows that we can entrust them to the Lord and move on.

Esther 2:19–3:15

🌿

WHEN THE VIRGINS were assembled a second time, Mordecai was sitting at the king's gate. ²⁰But Esther had kept secret her family background and nationality just as Mordecai had told her to do, for she continued to follow Mordecai's instructions as she had done when he was bringing her up.

²¹During the time Mordecai was sitting at the king's gate, Bigthana and Teresh, two of the king's officers who guarded the doorway, became angry and conspired to assassinate King Xerxes. ²²But Mordecai found out about the plot and told Queen Esther, who in turn reported it to the king, giving credit to Mordecai. ²³And when the report was investigated and found to be true, the two officials were hanged on a gallows. All this was recorded in the book of the annals in the presence of the king.

³:¹After these events, King Xerxes honored Haman son of Hammedatha, the Agagite, elevating him and giving him a seat of honor higher than that of all the other nobles. ²All the royal officials at the king's gate knelt down and paid honor to Haman, for the king had commanded this concerning him. But Mordecai would not kneel down or pay him honor.

³Then the royal officials at the king's gate asked Mordecai, "Why do you disobey the king's command?" ⁴Day after day they spoke to him but he refused to comply. Therefore they told Haman about it to see whether Mordecai's behavior would be tolerated, for he had told them he was a Jew.

⁵When Haman saw that Mordecai would not kneel down or pay him honor, he was enraged. ⁶Yet having learned who Mordecai's people were, he scorned the idea of killing only Mordecai. Instead Haman looked for a way to destroy all Mordecai's people, the Jews, throughout the whole kingdom of Xerxes.

⁷In the twelfth year of King Xerxes, in the first month, the month of Nisan, they cast the pur (that is, the lot) in the presence of Haman to select a day and month. And the lot fell on the twelfth month, the month of Adar.

⁸Then Haman said to King Xerxes, "There is a certain people dispersed and scattered among the peoples in all the provinces of your kingdom whose customs are different from those of all other people and who do not obey the king's laws; it is not in the king's best interest to tolerate them. ⁹If it pleases the king, let a decree be issued to destroy them, and I will put ten thousand talents of silver into the royal treasury for the men who carry out this business."

¹⁰So the king took his signet ring from his finger and gave it to Haman son of Hammedatha, the Agagite, the enemy of the Jews. ¹¹"Keep the money," the king said to Haman, "and do with the people as you please."

¹²Then on the thirteenth day of the first month the royal secretaries were summoned. They wrote out in the script of each province and in the language of each people all Haman's orders to the king's satraps, the governors of the various provinces and the nobles of the various peoples. These were written in the name of King Xerxes himself and sealed with his own ring. ¹³Dispatches were sent by couriers to all the king's provinces with the order to destroy, kill and annihilate all the Jews—young and old, women and little children—on a single day, the thirteenth day of the twelfth month, the month of Adar, and to plunder their goods. ¹⁴A copy of the text of the edict was to be issued as law in every province and made known to the people of every nationality so they would be ready for that day.

¹⁵Spurred on by the king's command, the couriers went out, and the edict was issued in the citadel of Susa. The king and Haman sat down to drink, but the city of Susa was bewildered.

MORDECAI HAPPENED TO overhear a plot to assassinate Xerxes while he was "sitting at the gate." This phrase refers to holding an official position in the court. The gate entering into the walled palace complex was a large building in which legal, civil, and commercial business was transacted. If archaeological evidence from Susa has been correctly interpreted, the gate built by Xerxes' father and predecessor, Darius, measured 131 by 92 feet.[1] This gate was a large building consisting of a central hall that led into the royal compound and two rectangular side rooms.[2] The central hall was supported by four columns with trilingual inscriptions on the bases that read, "Xerxes the King says, 'By the grace of Ahuramazda, the Gate, Darius the King made it, he who was my father.'"[3] The excavation of this gate and the square in front of it correspond well to the details of the palace given by the author of Esther (cf. 4:6), indicating that the author was familiar with the palace complex at Susa.

Mordecai foiled the assassination plot by reporting it to Queen Esther, who in turn reported it to Xerxes, giving due credit to Mordecai. All of this was recorded in the annals of the king. Herodotus refers to an official list recorded in the Persian archives naming the king's "benefactors."[4] Acts of loyalty were usually rewarded immediately and generously by Persian kings, but Mordecai's reward was apparently overlooked. Although this attempt on Xerxes' life was foiled, Herodotus reports that a subsequent attempt succeeded when the king was assassinated in his bedroom in 465 B.C.

At this point, a new character is introduced into the story: Haman the Agagite. Xerxes had promoted Haman to a high position, though no explanation of why he deserved this honor is given. Given Mordecai's demonstrated loyalty to the king, promotion would have been an appropriate reward. The author places the promotion of Haman just where the original readers would have expected a report of Mordecai's reward as a benefactor of the king. Haman's introduction forms an unexpected twist when juxtaposed with Mordecai's unrewarded loyalty.

---

1. Edwin M. Yamauchi, *Persia and the Bible*, 299.

2. Prudence O. Harper et al., eds., *The Royal City of Susa: Ancient Near Eastern Treasures in the Louvre* (New York: Metropolitan Museum of Art, 1992), 216.

3. Yamauchi, *Persia and the Bible*, 300.

4. LCL: *Herodotus* 8.85.

A subtheme in this conflict between Mordecai and Haman is again that of respect commanded and respect refused. All the officials at the king's gate knelt and paid honor to Haman because the king had commanded it—all of them, that is, except Mordecai. Mordecai's refusal to give Haman the honor commanded by the king is left unexplained. Perhaps he resented Haman's promotion when he himself deserved, but had not received, a reward for his loyalty to the king. However, as much as five years may have passed (cf. 2:16 and 3:7), and if this was Mordecai's reason for not bowing to Haman, it apparently was not obvious to his colleagues. They asked him repeatedly to explain himself, but he refused. The text does not say he refused to pay homage because he was a Jew, although that is implied. His colleagues reported his behavior to Haman to see if Mordecai the Jew would be given an exception to the king's command (3:4). This suggests a lurking tension between the Jews and Gentiles of the court.

Interpreters throughout the ages have offered explanations for Mordecai's refusal. It is known from other sources that in general, Jews did bow to pagan officials of the Persian court. It was not a religious act but one of court protocol, much as moderns still curtsey or bow to the British queen. This suggests that Mordecai's refusal was not religiously motivated, but personal and specific to Haman. However, interpreters have been quick to exonerate Mordecai's behavior by ascribing a religious motivation. In the Greek version of the story, Mordecai explicitly says that it was not from hybris or arrogance that he refused to bow to Haman, but that he might not give the glory due to God to any man.[5] Some interpreters have suggested that Haman, being a pagan, wore an emblem of an idol on his garment to which Mordecai refused to pay homage.

In Hebrew narrative the characteristic described when a character is introduced is key to understanding his or her role in the story. When Mordecai is introduced in 2:5, he is identified not as a wise man or as an official in the court, but as a Jew of the tribe of Benjamin. When Haman is introduced, he is identified as an Agagite. The author implies that the perennial relationship of enmity between the Jews and the

---

5. A modern English translation of this ancient Greek version of Esther, including the six additional chapters, is found in the NRSV; see *The New Oxford Annotated Bible with the Apocrypha* (New York: Oxford Univ. Press, 1994), AP 41–56.

Agagites is mirrored in the personal relationship between Mordecai and Haman. The original readers would expect the relationship to be characterized by conflict and aggression.

Agag was the king of the Amalekites at the time Saul (also of the tribe of Benjamin) was the first king of Israel (1 Sam. 15). The Amalekites were a nomadic people of the southern desert region who frequently raided Israel from the beginning of its history. This heathen nation had the dubious distinction of being the first people of the world to attack and try to destroy God's newly formed covenant nation. Because of this, God promised Moses that he would completely erase the memory of the Amalekites from under heaven and would be at war with them from generation to generation (Ex. 17:8–16). In Deuteronomy 25:17–19, God commanded Israel, once they were settled in the land, to be agents of his promise and so war against the Amalekites as to blot out their memory forever.

In the years between Moses and King Saul, God gave Israel the land as promised. When Saul came to power, God instructed him through the prophet Samuel to "attack the Amalekites and totally destroy everything that belongs to them," and to "put to death men and women, children and infants, cattle and sheep, camels and donkeys" (1 Sam. 15:1–3). Saul did attack the Amalekites as commanded, but he took Agag their king alive and spared his life along with the best of the sheep and cattle, in disobedience to God's command.

Over the centuries after Saul spared Agag's life, other perennial enemies of Israel were called Agagites, even though they had no ethnic relationship to the Amalekites. In the first century of this era, for example, Jewish writers referred to the Romans as Agagites. In our own time, the Palestinians in Israel are sometimes referred to by that ancient appellation. The *New York Times* reported on a violent incident in Israel by saying that "a core of militant Jews has preached a doctrine of intolerance, often with the Arab as the biblical enemy Amalek."[6]

Rabbinic tradition held that Haman was in fact a descendant of Agag. However, as the use of the appellation illustrates, Haman need not have been genetically descended from the Amalekites to have earned the name *Agagite*. By using this term, the author is characterizing him as anti-Semitic, an enemy of the Jews. The original readers

---

6. "An Ideology Takes Up Arms Against Peace," *New York Times* (Feb 27, 1994), sec. 4, 1.

would have understood this one clue as introducing yet another episode of the age-old conflict between Israel and the powers that sought to destroy her. God's promise to protect Israel and to be at war with Amalek in every generation was given within the context of the Sinai covenant (Ex. 17:8–16). But would that promise still stand for the Jews living in exile precisely because they had violated that covenant? Could they expect God to be faithful to his covenant promises when they had failed to keep theirs? In other words, was the covenant between God and his people still in effect? This is the underlying question that would have generated plot tension in the minds of the original readers.

Haman's name sounds something like the Hebrew word for wrath (Heb., *ḥemah*), an apt description of his temperament and role in this story. Once he knew that Mordecai was a Jew, Haman's pride-driven wrath was turned against all the Jewish people in the empire. Since the text does not give any specific reason for this, the reader is left to infer anti-Semitism as first expressed in the ancient conflict between Israel and Amalek.

Esther had been queen for five years when Haman skillfully manipulates the king to gain support for his evil plan. He begins by bringing an accusation certain to arouse the king's attention—that there is "a certain people" who do not obey the king's laws. It may have been true that the Jews observed certain distinctive customs even in Persia, but in narrative fact it is only Mordecai who does not obey the king, and then only one specific command—to bow to Haman. Haman carefully avoids mentioning that these people are the Jews, and the king is apparently too apathetic to ask which people are so charged.

Haman then appeals to the king's need to replenish the treasury depleted by Xerxes' disastrous war with Greece. Herodotus reports that the annual revenue of the Persian empire under Xerxes' father, Darius, was 14,560 thousand talents.[7] This revenue was generated by receiving tribute (i.e., taxes) from the satrapies. Haman's offer to provide ten thousand talents of silver (about 300 tons) represents a substantial contribution to the royal coffers. Haman may have thrown out an exaggerated figure of ten thousand talents to sell his idea. Presumably, whatever revenue he promises will come by plundering the possessions of those killed (cf. 3:13).

---

7. LCL: *Herodotus* 3.95.

Haman, like others before him, informs the king what is in the king's own best interest. Xerxes, whose word is irrevocable law, was first advised by Memucan on how to deal with Vashti. Then his personal attendants suggested how a new queen should be chosen. In both previous cases, the machinery of the entire empire was put in motion by the advisors' manipulation of the king. In this scene also, the king blindly allows Haman to use the royal power to his own ends. The signet ring used to sign and seal official documents is given to Haman, vesting him with the full authority of the throne to do as he wishes. Whoever possessed the signet ring effectively held the king's authority (cf. 3:12).

To determine the propitious time for an attack on the Jews, Haman consults the *pur* (pl., *purim*) or lot. Archaeologists have unearthed samples of *purim*, which were clay cubes inscribed with either cuneiform characters or dots that look almost identical to modern dice.[8] "Casting the lot" literally meant throwing the dice. But unlike their modern use, the ancient lot was used not for gambling but for divination. It was a way of asking the gods for answers to questions about the future.

Purim is a Hebrew pluralized form of an Akkadian word used to refer to this cube-shaped object of divination. This word is found only in the book of Esther, and when the author first uses it (3:7), he also gives his readers the equivalent Hebrew word used to refer to the cube (*goral*), which the NIV translates as "lot." The *pur* or *goral* was used also by ancient Israel to query Yahweh. For instance, Joshua cast lots before the Lord to learn how to assign the land to the various tribes (Josh. 18:6).

Haman casts the lot in the first month, Nisan, the month the Jews celebrate Passover. It falls on the twelfth month, Adar. Haman will have to wait eleven months for the propitious day to attack the Jews, but immediately he sends out the decree sealing their fate. The edict of death is sent out on the thirteenth day of the first month, which ironically is the very eve of Passover (cf. Ex. 12:18; Lev. 23:5; Num. 28:16). The decree orders the citizens of Persia to take up arms against their Jewish neighbors, killing young and old, women and children, exactly eleven months later, on the thirteenth day of the twelfth month.

Passover commemorates the deliverance of Israel from Egypt, the event that constituted the founding of God's covenant people as a

---

8. For photographs of the lots used in the ancient Near East, see William W. Hallo, "The First Purim," *BA* 46/1 (1983): 19–29.

nation. It celebrates the existence of the Jews as a people and their special relationship to God. The joy of this holiday is turned to sorrow in Persia when the decree is delivered on Passover, calling for their annihilation simply because they are Jews. The coincidence of the decree with Passover is tragically ironic, but serves to heighten the glory of the subsequent deliverance and links it to the ancient covenant of Sinai.

When he was first introduced in 3:1, Haman is referred to as "son of Hammedatha, the Agagite." That appellation is repeated here, but with the additional phrase "the enemy of the Jews." In this chilling scene, all of the power of the Persian empire is about to come down on the Jewish people because of Haman's overweening pride.

GOD'S PROVIDENCE THROUGH life's injustices. Haman's prideful demand of Mordecai's respect and Mordecai's refusal to give it precipitate this threat of genocide. Notice that the king had to command his lower officials to pay honor and respect to Haman. This is another example of how the power of the empire was used to demand respect, just as Memucan's immoderate need for honor and respect motivated the king's decree in chapter 1 that wives everywhere respect their husbands.

In chapter 1, Memucan's similar fear of losing respect drove him to escalate an incident between Xerxes and Vashti to empire-wide proportions through the issuing of a royal decree. The disobedience of one woman, Vashti, had reverberations for all the women of the empire. A similar pattern is seen in this episode, where an incident involving two individual people escalates to empire-wide proportions. The disobedience of one Jew, Mordecai, brings an edict against all the Jews of the empire. A subtheme of the Esther story is that when such maniacal need for honor and respect is coupled with absolute power, the result is oppression and injustice.

"You are always righteous, O LORD, when I bring a case before you. Yet I would speak with you about your justice: Why does the way of the wicked prosper? Why do all the faithless live at ease?" (Jer. 12:1). This question no doubt crossed Mordecai's mind when Haman the Agagite was promoted to live in the power and wealth of being second only to the king himself. Readers familiar with the custom that Persian kings liberally rewarded their benefactors would have noticed at the end of chapter 2 that Mordecai's unrewarded good deed, which saved Xerxes' life, was an injustice. The circumstances of Mordecai the Jew, one of God's people, and Haman the Agagite, an enemy of God, surely gives rise to the question so eloquently expressed in Jeremiah 12:1.

Esther became queen in the seventh year of Xerxes' reign (2:16–17), and Haman conspires against the Jews in the twelfth year (3:7). Sometime within this five-year period, Mordecai foiled the assassination plot and Haman rose to power. While Mordecai went unrewarded for quite some time, the man who would eventually attempt to eliminate the Jews was rising to a position in the court where he had the power to actually make good on such a threat. But had Mordecai been rewarded immediately as was custom, there would have been no opportunity for the deferred reward to become a crucial link in the deliverance of the Jews from the threat of genocide.

Haman has risen to his position of power, but both Esther and Mordecai are also now in position to be agents of the later deliverance of their people. But of course, they cannot see what is ahead. Both Esther and Mordecai have come to this place through the injustice and wickedness of others. Yet even so, they both had made decisions to live as they did in the Persian court. These unfolding events begin to show the inscrutable interplay between circumstances thrust upon us, sometimes unjustly, and those the result of our own behavior, often flawed. God's providence marvelously moves through both in his own good time.

The lot. Haman's casting of the *pur* or *goral* introduces the element of destiny into the story. The word *goral* was used not only as a noun to refer to the cubes thrown in divination, but also to the destiny or choice that they indicated. In Psalm 16:5–6 David praises the Lord because "you have assigned me my portion and my cup; you have made my lot [*goral*] secure. The boundary lines have fallen for me in pleasant places; surely I have a delightful inheritance." Using a literary allusion to Joshua's division of the Promised Land by casting lots, David, now king of that land, reflects on the security found in the Lord alone. It is the Lord who has secured David's destiny.

In Proverbs 16:33 the *goral* (lot) is mentioned again: "The lot is cast into the lap, but its every decision is from the LORD." Haman cast the lot to secure a date for the successful annihilation of the Jews, but it was Yahweh, the God of the Jews, who determined how it fell. Even the date of the planned annihilation of God's people was determined neither by Haman's gods nor by chance; it was determined by Yahweh, according to the ancient covenant he had made with Israel when he brought them out of Egypt. At the Exodus, commemorated by the Passover, God saved his people from destruction by the Amalekites and promised to do so from generation to generation (Ex. 17:8–15).

To the Jewish reader, Haman's casting of the *pur* and the resulting edict of death on Passover eve would be profoundly ironic, suggesting the critical question: "Would God still deliver his people, now in exile in Persia, even though they had violated the very covenant in which he promised protection?" In other words, the knowledgeable reader would be asking whether the covenant with Yahweh, celebrated by Passover, was still in effect for the Jews of Persia. Because the remnant of Jews who had returned to Jerusalem to rebuild the city and the temple were nevertheless still under Persian rule, their fate, too, was being cast in faraway Susa.

Threats against God's people. History has shown that there is a force at work in the world bent on destroying God's people and thwarting God's promises. It can unleash the power of the world's greatest and mightiest nations by using the depraved nature of those entrusted with that power. This episode from Esther shows that the security of God's people is fragile as they live under worldly rulers. Because of an interpersonal conflict between two individuals, the existence of the whole nation of God's people is jeopardized. The world is shown to be a dangerous place, a place where "it is not in the king's best interest" to tolerate the people of God.

A situation similar to this story from Susa occurred in the life of the early church when first-century Christians felt the full force of Roman might. The Roman emperors demanded "respect" by issuing a decree that an offering of incense must be burnt in their honor. All good citizens of the empire would in this way express their appreciation for the benefits and well-being the Roman emperor provided. When Christians saw that demand to be in conflict with their allegiance to Jesus Christ and refused to pay such honor, the charge brought against them was treason, a political crime punishable by death. It was not in the emperor's best interest to let such "traitors" live, though their only offense was a refusal to offer the "respect" demanded.

The New Testament book of Revelation portrays the worldly power of the Roman empire as an ugly beast who demanded "worship" and who received his authority from the dragon. "The beast was given a mouth to utter proud words and . . . to make war against the saints and to conquer them. And he was given authority over *every tribe, people, language and nation*" (Rev. 13:5, 7, emphasis added). Everyone whose name was not written in the book of life, those who did not belong to the Lamb, bowed down and worshiped the beast. Those who refused to bow put their lives in jeopardy.

Satan, the dragon, drives the beast of world empires to demand "respect" and to destroy those who refuse it. When he was in the desert, Jesus himself endured Satan's demand to be worshiped. In Luke 4:5–8, Satan displayed "all the kingdoms of the world" and said to Jesus, "I will give you all their authority and splendor, for it has been given to me, and I can give it to anyone I want to. So if you worship me, it will all be yours." Jesus answered, "It is written: 'Worship the Lord your God and serve him only.'" Jesus refused to bow down to Satan, and consequently, the worldly powers of the Jewish aristocracy consorting with the Roman regime were eventually turned against him at his crucifixion.

An assault on God's covenant people at any time in human history is really an attack on the authority, power, and character of God himself. Although neither God nor Satan is mentioned in the book of Esther, there is a force at work directing the mighty power of Persia against God's people. It is a force that demands to be "respected" and "honored," a force that is willing to destroy those who refuse. However, an even greater power is concurrently at work protecting, preserving, and saving the Jews from destruction. Both the power that would destroy and the greater power that would deliver from destruction are veiled in the actions of Haman and Xerxes, of Mordecai and Esther.

Satan's rebellion against God and his people is played out in the lives of people whose individual decisions have far-reaching consequences. Although Mordecai did not refuse to pay homage to Haman for explicitly religious reasons, in the Esther story, he (and Vashti?) stands on the side of those who refuse to bow to the beast and who, as a result, suffer the crushing force of earthly powers driven by Satan.

GOD'S MYSTERIOUS WORKING. Most of us like to think that through thoughtful planning and wise living we can successfully direct the course of our lives. While much of the time life might cooperate with our plans, all of us can probably look back and see how circumstances beyond our control have redirected our lives, whether for good or for sorrow. Our sense of ultimately being in control is at times revealed by life's circumstances to be an illusion.

Whether we like it or not, we often feel caught in circumstances beyond our control. Life is full of seemingly insignificant events that in retrospect we recognize as changing the course of our lives. Every new day brings circumstances and decisions, and we cannot know how one event will lead to another. Only God knows the end of a matter before it has even begun. The author of Esther is demonstrating the workings of divine providence. God works mysteriously, patiently, and inexorably through a series of "coincidental" events and human decisions, even those based on questionable motives and evil intents. All of the "chance" events in life are really working toward the end that God has ordained.

Esther suffered the humiliation of being taken into the king's court to be sexually used. Apparently no one considered what plans she might have had for her life, plans perhaps to be a godly wife with a home and family.[9] Her plans for her life were forever changed when the king's men seized her from her home. Mordecai suffered the humiliation of being deprived of his rightful reward after putting himself at risk to save the king's life when he reported the treacherous eunuchs. To add insult to injury, Haman was all the while gaining the power that would eventually be turned against Mordecai and his people. There is the sad irony that when the wicked do prosper, God's people are often overlooked and unrewarded.

It is frustrating when our best plans are overturned and our good deeds and hard work go unnoticed and unrewarded. Most bitterly, we often see others prosper who are less deserving, at least in our own opinion. Such injustice hurts, but the example of Esther and Mordecai give us reason to bear such situations with patience and grace. Mordecai's forbearance when he did not receive the expected reward allowed that

---

9. One way to take the wording of the Greek version suggests that Mordecai was raising Esther to one day be his own wife.

injustice to lead to greater good when it was finally put right. God is invisibly at work, making even life's greatest disappointments a link in a chain of good things yet to come. We cannot see the end of things from the middle and must walk by faith, not by sight. The Lord will bring a greater good, his perfect plan, out of all the frustration we feel and out of all the evil we experience. When all is said and done, God uses even injustice to fulfill his promises to us. As Joseph explained to his brothers, "You intended to harm me, but God intended it for good" (Gen. 50:20).

Paradoxically, Satan channeled wrath against Jesus through human agents who nailed him to the cross, but it was simultaneously God's work of atonement. The apostle Peter preached that the human agents involved in that action were ignorant of their role and were acting from their own instincts and interests (Acts 3:17). Nevertheless, "this is how God fulfilled what he had foretold through all the prophets" (Acts 3:18). When Peter and John were released after being arrested in Jerusalem, they led the church in a prayer that indicted all the worldly powers for the death of Jesus (Acts 4:27–29):

> Indeed Herod and Pontius Pilate met together with the Gentiles and the people of Israel in this city to conspire against your holy servant Jesus, whom you anointed. *They did what your power and will had decided beforehand should happen.* Now, Lord, consider their threats and enable your servants to speak your word with great boldness. (emphasis added)

It was not in spite of the greatest injustice and most concerted evil against Jesus that God achieved his work of atonement, but through those very acts of injustice and evil. What mind-boggling mystery!

God's absolute sovereignty is displayed magnificently in the great paradox that even Satan's wrath and retribution working through worldly powers is nevertheless constrained by God's eternal decrees. God works concurrently through the very forces that Satan means for evil to bring about his perfect good. It was with this confidence that the early church prayed for boldness to preach the gospel while facing life-threatening opposition. With this same confidence, Christians today can face the powers of evil arrayed against them.

Encouragement for persecuted Christians. The book of Revelation was written to encourage Christians who, like the Jews of Susa, found their existence threatened when the government under which they lived turned beastly. American Christians probably cannot fully appreciate this situation, for there has never been a time in our nation's history when the government has issued a decree outlawing the church or demanding a "respect" that compromises allegiance to Christ. Unfortunately, this has not been the experience of Christians in other parts of the world. One source reports that in this century alone, an average of 300,000 Christians have been martyred each year.[10]

Because Christians (and Jews) throughout history have typically been executed on the charges of political treason rather than for religious piety, it is sometimes debated whether such numbers include Christians killed for reasons other than faith. Regardless of the precise number of those martyred, the church around the world still suffers in many ways at the hands of governments who are ideologically antithetical to the fundamental principles of Christianity. The prayer of the earliest Christians, "Now, Lord, consider their threats and enable your servants to speak your word with great boldness," must still be the prayer of the church today, offered up with a confidence in God's powerful providence.[11]

The book of Revelation shows that despite the terrible power world empires now hold, the true King of kings will have the victory over these ungodly empires of the world. Christians are to live faithfully for that day, even under the shadow of persecution and death. After describing the beast and his satanic power, John acknowledges that, like their Lord, Christians will suffer and die when the government turns against them, just as the Roman empire did. However, because Jesus arose never to die again, we are safe in Christ even when the beast threatens to devour us. "He who has an ear, let him hear. If anyone is to go into captivity, into captivity he will go. If anyone is to be killed with sword, with the sword he will be killed. This calls for patient endurance and faithfulness on the part of the saints" (Rev. 13:9–10).

God intends to save and protect his people in Christ (e.g., Rom. 8:28) and ultimately to destroy those who wickedly remain opposed to Christ. There is no power, no enemy, that can thwart God's electing purpose. We, too, like David in Psalm 16, can praise God because he has made our lot secure in Christ.

---

10. *World Christian Encyclopedia*, ed. David Barrett (New York: Oxford Univ. Press, 1982), quoted by Timothy K. Jones in "Dying for Jesus," *CT* (March 19, 1990), 12.

11. See the "Theological Postscript" at the end of this commentary for a brief discussion of the significance of prayer in relation to divine providence.

Esther 4:1-17

WHEN MORDECAI LEARNED of all that had been done, he tore his clothes, put on sackcloth and ashes, and went out into the city, wailing loudly and bitterly. ²But he went only as far as the king's gate, because no one clothed in sackcloth was allowed to enter it. ³In every province to which the edict and order of the king came, there was great mourning among the Jews, with fasting, weeping and wailing. Many lay in sackcloth and ashes.

⁴When Esther's maids and eunuchs came and told her about Mordecai, she was in great distress. She sent clothes for him to put on instead of his sackcloth, but he would not accept them. ⁵Then Esther summoned Hathach, one of the king's eunuchs assigned to attend her, and ordered him to find out what was troubling Mordecai and why.

⁶So Hathach went out to Mordecai in the open square of the city in front of the king's gate. ⁷Mordecai told him everything that had happened to him, including the exact amount of money Haman had promised to pay into the royal treasury for the destruction of the Jews. ⁸He also gave him a copy of the text of the edict for their annihilation, which had been published in Susa, to show to Esther and explain it to her, and he told him to urge her to go into the king's presence to beg for mercy and plead with him for her people.

⁹Hathach went back and reported to Esther what Mordecai had said. ¹⁰Then she instructed him to say to Mordecai, ¹¹"All the king's officials and the people of the royal provinces know that for any man or woman who approaches the king in the inner court without being summoned the king has but one law: that he be put to death. The only exception to this is for the king to extend the gold scepter to him and spare his life. But

thirty days have passed since I was called to go to the king."

¹²When Esther's words were reported to Mordecai, ¹³he sent back this answer: "Do not think that because you are in the king's house you alone of all the Jews will escape. ¹⁴For if you remain silent at this time, relief and deliverance for the Jews will arise from another place, but you and your father's family will perish. And who knows but that you have come to royal position for such a time as this?"

¹⁵Then Esther sent this reply to Mordecai: ¹⁶"Go, gather together all the Jews who are in Susa, and fast for me. Do not eat or drink for three days, night or day. I and my maids will fast as you do. When this is done, I will go to the king, even though it is against the law. And if I perish, I perish." ¹⁷So Mordecai went away and carried out all of Esther's instructions.

MORDECAI REACTS WITH great emotion when he hears that the personal conflict between himself and Haman has brought the entire Jewish nation into jeopardy. Haman's plan to annihilate all the Jewish people is way out of proportion to Mordecai's offense. Apparently Mordecai's behavior had merely given Haman the excuse to put his power behind his anti-Semitism. Whether or not Haman was a genetic descendent of the Amalekites, he is displaying the same contempt for God's people that Moses and the Israelites experienced on their way to the Promised Land (Ex. 17:8–16; see comments on Est. 2:19–3:15).

Upon hearing of the king's decree, Mordecai tears his clothes and puts on sackcloth and ashes in an act of deep mourning and distress. This gesture was common throughout the biblical period. Joshua and Caleb tore their clothes when they heard the people wanted to return to Egypt rather than to enter the land God had promised to give them (Num. 14:6). David ripped his clothing on several occasions, for instance, after hearing of the deaths of Saul (2 Sam. 1:11), Abner (3:31), and Amnon (13:31). Eliakim and Shebna tore their clothing when Jerusalem was threatened by the Assyrians (Isa. 36:22). Ezra used this same gesture to express his distress that God's people, including the priests and Levites, had intermarried with pagan Gentiles (Ezra 9:3). The Persians in Susa would have recognized the significance of Mordecai's behavior, for they, too, tore their clothes in grief when they were defeated by the Greeks in battle at Salamis.[1]

Although apparently separated from direct contact with Mordecai during the first five years of her marriage to Xerxes, Esther remains concerned for him. His distress distresses her, and she sends clothing to him to replace his sackcloth. However, it is only when he refuses to accept her gift that she attempts to find out what is actually troubling her cousin.

When Esther's attending eunuch, Hathach, however, brings Mordecai's entreaty that she go to the king to plead for "her" people, she begs off, explaining that she no longer routinely sees the king. Moreover, as Mordecai well knows, she cannot go to the king uninvited without risking her life, for unless Xerxes extends his golden scepter, her life will be taken on the spot. Surely Mordecai does not mean to suggest she jeopardize herself like that!

Herodotus attests that the Persian kings enforced a law first instituted by Deioces the Mede forbidding anyone to approach the king without a summons.[2] The correct protocol was to request an audience with the king through his messenger-eunuchs and await an invitation for an audience. There were only seven men in the court known as the king's "Friends," who were permitted "to see the face of the king." Herodotus explains that only they could enter the king's presence unannounced, except when he was sleeping with a woman.

Haman had access to the king, but Esther did not. Apparently she does not expect to see the king anytime soon, since he has not summoned her for thirty days. She chooses not to request an audience, perhaps expecting to be ignored. Apparently five years into her marriage, the king's desire for her has cooled. Or given her mission, perhaps she does not wish to arouse the suspicions of the court by requesting an audience. Whatever her fears, it seems likely that the ruthless King Xerxes will not extend the golden scepter if the queen's death would be somehow expedient to his other interests.

---

1. LCL: *Herodotus* 8.99.
2. Ibid., 1.99; 3.77, 84.

Mordecai replies to Esther, "If you remain silent at this time, relief and deliverance for the Jews will arise from another place ... and who knows but that you have come to royal position for such a time as this?" Mordecai pointedly remarks that even if the queen should decide to continue to hide her Jewish identity, as he himself had previously advised, she will face certain death, but the Jews will be helped "from another place." Some commentators have seen in this phrase an allusion to God's intervention, should human agency fail. The reason the phrase "from another place" can be construed as a veiled reference to God is because in rabbinical Hebrew God is sometimes referred to as "the Place" (see *Genesis Rabba* [§68], where God is referred to as "the Place" in which all creation exists). This rabbinical idiom, however, dates from a later age; in any case, Mordecai does not say that help for the Jews will arise from "the Place," but simply from "another place." Mordecai is expressing his confidence that the Jews will not face annihilation, but will be helped through some other human agent.

Modern interpreters are not the only ones to see in this phrase a possible allusion to God. One of the two ancient Greek translations of Esther rephrases Mordecai's statement this way: "If you neglect to help your people, then God will be their help and salvation, but you and your father's house will perish."[3] However, this does not necessarily mean that "from another place" was understood by the Greek translator as a reference to God. God is referred to many places throughout the Greek versions of Esther where he is not in the Hebrew text (from which the NIV was translated). The reading in the Greek may simply be one of the many places where a reference to God is added independently from how the Hebrew read.

If "from another place" is a euphemism for God, Mordecai's statement means that if Esther fails to act, God himself will intervene. This understanding is problematic, for it is not a choice between Esther's delivering the Jews or God's delivering them. Rather, it is a question of what human agency God will use to deliver the Jews since they

---

3. This reading is found in 4:9 of a Greek version of Esther known as the Alpha-text; the LXX of Esther, also a Greek version, follows the Hebrew and therefore reads as the NIV. An English translation of the Greek Alpha-text of Esther may be found as an appendix in David J. A. Clines, *The Esther Scroll: The Story of the Story* (Sheffield: JSOT Press, 1984).

have no king. Mordecai's point is that the Jews will be delivered some-how, but that Esther's doom is certain if she fails to act.

In Mordecai's thinking, Esther's life *may be* in jeopardy if she goes to the king uninvited, but her doom *is certain* if she does not. Mordecai's remark is unsettling. If Esther fails to act as he is suggesting, is he threatening to reveal her identity as a Jew, thus bringing her under Haman's decree? Or is he invoking divine judgment on her for her apparent apathy toward her people? Esther probably wondered the same thing.

Ronald Pierce sees Mordecai as actually threatening Esther's life in this passage. He points out that Mordecai is certain that if Esther refuses, help will arise from another place, and the Jews will be deliv-ered; but even so, Esther will die.[4] Pierce interprets this to mean that Mordecai is prepared to take things into his own hands and kill Esther if she betrays her people in this dire hour. Therefore, he sees no reason to applaud Esther's bravery for going to the king because she has at least a chance of surviving an uninvited audience with her husband, while apparently no chance of surviving Mordecai's threat if she refuses. The author leaves the reader with tantalizing ambiguity.

Mordecai's words also suggest that there is a purpose in all that has happened that exceeds Esther's own interests. He asks, ". . . and who knows but that you have come to royal position for such a time as this?" Mordecai points out that all of the previous circumstances of Esther's life that led her to the Persian throne may have been just for this moment when she can intercede for her people.

It is only after hearing this remark containing both a veiled threat and a suggestion of a greater purpose that Esther decides to act as Mordecai wishes. Perhaps she believes Mordecai's veiled threat and thinks it safer to take her chances with Xerxes. Or perhaps she glimpses a greater vision of the purpose for her life, regardless of the outcome ("If I perish, I perish"). The author does not let us in on Esther's thoughts. In either case, this is the last time in the story that Morde-cai commands Esther. After deciding to go to the king, she gives Mordecai a command, which he "went away and carried out." Esther commands Mordecai to call the Jews of Susa to a fast.

---

4. Ronald W. Pierce, "The Politics of Esther and Mordecai," *BBR* 2 (1992): 87.

THE BOOK OF **Esther and the prophet Joel.**
Biblical authors often use phrases from the
other biblical books known to them, which
would presumably also be known to the orig-
inal readers. For instance, in addition to quoting full sentences from the
Old Testament, the New Testament writers copiously use brief phrases
from the Old Testament that would have been familiar to their readers. Richard Hays has pointed out how these "echoes" of the Old Testament can inform our interpretation:

> When a literary echo links the text in which it occurs to an ear-
> lier text, the figurative effect of the echo can lie in the unstated
> or suppressed (transumed) points of resonance between the two
> texts.... Allusive echo functions to suggest to the reader that text
> B should be understood in light of a broad interplay with text A,
> encompassing aspects of A beyond those explicitly echoed....
> Metalepsis ... places the reader within a field of whispered or
> unstated correspondences.[5]

The Hebrew phrase translated in the NIV of Esther 4:3 as "with fasting, weeping and wailing" occurs in both 4:3 and in Joel 2:12.[6] (Of
course, the individual words of this phrase occur many other times in
the Old Testament.) This phrase forms an intertextual link between
Esther and Joel. The author of Esther, in other words, tells this episode
of the story using an allusive echo of Joel 2. Metalepsis thus places the
readers of Esther 4 within "a field of whispered or unstated corre-
spondences" between the events of this chapter and the words of the
prophet in Joel 2. If this echo is intentional, the author of Esther
assumes his readers are familiar enough with Joel's words to recognize
them and invites his readers to interpret Esther 4 in light of its broad
interplay with Joel 2.[7]

---

5. Richard B. Hays, *Echoes of Scripture in the Letters of Paul* (New Haven: Yale Univ. Press,
1989), 20.

6. However, in Joel 2:12 the NIV translates this phrase "with fasting and weeping and
mourning." It may have been true that the original readers of the Esther story would have
recognized this Hebrew phrase as alluding to Joel's prophecy, but most modern readers will
not make the connection.

7. Because metalepsis is a literary phenonmenon, the allusive echoes of Joel 2 in Esther
would be further evidence for dating the book of Joel. Some scholars date Joel as early as
the ninth century B.C.; others not until the postexilic period, when Esther itself was being

In the threat of impending judgment, the Lord commands his people through the prophet Joel (see Joel 2:12–14):

> "Even now," declares the LORD,
>> "return to me with all your heart,
>> with *fasting and weeping and mourning*."
> Rend your heart
>> and not your garments.
> Return to the LORD your God,
>> for he is gracious and compassionate,
> slow to anger and abounding in love,
>> and he relents from sending calamity.
> *Who knows?* He may turn and have pity
>> and leave behind a blessing. . . . (emphasis added)

Since the same Hebrew phrase found in the Lord's exhortation through the prophet Joel occurs in Esther 4:3 to describe the response of Mordecai and the Jews to the edict of death, the author, without explicitly mentioning divine judgment, casts Haman's pogrom as an occasion for the Jewish people, in exile for their sin, to turn to their Lord, who may relent from sending this calamity on them. The very next statement Joel makes, "Rend your heart and not your garments," resonates with Mordecai's reaction to Haman's edict. The invitation in Joel 2 to turn to the Lord in repentance is invoked by the allusive echo in Esther. The author of Esther portrays the Jews' response of "fasting, weeping and wailing" in the face of this calamity as the repentance called for by Joel.

Prayer is usually assumed to accompany fasting in biblical idiom. Some commentators infer that the Jewish people naturally prayed for deliverance as they fasted, especially since Esther requests a fast "for me" (v. 16), presumably a request for intercessory prayer.[8] Ronald Pierce takes the opposite view, that while readers would expect prayer to be mentioned in the same breath as fasting, its conspicuous absence is a

---

written. At first glance, metalepsis of Joel in Esther may be taken to support the earlier dating of Joel. However, the book of Esther was written after the reign of Xerxes, so even given a late date, Joel could be postexilic and still precede the book of Esther. Furthermore, if Joel was a postexilic prophet, his words may have been well known among the Jewish people even before the book of Joel was inscripturated. Therefore, while possibly supporting an early date for Joel, metalepsis in Esther does not demand it.

8. The Greek translators of the LXX, and modern interpreters such as Joyce Baldwin, Fredric Bush, Carey A. Moore, and Lewis B. Paton, hold this view.

further indication of the prayerlessness of secularization.[9] Notice, however, that prayer is also not explicitly mentioned in the call to repentance in Joel 2.

If the people fast, weep, and mourn, Joel says, "Who knows? He [the LORD God] may turn and have pity." Thus Mordecai's statement, "and who knows but that you have come to royal position for such a time as this?" again echoes Joel's, suggesting that Esther's royal position is the means by which the Lord God might "turn and have pity" on his people, "relenting from sending calamity."

The prophecy of Joel continues (Joel 2:15−16a):

Blow the trumpet in Zion,
> declare a holy fast,
> call a sacred assembly.
Gather the people,
> consecrate the assembly. . . .

Whether Esther was mindful of Joel's prophecy or not, she in effect "blows the trumpet in Zion," commanding Mordecai to call a fast for all the Jews of Susa, to see if the Lord may relent from sending this calamity on her people. For the first time in this story Esther identifies herself with God's people and responds to the prophetic call to repentance by joining with the Jews of Susa in this fast.

Identity crisis for Esther. When the situation had come to a crisis, Esther was brought to a defining moment in her life by circumstances over which she had no control. Mordecai said to Esther, "If you remain silent at this time, relief and deliverance for the Jews will arise from another place ... and who knows but that you have come to royal position for such a time as this?" It was for "such a time as this" that she was forced to choose between identifying herself with God's covenant people or continuing to live as a pagan in the king's court. Apparently no one in the court, including her own husband, knew that she was a Jew. To save her people would mean revealing her own identity as well. She would be admitting that she had not been living as a devout Jew should live. Furthermore, she would be identifying herself as a target of destruction under Haman's decree and an easy mark in the treacherous Persian court.

---

9. R. Pierce, "The Politics of Esther and Mordecai," 88.

In this moment, Esther has to decide who she really is. As L. Ryken points out, Esther is the only person in the story with two names—her Hebrew name, Hadassah, and her Persian name, Esther. He reads this as an indication of the identity crisis with which she is faced when, after being raised as a Jew, she is thrust into the king's court where she must live as a pagan.[10] Her Jewish character led her to obey Mordecai, which meant, paradoxically, that she must deny that character and live as a pagan. She found favor in the court of King Xerxes, enabling her to become an agent through whom God would fulfill his ancient promise to her people, whether she was aware of it or not. Nevertheless, she had to overcome herself in order to do what God had created her and positioned her to do.

Up to this point in the story, while Esther was pretending to be a pagan, she was controlled by her circumstances. She has been passive in the story, not initiating action, but following along the path of least resistance. Then comes that defining moment when she is faced with taking responsibility for the life God has given her by identifying herself with the people of God. According to Ryken, it is through this traumatic ordeal that Esther, "initially a beautiful young woman with a weak character, becomes transformed into a person with heroic moral stature and political skill."[11]

If Esther decides to remain silent and to continue to live as a pagan, God will use some other means to fulfill his covenant promises. Deliverance will arise from another place. Yet God has placed Esther in that era of history, in that city of Persia, and even in that bedroom of Xerxes, so that when the moment comes, he can fulfill the ancient promise through her. In this scene the interaction of human responsibility with divine sovereignty is eloquently pictured. Esther comes to this defining moment through her past decisions, whether they are right or wrong. The decision she now faces will irrevocably define her future and determine the destiny of her people as well. Her predecessor, Vashti, was deposed for taking her own initiative. If the king's ardor has cooled toward Esther, given the intrigues of royal polygamy, perhaps Xerxes will find it expedient to allow Esther to die one way or another. She has good reason to be afraid of the consequences of her decision.

---

10. Leland Ryken, *Words of Delight: A Literary Introduction to the Bible*, 116–20.
11. Ibid., 119.

While her people fast with her, Esther overcomes herself and finds the courage to reveal her identity as a Jew before Xerxes regardless of the consequences. Whether or not she is mindful of the covenant and its promises, her decision to identify with God's people is a decision to risk being an agent through whom God can fulfill those promises.

Who is the main character in the story? This development in Esther's character suggests that the author understands her to be the main character of the story. The question of whether Mordecai or Esther is the main character has been debated. An informal poll I took of about fifteen seminary students reading the book in Hebrew showed that about half thought Mordecai was the main character and half, Esther.

Scholars, too, have debated this question. A literary analysis of characterization in the book suggests that the three couples, Vashti and Xerxes, Zeresh and Haman, and Esther and Mordecai, function as literary foils, that is, pairs that are intended to be compared and contrasted.[12] As a literary character, Esther's development is complex and progressive throughout the story in contrast to Mordecai, who shows no character development through his rise to power. This suggests that in the author's mind, Esther is the main character on whom he expects his readers to focus.

Esther's decision to go to the king begins a role reversal with Mordecai. Although he continues to play a prominent role in the story, it is only because Esther facilitates his involvement. It is Esther, not Mordecai, who plans the strategy to unmask Haman and prevent the genocide, and it is Esther, not Mordecai, who finally has to courageously face the king. Furthermore, although it is not known that the author of the book assigned its name, the book is, after all, called "Esther," not "Mordecai." Someone must therefore have considered Esther to be the main character. Given that Esther is the main character of the story, the author invites his readers to reflect on her character development, comparing it perhaps with our own.

After her decision to identify herself with God's people, Esther becomes the active agent, commanding Mordecai, planning a strategy to save her people, and even confronting Haman to his face. Her

---

12. Wilma McClarty, "Esther," in *A Complete Literary Guide to the Bible*, Leland Ryken and Tremper Longman III, eds., 216–29.

decision energizes her, gives her purpose, and emboldens her to face a threatening and uncertain future. There is first a great reversal in Esther's own life, through which consequently comes the great reversal of the destiny for her people. The defining moment in her own life is at the same time a crucial moment through which God will sovereignly fulfill his promise to his people in Persia. This is where wisdom and encouragement for Christian living is found in the example of Esther's life.

The Bible from Genesis to Revelation is the story of God's reconciling fallen humanity to himself in Jesus Christ. Other than Jesus himself, the people in the biblical stories are no paragons of virtue. Each of them has serious character flaws and questionable motives. Because of this, we must be cautious and discerning before imitating the specific behaviors of any biblical person, particularly those of the Old Testament. As Christians our exemplary role model is Jesus, and the basis for ethical living the fruit of the indwelling Holy Spirit (Gal. 5).

Each of the biblical characters is shown in relationship to God and his people. Some end up rejecting God and opposing his work. Those who are reconciled to God become testimonies of God's redemptive work in history, and to that extent are examples to be followed. The author of the Esther story does not hold up Esther or Mordecai as exemplary role models in their specific behaviors. But his story does show that there are two opposing sides represented by God's people, albeit scattered in exile, and the rest of humanity, who by opposing God's people end up opposing God himself.

Esther seems caught between the Gentile world of the pagan court and the Jewish world in which she was raised. By showing all the good that came from her decision to identify with God's covenant people, the biblical author implicitly invites his readers to consider where they are in relationship to God. Thus, as readers today we can gain insight and wisdom in the example of Esther as she resolves the tension in her identity by deciding to cast her lot with God's covenant people.

DEFINING MOMENTS. IT is unlikely that any of us will ever be in Esther's dire predicament, but every one of us faces defining moments in our own lives. Certainly the most fundamental of them comes when we hear the gospel of Jesus Christ and decide how to respond to it. The gospel confronts us with the decision either to continue to live as pagans or to identify ourselves with God's people, the church. Our choice defines who we are and with what people we identify. The decision to be identified with Christ energizes our lives. It gives us a purpose bigger than our own concerns and problems and a hope that goes beyond our own death. It transforms us into people moved by the Holy Spirit, human agents of God's grace and love in the world.

However, the new birth is only the beginning of decisions. It is followed by a continuous sequence of defining moments throughout life as we daily face decisions that demand we choose either to identify ourselves with Christ by obedience to his Word or to live as pagans in that moment. Only if we live as Christ commands, in every moment and every decision, will we be the agents through whom the promises of the new covenant are fulfilled. By the winsome testimony of our words and our lives, others are called to come to Christ and to identify with his people. By sustained obedience to God's Word, which the apostle Paul calls "the renewing of your mind" (Rom. 12:2), God's promise of his transforming work in our own lives is realized and touches the lives of others in ways we can neither control nor predict.

Motivation to live as God's child. However, it sometimes happens that even after coming to Christ, some Christians continue to think and live like pagans. At decision points, they take the path of least resistance instead of making the hard choice to obey God's unpopular Word. How long can one live like a pagan before one's true identity is revealed?

It seems to be human nature that sometimes we will do the right thing only when it becomes too painful to continue to do the wrong thing! Esther finds herself between a rock and hard place. Her life is in jeopardy by whichever choice she makes. She decides finally to identify with God's people only after feeling too threatened by the alternative. It is interesting to see that even though Esther's decision to "fast, weep, and mourn" with her people is made under duress, she does nevertheless end up identifying herself with God's covenant people. She leads her people to do what God commanded his people to do through the prophet Joel in the face of such calamity. In spite of its flawed quality, Esther's right decision enables her to become the agent through whom her people actually are delivered, in fulfillment of the ancient promise.

It is encouraging to realize that even if we turn to God reluctantly and perhaps even for the wrong reasons, we are still putting ourselves in a position to receive God's promise of mercy. The Lord's hand may graciously lead and guide his people who are living like pagans in the court of the king, but those defining moments will come around when each must decide whether or not to identify with God's people through obedience to his Word.

Some defining moments may come unexpectedly and pass quickly, yet with far-reaching consequences. That moment of opportunity when a student must decide whether to cheat on an exam, or a taxpayer on her tax return, or a husband on his wife, defines the person one way or the other, depending on the decision made. The incident becomes a part of who that person is within himself or herself, even if the decision never becomes known to others. The cumulative effect of many such defining moments in the past determines who we truly are at this moment.

Then there are those predictably big defining moments, such as when a profession or a marriage partner is chosen. There is probably no larger a defining moment than when we decide how we will spend our lives and with whom. Recently I met a woman who told me that in college her great desire was to be a foreign missionary. "But then I got engaged to a man who wasn't a Christian, and . . . you know . . . ," her voice trailed off with a fleeting look of embarrassment and regret.

Perhaps, like Esther, you have been brought to this moment in your life by circumstances over which you had no control, combined with flawed decisions you made along the way. Perhaps instead of living for God, you have so concealed your Christian faith that no one would even identify you as a Christian. Then suddenly you find yourself facing calamity, either in the circumstances of your life with others or just within your own inner emotional world. Regardless of the straits you find yourself in, turn to the Lord. Rend your heart, not your garment; "fast, weep, and mourn," and return to the Lord your God. His purposes are greater than yours. And, who knows? Perhaps you have come to your present situation for such a time as this.

Esther 5:1–14

ON THE THIRD day Esther put on her royal robes and stood in the inner court of the palace, in front of the king's hall. The king was sitting on his royal throne in the hall, facing the entrance. ²When he saw Queen Esther standing in the court, he was pleased with her and held out to her the gold scepter that was in his hand. So Esther approached and touched the tip of the scepter.

³Then the king asked, "What is it, Queen Esther? What is your request? Even up to half the kingdom, it will be given you."

⁴"If it pleases the king," replied Esther, "let the king, together with Haman, come today to a banquet I have prepared for him."

⁵"Bring Haman at once," the king said, "so that we may do what Esther asks."

So the king and Haman went to the banquet Esther had prepared. ⁶As they were drinking wine, the king again asked Esther, "Now what is your petition? It will be given you. And what is your request? Even up to half the kingdom, it will be granted."

⁷Esther replied, "My petition and my request is this: ⁸If the king regards me with favor and if it pleases the king to grant my petition and fulfill my request, let the king and Haman come tomorrow to the banquet I will prepare for them. Then I will answer the king's question."

⁹Haman went out that day happy and in high spirits. But when he saw Mordecai at the king's gate and observed that he neither rose nor showed fear in his presence, he was filled with rage against Mordecai. ¹⁰Nevertheless, Haman restrained himself and went home.

Calling together his friends and Zeresh, his wife, ¹¹Haman boasted to them about his vast wealth, his many sons, and all the ways the king had honored him and how he had elevated him above the other nobles and officials. [12]"And that's not all," Haman added. "I'm the only person Queen Esther invited to accompany the king to the banquet she gave. And she has invited me along with the king tomorrow. [13]But all this gives me no satisfaction as long as I see that Jew Mordecai sitting at the king's gate."

[14]His wife Zeresh and all his friends said to him, "Have a gallows built, seventy-five feet high, and ask the king in the morning to have Mordecai hanged on it. Then go with the king to the dinner and be happy." This suggestion delighted Haman, and he had the gallows built.

IN CHAPTER 1, Vashti risked her life by refusing to appear before Xerxes when summoned (1:12). In another of the story's ironies, Esther now risks her life by appearing before the same king unsummoned (cf. 4:11). Archaeological evidence shows that her trepidation was not unwarranted. Two bas-reliefs have been excavated from Persepolis showing a Persian king seated on his throne with a long scepter in his right hand. An attendant standing behind the throne is a Median soldier holding a large ax.[1] The threat of death and the hope of life are equally present as Esther summons the courage to approach the king.

After three days of fasting, Esther does not just try to make herself beautiful for her uninvited audience with the king, she appears before him in her *royal* robes. At the same time as she decides to identify with her people, she also claims her authority and power as the Queen of Persia in going before the king. The threat of death passes when Xerxes extends the golden scepter to her, granting her protected access into his presence.

For the first time in the story, Esther is directly addressed as "Queen Esther" when Xerxes offers her up to half of the kingdom (v. 3). This expression was an idiom commonly used by ancient royalty and was not intended to be taken literally. It simply meant that the king was dis-

---

1. For a photo of this relief see Edwin M. Yamauchi, *Persia and the Bible*, 360.

posed to be generous in meeting a request. Xerxes' offer bodes well for the future of the Jews of Persia. Centuries later, John the Baptist died when Herod also offered "up to half my kingdom" to the daughter of Herodias (Mark 6:23). On that occasion in the presence of all his officials, Herodias knew that Herod would not risk losing face by denying her request for John's head. Esther, however, is meeting the king in the privacy of his throne room; rather than demanding Haman's head, she chooses a more oblique approach.

In answer to the king's direct question, Esther invites the king to a festive meal and asks him to summon Haman as well. This pleases the king, and both he and Haman go to the banquet Esther has prepared. Esther now has Xerxes and Haman, the two most powerful men of the Persian empire, responding to her initiative.

At the banquet while the king is drinking wine, he again asks Esther why she appeared uninvited in her royal robes in the throne room. Previously in the story when Xerxes was drinking wine, Vashti ended up losing her royal position and power. Will the same happen to Queen Esther? Using a delay tactic, Esther again asks only that Haman and the king come to a second banquet on the next day. At that time Esther assures the king she will present her request. The suspense is heightened, not only for the king, but also for the reader.

Haman's prideful excitement at being invited to a private dinner of the king and queen is marred when Mordecai shows no gesture of deference as Haman leaves the palace. Emboldened by the presumption that he stands solidly in the favor of both King Xerxes and Queen Esther, Haman takes the advice of his wife. Zeresh counsels him simply to eliminate immediately the cause of his dissatisfaction. Haman builds a gallows of extraordinary size, seventy-five feet high, not realizing that its size is the measure of his own pride.

Zeresh's advice is reminiscent to that of Jezebel when her husband, King Ahab, was sulking like a spoiled child (1 Kings 21:1—16). Like Haman, all of Ahab's power and entitlements failed to satisfy because he wanted just one more thing, the vineyard owned by Naboth. Jezebel's solution was to arrange the murder of Naboth so that Ahab could have what he wanted. With similar reasoning, Zeresh counsels Haman simply to kill Mordecai. The satisfaction of human pride in its demand for honor and respect outweigh the value of human life in the pagan world of Persia.

The irony of this scene builds on that of chapter 1. Haman's haste to elicit and follow the evil advice of his wife and friends (5:14) contrasts with the king's order that "every man should be ruler over his own household" (1:22). By commanding respect through the brute exercise of power, the king and Haman may be able to save face, but reality laughs behind their backs.

IN THIS SCENE Esther emerges as the dominant character in the rest of the story and as the power that drives the resolution of the plot. She begins to take the initiative and make decisions that will ultimately issue at the end of the story with the statement, "Esther's decree confirmed these regulations about Purim, and it was written down in the records" (9:32). As the four major characters are introduced in the story, one would least expect Esther, the woman who hid her Jewish identity, to emerge as a respected leader among the Jewish people on whose authority Purim still stands.

The transformation of Esther's character from a person of "weak character" to one with "heroic moral stature and political skill"[2] proceeds from that defining moment when she decides to identify herself with God's covenant. Esther is referred to by name thirty-seven times in the story. In only fourteen of those references she is "Queen Esther." All but one of those fourteen references to her as "Queen Esther" occurs after 5:1. Esther assumes the dignity and power of her royal position only after she claims her true identity as a woman of God.

It was "on the third day" after Esther's decision to identify herself with God's people that she appears in royal splendor before the king. A Jewish midrash on this scene points out that "Israel are [sic] never left in dire distress more than three days."[3] In this midrash, the "miracle" of deliverance through Mordecai and Esther is compared to events in the lives of Abraham, Jacob, and Jonah, which also involved three days (cf. Gen. 22:4; 31:22; Jonah. 1:17). It links this miracle to the Jewish tradition that the dead will "come to life only after three days"

---

2. Leland Ryken, *Words of Delight: A Literary Introduction to the Bible,* 118.

3. *Midrash Rabbah Esther,* Maurice Simon, trans. (London: Soncino, 1939), 112. A midrash is a commentary on biblical passages that has accumulated through the centuries among the Jewish rabbis.

from the start of the final judgment.[4] This idea is based on Hosea 6:2: "After two days he will revive us; on the third day he will restore us, that we may live in his presence."

The deliverance of God's people from death and destruction is initiated "on the third day" after Esther's decision, when Xerxes extends to her the golden scepter. Had the king not extended this mercy, her execution or banishment would have been a ominous portent of the things to come for the Jews. But on the third day in the throne room of the king, Esther was granted life instead of death. The golden scepter foreshadows the deliverance of her people, initiated by this audience with the king.

Christians and Jews alike would probably be reluctant to see in the ruthless and pagan king Xerxes a type of God himself. However, it is not necessary to cast aspersion on God's character in order to see some picture of grace portrayed in this scene of Esther's story. Martin Luther, for example, associated the king's scepter with the gospel of Jesus Christ. In his exegesis of Psalm 2:9 ("you will rule them with an iron scepter") he writes, "This is the rod before whose tip, in the hand of Joseph, Jacob bowed (Gen. 47:31) and whose point the blessed Esther kissed (Esther 5:2)."[5]

On the third day the Persian king, whose word was irrevocable law, extends the golden scepter to Esther, lest she die for coming into his presence unsummoned. Esther approaches the king and completes this gracious gesture by touching the tip of the scepter. Her safety in his presence is thereby guaranteed. This scene pictures a gracious act of a king who holds life-and-death power. Had God not extended the cross of Jesus Christ to the world, all would die in his presence. "On the third day" after the final judgment transpired on the cross, Jesus Christ arose to imperishable life, guaranteeing safety to enter God's presence to all who reach out in faith to touch that cross-shaped scepter.

Contemporary Significance

IN CHAPTER 4, Esther's decision to identify herself with God's people was compared to coming to faith in Jesus Christ. Each of us comes to defining moments when we must decide whether to continue to live as pagans or to take our stand with

---

4. Ibid.
5. Jaroslav Pelikan, ed., *Luther's Works*, vol. 14 (St. Louis: Concordia, 1958), 336.

God's covenant people in Christ. Esther's decision put her life at great risk. Yet it is also that very decision that gave her the strength and courage to face the risk of going to the king uninvited. Esther's decision empowered her to action that ultimately led to the deliverance of her whole people. As a result of her decision to identify with God's people, she was personally transformed to the full dignity, courage, and power to be what she was, the Queen of Persia.

We have the benefit of knowing the end of the story and how Esther's decision led her to power and fame. But at the time Esther made that decision, she did not know how her story would end. At that point her decision could have just as well ended her life, either in the king's throne room or during the execution of Haman's decree. Moreover, Esther may or may not have known the Hebrew Scriptures; but even if she did, God's promise to protect his people was a promise collectively to the nation. Esther had no promise from God for her personal, individual safety. In other words, Esther could not have known at the time she decided to risk her life that it was that very decision that would fulfill her personal destiny as well as the destiny of her people.

In the original decision of "conversion" to Jesus Christ and in all subsequent decisions, we become the women or men God has created us to be by aligning ourselves with his covenant in Christ. As Paul wrote in Galatians, that covenant issues in the life-changing work of the Holy Spirit within us. Like Esther, we too need a transformation of our character so that we may no longer live as pagans. Obeying laws can never effect true transformation, because while we may conform our behavior to law, law by its very nature (even God's law) is powerless to transform our character. Character transformation is a work of the Holy Spirit, who brings to fruition the qualities of love, joy, peace, patience, kindness, goodness, faithfulness, gentleness, and self-control in those who belong to Jesus Christ (Gal. 5:22–23). Without this transformation of character by the Holy Spirit, none of us can attain the full potential of our humanity. Without the work of God's Spirit, we cannot be the persons God created us to be, nor can we attain fully to the purpose of our lives as agents of God's redemptive work in history.

Esther's decision reached far beyond her own identity, enabling her to be the agent through whom God would deliver a whole nation of people. At the same time, her decision also made her the agent through whom death and destruction would come to Haman. Esther's defining moment was truly a life-and-death decision that went far beyond her own life to touch the lives of others.

As soon as Esther identified herself to the king as a Jew, she came under Haman's edict of death. The dark powers and principalities of this world are against the Christian church just as they were against Jesus and God's covenant people before him. When a woman or man takes a stand with Jesus Christ, he or she becomes part of a people who are targeted in spiritual battle by those who want to destroy the work of Christ in history. This is the point the apostle Peter makes when writing to certain Christians of the first century who had lost social and political standing in their polytheistic culture (1 Peter 4:12—19):

> Dear friends, do not be surprised at the painful trial you are suffering, as though something strange were happening to you. But rejoice that you participate in the sufferings of Christ, so that you may be overjoyed when his glory is revealed. If you are insulted because of the name of Christ, you are blessed, for the Spirit of glory and of God rests on you. If you suffer, it should not be as a murderer or thief or any other kind of criminal, or even as a meddler. However, if you suffer as a Christian, do not be ashamed, but praise God that you bear that name. For it is time for judgment to begin with the family of God; and if it begins with us, what will the outcome be for those who do not obey the gospel of God? And,

> > "If it is hard for the righteous to be saved,
> >   what will become of the ungodly and the sinner?"

> So then, those who suffer according to God's will should commit themselves to their faithful Creator and continue to do good.

In spite of the overwhelming threat against them, the Jewish nation exiled in Persia was delivered because one person took her stand as a woman of the covenant. As we take our stand with Christ, we may experience suffering simply because we are Christians. American Christians generally do not face the forms of physical and mental suffering from persecution experienced by many of our brothers and sisters around the globe and throughout the ages. However, anyone who dares to believe in miracles in this post-Enlightenment, scientific age does potentially face a loss of standing simply for believing the foundational truth of Christianity, the bodily resurrection of Jesus.

Social ostracization and academic marginalization are modern forms of persecution against Christians. But we must remember that the reason for such suffering is at the same time the only hope of our deliverance. Because Christ triumphed in resurrection life over the ultimate evils of hell, death, and the grave, our union with him guarantees that same victory to us.

Esther 6:1–14

❧

THAT NIGHT THE king could not sleep; so he ordered the book of the chronicles, the record of his reign, to be brought in and read to him. ²It was found recorded there that Mordecai had exposed Bigthana and Teresh, two of the king's officers who guarded the doorway, who had conspired to assassinate King Xerxes.

³"What honor and recognition has Mordecai received for this?" the king asked.

"Nothing has been done for him," his attendants answered.

⁴The king said, "Who is in the court?" Now Haman had just entered the outer court of the palace to speak to the king about hanging Mordecai on the gallows he had erected for him.

⁵His attendants answered, "Haman is standing in the court."

"Bring him in," the king ordered.

⁶When Haman entered, the king asked him, "What should be done for the man the king delights to honor?"

Now Haman thought to himself, "Who is there that the king would rather honor than me?" ⁷So he answered the king, "For the man the king delights to honor, ⁸have them bring a royal robe the king has worn and a horse the king has ridden, one with a royal crest placed on its head. ⁹Then let the robe and horse be entrusted to one of the king's most noble princes. Let them robe the man the king delights to honor, and lead him on the horse through the city streets, proclaiming before him, 'This is what is done for the man the king delights to honor!'"

¹⁰"Go at once," the king commanded Haman. "Get the robe and the horse and do just as you have suggested for Mordecai the Jew, who sits at the king's gate. Do not neglect anything you have recommended."

¹¹"So Haman got the robe and the horse. He robed Mordecai, and led him on horseback through the city streets, proclaiming before him, "This is what is done for the man the king delights to honor!"

¹²Afterward Mordecai returned to the king's gate. But Haman rushed home, with his head covered in grief, ¹³and told Zeresh his wife and all his friends everything that had happened to him.

His advisers and his wife Zeresh said to him, "Since Mordecai, before whom your downfall has started, is of Jewish origin, you cannot stand against him—you will surely come to ruin!" ¹⁴While they were still talking with him, the king's eunuchs arrived and hurried Haman away to the banquet Esther had prepared.

THIS IS ARGUABLY the most ironically comic scene in the entire Bible. While Haman plots Mordecai's outrageous death, the king plans to honor Mordecai's faithful service. An unsuspecting Haman enters the king's court, where he magnificently trips over his own pride. "Who is there that the king would rather honor than me?" he muses. If ever there was a picture of pride going before the fall, Haman is it.

Haman's splendid humiliation results from a series of coincidences, each believable in itself, and yet a series that is completely out of Haman's control. The mighty Haman is rendered powerless by a "chance event" when the king just happens to have a sleepless night. He just happens to have the chronicles of his reign read to him. The story of Mordecai's loyalty just happens to come to his attention at the same moment when Haman just happens to be plotting Mordecai's death.

After the king's intriguing banquet with Esther, he is unable to sleep. Xerxes decides to review court business. "The book of the chronicles" was the official record of the Persian kings, in which every official transaction of the court was recorded. From this official transcript the king would draw up a list of those who were to be rewarded for faithful service to the throne.

It was important that Persian kings publicly reward those who were loyal as a means of promoting their own safety in such treacherous times. Herodotus records examples of two such honors. In one instance Xerxes granted land to two ships' captains who had assisted in a battle against the Greeks and recorded one of them in the list of the "King's Benefactors."[1] In another incident, a man was made governor of Cilicia for saving the life of Xerxes' brother.[2]

The king was mortified to find that nothing had been done to honor Mordecai publicly, who some five years before had foiled an assassination plot against him (cf. 2:16; 3:7). Why the king was reviewing his official transcripts from years earlier is not explained—another chance event. Mordecai had no doubt been keenly disappointed by this oversight. His willingness to overlook the slight and continue faithfully to serve the king gives insight into his character.

Haman's proposal for what "should be done to the man the king delights to honor" may seem unusual by modern standards. Believing the honors would go to himself, Haman could not ask for a promotion because he was already second only to the king in his authority over the empire. He apparently had all the wealth and luxury such a high-ranking position could afford in opulent Persia. His request to wear the king's robe and ride the king's horse was intended both to honor the king and to reinforce Haman's relationship with him.

There is some evidence from ancient historians that the Persian royal robes, as well as the king's bed and throne, were believed to have the power to impart the benefits of royalty in an almost magical way. However, even without the invocation of magic, a man permitted to wear the king's robe would be vested with a certain dignity and prestige in the eyes of his peers because of the close association with the king. To put it in modern terms, there would be nothing magical about the President of the United States allowing his personal jet, Air Force One, to transport one of his associates, in effect elevating that person's power and prestige in the public eye.

A similar episode involving royal robes symbolically predicted King David's rise to power. Prior to the Persian period in Israel's history, Jonathan, the royal prince and heir of Israel's throne, symbolized his

---

1. LCL: *Herodotus* 8.85.
2. Ibid., 9.107.

covenant with David by giving him the robes he was wearing (1 Sam. 18:1–5). The very next sentence tells us that David was thereafter so successful that he was given a high rank in Saul's army. Eventually David himself wore the royal robes of Israel's king, sitting on the throne that would have been Jonathan's had Saul's dynasty continued.

For Haman no other honor was left to him but to partake of the king's own power, prestige, and stature. To have such an intimate gesture bestowed instead on Mordecai, the Jew, is a crushing humiliation. More importantly, it foreshadows the reversal of fortune that is about to inexorably unfold before Haman's horrified eyes. When he plotted the destruction of "a certain people" (3:8), he failed to mention their identity to the king or to his wife and friends. When Haman's wife, Zeresh, and his friends later learn that Mordecai is Jewish, they reverse their earlier advice. Not only will Haman's plan against Mordecai be frustrated, but Haman himself will come to ruin for the attempt. The full extent of Haman's tragic miscalculation begins to emerge.

FEASTS. THE KING'S sleepless night is the pivot point of the literary structure of the story around which the great reversal of destiny occurs. The literary structure of this book is defined by the recurrence of the primary literary motif, the *misteh*—the Hebrew word most often translated in the NIV as "feast" or "banquet."[3] This Hebrew word, which occurs twenty times in the book of Esther and only twenty-four times in all the rest of the Old Testament, usually refers to eating and drinking on special occasions. This dominant motif of feasting is appropriate, since the Esther story explains the origin of Purim, a Jewish feast day. It further explains why Purim was celebrated on two different, consecutive days.

As several commentators have noted, the story of Esther both begins and concludes with pairs of feasts, with other pairs of feasts intervening.[4] In chapter 1 Xerxes gives *two* consecutive feasts; in chapter 9 the Jews observe *two* consecutive feast days to celebrate their

---

3. "Banquet" in 1:3, 5, 9; 2:18; 5:4, 5, 8, 12; 6:14; 7:8; "dinner" in 5:14; "feasting" in 8:17; 9:17, 18, 19, 22.

4. See Sandra Berg, *The Book of Esther: Motifs, Themes and Structure* (SBLDS 44: Missoula, Mont.: Scholars, 1979).

deliverance. These two pairs of feasts mirror each other. For instance, Xerxes' first feast is for the nobility throughout the empire; the first of the Purim feast days is celebrated by the Jews throughout the empire. Xerxes' second feast is for the residents of Susa; the second day of the Purim feast is celebrated by the Jews residing in Susa.

When the several banquets in the Esther story are listed, they appear to form pairs, as indicated in the following diagram by the letters (i.e., A^1 and A^2 are a pair):

Banquets and Feasting in Esther

1. Xerxes' banquet for the nobles of the empire (1:2–4) — A^1
2. Xerxes' banquet for all men in Susa (1:5–8) — B^1
3. Esther's coronation banquet (2:18) — C^1
4. Esther's first banquet for the king and Haman (5:1–8) — D^1
5. Esther's second banquet for the king and Haman (7:1–9) — D^2
6. Feasting in celebration of Mordecai's promotion (8:17) — C^2
7. The first day of Purim feasting throughout empire (9:17, 19) — A^2
8. The second day of Purim feasting in Susa (9:18) — B^2

Since the book both begins and ends with pairs of feasts, it is striking that Esther also gives not one, but *two* banquets for the king and Haman. Haman's downfall begins between the first and second of Esther's banquets, when the king has a sleepless night. Thus there are three pairs of feasts that mark the beginning, the climax, and the conclusion of the story.

Peripety. These three pairs of feasts define the rise and fall of a plot that is characterized by peripety—a literary term that refers to a sudden turn of events in a story that reverses the intended and expected action (see comments on "Literary Structure" in the Introduction). The deliverance of the Jewish people against all odds is a reversal of destiny. Peripety in Esther is achieved by a literary device called chiasm, where each element of the chiasm not only corresponds to its parallel, but in reverse order. The use of this literary structure to achieve peripety in Esther is a good example of the interplay between content and literary form (see chart on next page).

The narrative tension of the conflict between the Jews of Persia and their enemy, Haman, is not simply resolved, it is resolved through reversals. Haman's plan could have simply been stopped and the status quo preserved. Instead, there is a great reversal of fortune. An event

Chiastic Structure of Reversals in Esther	
3:10 - the king gives Haman his ring	8:2 - the king gives Mordecai the same ring
3:12 - Haman summons the king's scribes	8:9 - Mordecai summons the king's scribes
3:12 - letters written, sealed with ring	8:10 - letters written, sealed with same ring
3:13 - the Jews, even women and children, to be killed on one day	8:11 - the enemies, even women and children, to be killed on one day
3:14 - Haman's decree publicly displayed as law	8:13 - Mordecai's decree publicly displayed as law
3:15 - couriers go out in haste	8:14 - couriers go out in haste
3:15 - the city of Susa is bewildered	8:15 - the city of Susa rejoices
4:1 - Mordecai wears sackcloth and ashes	8:15 - Mordecai wears royal robes
4:1 - Mordecai goes through city crying	6:11 - Mordecai led through the city in honor
5:14 - Zeresh advises Mordecai's death	6:13 - Zeresh predicts Haman's ruin

intended to harm the Jews actually results in the opposite, against every expectation. Instead of being destroyed, the Jewish people are not only delivered, but empowered through the high rank of Esther and Mordecai. The empowered destroyer, Haman, not only loses his power, but is himself destroyed. In 9:1, the author explicitly states the theme of deliverance as a reversal:

> On the thirteenth day of the twelfth month, the month of Adar, the edict commanded by the king was to be carried out. On this day the enemies of the Jews had hoped to overpower them, but now *the tables were turned* and the Jews got the upper hand over those who hated them. (emphasis added)

Chapter 6 contains the first of the many reversals to follow. On the very day Haman goes to the king seeking permission to kill Mordecai (6:4), Haman ends up not only not killing Mordecai, but publicly honoring him in the king's name (6:11).

The three pairs of feasts focus the structure of the story on the pivot point of the peripety around which these reversals occur. The author's attention to rhetorical symmetry is also expressed by referring to the annals of the king three times—at the beginning of the story (2:23), in the middle (6:1), and at the end (10:2).

The Literary Structure of Esther

"... their sorrow was turned into joy and
their mourning into a day of celebration" (9:22)

Peripety: a sudden turn of events that reverses the expected or intended outcome.

↑ Conflict

"That night the king could not sleep ..."
6:1

Esther's 1st banquet	Esther's 2nd banquet
5:4	7:1

The king celebrates   The Jews celebrate
two banquets 1:4, 5   two feast days 9:16—18

plot movement →

One might expect the pivot point of peripety in narrative to fall on the scene of highest narrative tension. The point of highest dramatic tension is usually a scene involving two or more of the characters, typically the protagonist (hero) facing off with the antagonist (villain). In the story of Esther, her uninvited audience with the king is certainly a scene of high dramatic tension, but it does not bring the plot to its climax. Rather, it reaches its climax during the second banquet, when Esther confronts Haman (the antagonist) to his face. Therefore, standard literary form indicates that this scene of narrative climax shows Esther to be the protagonist, or heroine, of the story, rather than Mordecai, for it is she who faces off with the antagonist.

Notice, however, that the pivot point of the peripety in Esther is not located at the climax of the narrative. Instead, the pivot point of this peripety is the seemingly insignificant event recorded in 6:1, when the king had a sleepless night. As insignificant as this ordinary event may appear, it is with this event that the tables begin to turn and the reversals begin to occur. The Feast of Purim celebrates this grand reversal in the month of Adar because it was a month "when their sorrow was turned into joy and their mourning into a day of celebrating" (9:22).

By making the pivot point of the peripety an insignificant event rather than the point of highest dramatic tension, the author is taking the focus away from human action. Had the pivot point of the peripety been at the scene where Esther approaches the king uninvited or where Esther confronts Haman, the king and/or Esther would have been spotlighted as the actual cause of the reversal. By separating the pivot point of the peripety in Esther from the point of highest dramatic tension, the characters of the story are not spotlighted as the cause of the reversal. This reinforces the message that no one in the story, not even the most powerful person in the empire, is in control of what is about to happen. An unseen power is controlling the reversal of destiny. The Greek translation makes this implicit truth explicit with the statement, "The Lord took sleep from the king that night" (LXX of 6:1, pers. trans.).

THE MONOTHEISTIC WORLDVIEW **of the author of Esther.** This structure of peripety in Esther is not simply a literary device that produces an aesthetically pleasing story. The literary form of the story and its content mutually interact to create its meta-message. The structure of peripety deeply reflects the worldview of the author and provides the framework within which we can understand the theological implications of the Esther story.

In spite of having all the power of the Persian empire at his disposal, Haman's carefully laid plans were turned against him simply because the king had a sleepless night! The author is suggesting that beneath the surface of human decisions and actions is an unseen and uncontrollable power at work, which can be neither explained nor thwarted. In ancient polytheistic culture, the gods controlled fate. With a pantheon of competing gods and goddesses, human affairs could be turned upside down if one god overpowered another. Fate was therefore capricious, because one could never be sure which god or goddess was in control of one's situation. The author of Esther wrote from the perspective of the Jews, who were monotheistic. By constructing this story using peripety, what is the divinely inspired author of Esther trying to say about how God rules?

If there is but one God, does he change his mind from day to day or week to week, making human events lead first in one direction and then in another? Read in a polytheistic context, the story suggests that Yahweh, the God of the Jews, had overpowered Haman's gods in this instance. Read from a monotheistic perspective, the story explains the reversal of fortune not as an ongoing tug-of-war between the gods, but as consistent with the powerful word of the one, true God. The author of Esther implies a consistency in God's rule of human history that is based on his word, not on circumstances. Regardless of how circumstances appear, God is ruling history according to the ancient covenant he made with Israel at Sinai.

The reversal of destiny that began when the king had a sleepless night implies that, despite their sin and despite their location away from Jerusalem, God's promise to Israel made at the beginning of their nation still stood. God was not capricious like the gods of the pagans. He was not locked in some struggle with other deities that gave him control only on certain days or in certain situations. All that had happened was consistent with the stated provisions of God's covenant. The Agagites would be destroyed, even though they seemed inviolable in their wealth and power.

Previously in Israel's history, God had used mighty miracles to deliver his people and to fulfill his promises. In the story of Esther God was using the ordinary events of life to realize his covenant promises to his people. He used even seemingly insignificant events, such as the king's sleepless night, and the decisions of less-than-perfect people to fulfill nevertheless the promises of his ancient covenant.

It is particularly appropriate for the pivot point of the peripety that reverses the expected outcome to occur at an ordinary and insignificant event in a book whose meta-message is about divine providence. God providentially directs the flow of human history through the ordinary lives of individuals to fulfill the promises of his covenant. What a great God we serve! Any deity worth his salt can do a miracle now and then. Our God is so great, so powerful, that he can work without miracles through the ordinary events of billions of human lives through millennia of time to accomplish his eternal purposes and ancient promises. God delivered an entire race of people in Persia because the king had a sleepless night, because a man would not bow to his superior, because a woman found herself taken to the bedroom of a ruthless man for a night of pleasure. How inscrutable are the ways of the Lord!

God's providence in our own lives. Is it not true that God has worked in your own life often through events that were unexpected and seemed insignificant at the time? Consider the chain of circumstances that led up to your own conversion to Christ. Perhaps you were randomly changing channels on the TV or radio when you happened to come upon a preacher whose message began a transformation in your life. Maybe you happened to pick up an evangelistic tract that opened your heart to the Lord. For others, it may have been a friend or casual acquaintance who happened to invite them to church or a home Bible study. That most significant work of God in your life came about through a chain of events, each of which probably seemed unimportant at the time.

Consider how God has guided and directed your life. How did you come to meet and marry your spouse? Why are you living in the place you are? What circumstances led to your current job? God's care and protection for his children seldom come by mighty miracles, but constantly and inexorably with the unfolding circumstances of each day, as one thing leads to another. Tiny miracles of God's providence direct your steps.

Of course, not all of life's circumstances are pleasant. Tragedies occur when, in God's providence, someone is in the wrong place at the wrong time. Life's circumstances can be tragic, ugly, and destructive, like the plot to annihilate the Jews of Persia initiated on the eve of Passover. The death of a loved one, serious illness, wayward children, broken relationships, shattered hopes and dreams—all are links in the uninterrupted chain of life. While none of these things is good in itself, even in the worst of life's circumstances God is working to fulfill his perfect promises. One thing leads to the next. The path to the joy God promises may wind through the swamps of suffering and despair.

Christians can face threatening circumstances with hope only because of the new covenant in Christ. The Jews of Persia were delivered because of the ancient covenant God had made with Israel on Mount Sinai. The peripety expressed in Esther was a deliverance against all odds from the destiny of death to a destiny of life. This life-and-death antithesis was inseparably bound up with Yahweh's ancient covenant. Before entering the Promised Land Moses set the covenant before the new generation of Israel, and in so doing set before them "life and prosperity, death and destruction" (Deut. 30:15–20). The reversal of destiny from death to life expressed by peripety in Esther actualized the covenant for the Jews of Persia.

The structure of redemptive history. The literary structure of peripety found in the book of Esther and its pivot point in an ordinary and insignificant event mirrors on a small scale the structure of all of redemptive history. Because of our sin, we are not living in the Garden of Eden, where the Lord walks and talks with us in the coolness of the day. Rather, we live in the exile of history, in a world where God is unseen. God has pronounced a sentence of death on us (Gen. 3), and every evidence of human circumstances demonstrates its efficacy. We should expect nothing but death, but we have seen the ultimate peripety, the ultimate reversal of expected ends, in another seemingly ordinary human event: the birth of a baby in Bethlehem and the execution of that man on a cross. The ordinary and the miraculous intersect in Jesus Christ. Because of the death and resurrection of Jesus Christ, our destiny has been reversed from death to life against all expectation. The cross of Jesus Christ is the pivot point of the great reversal of history, where our sorrow has been turned to joy.

Because the ancient covenant of Sinai is consummated in Jesus Christ,[5] God has made a covenant with those in Christ that cannot be thwarted by even the worst life brings against us. As the apostle Paul writes in Romans 8:35–39:

> Who shall separate us from the love of Christ? Shall trouble or hardship or persecution or famine or nakedness or danger or sword? As it is written:
>
> > "For your sake we face death all day long;
> > we are considered as sheep to be slaughtered."
>
> No, in all these things we are more than conquerors through him who loved us. For I am convinced that neither death nor life,

---

5. For one cogent explanation of how this is so, see O. Palmer Robertson, *The Christ of the Covenants* (Phillipsburg, N.J.: Presbyterian and Reformed, 1980).

neither angels nor demons, neither the present nor the future, nor any powers, neither height nor depth, nor anything else in all creation, will be able to separate us from the love of God that is in Christ Jesus our Lord.

In our darkest hours we can be assured of our final destiny of glory with Christ. We can be assured that the reversal of circumstance we so crave will one day be ours. By contrast, no matter how prosperous or powerful, those who are not in Christ will ultimately also suffer a reversal of fortune. Like Haman, they will find themselves caught in a web of destruction that hindsight will show to be of their own making. It can happen at any time.

Esther 7:1–10

S
O THE KING and Haman went to dine with Queen Esther, ²and as they were drinking wine on that second day, the king again asked, "Queen Esther, what is your petition? It will be given you. What is your request? Even up to half the kingdom, it will be granted."

³Then Queen Esther answered, "If I have found favor with you, O king, and if it pleases your majesty, grant me my life—this is my petition. And spare my people—this is my request. ⁴For I and my people have been sold for destruction and slaughter and annihilation. If we had merely been sold as male and female slaves, I would have kept quiet, because no such distress would justify disturbing the king."

⁵King Xerxes asked Queen Esther, "Who is he? Where is the man who has dared to do such a thing?"

⁶Esther said, "The adversary and enemy is this vile Haman."

Then Haman was terrified before the king and queen. ⁷The king got up in a rage, left his wine and went out into the palace garden. But Haman, realizing that the king had already decided his fate, stayed behind to beg Queen Esther for his life.

⁸Just as the king returned from the palace garden to the banquet hall, Haman was falling on the couch where Esther was reclining.

The king exclaimed, "Will he even molest the queen while she is with me in the house?"

As soon as the word left the king's mouth, they covered Haman's face. ⁹Then Harbona, one of the eunuchs attending the king, said, "A gallows seventy-five feet high stands by Haman's house. He had it made for Mordecai, who spoke up to help the king."

The king said, "Hang him on it!" [10]So they hanged
Haman on the gallows he had prepared for Mordecai.
Then the king's fury subsided.

THIS HIGHLY CHARGED scene begins innocu-
ously enough with: "So the king and Haman
went to dine with Queen Esther." Little did
either know what awaited them there! While
drinking wine Xerxes asks Queen Esther for the third time to reveal her
request and again assures her of his positive and generous response
(cf. 5:3, 6). Esther now begins the delicate and dangerous task of accus-
ing Haman without incriminating the king who had, after all, sealed
Haman's decree of death with his full knowledge and approval. She has
to incite the king against his friend and closest advisor without bringing the king's wrath down on herself. Once set in motion, the scene
moves with breathtaking speed toward Haman's destruction.

King Xerxes repeats exactly his words spoken at the previous banquet, "What is your petition?... What is your request?" In the king's
rhetoric, the two words "petition" and "request" refer to the one and the
same desire of Esther. Her reply is rhetorically structured exactly as was
his question: "... grant me my life—this is my petition. And spare my
people—this is my request." By framing her response using the king's
rhetoric, Esther is saying that her life and the life of her people are one
and the same. Her destiny is one with her people.

Esther continues her brief but skillful reply to the king, "I and my
people have been sold for destruction and slaughter and annihilation."
Esther quotes the exact words of Haman's edict (cf. 3:13), but by
using the passive voice, she delays mentioning Haman's name or the
fact that it was the king himself who sold the Jewish people for ten
thousand talents of silver (cf. 3:9, 11). This oblique tactic is not
unlike that used by Nathan the prophet when confronting David
with his sin in 2 Samuel 12. Nathan circumvented David's defense
mechanism by first arousing David's indignation and his resolve to
see justice done before revealing that David himself was the evil
man. The same tactic works for Esther, and Xerxes' indignation and
anger erupt with the demand that she tell him, "Who is he?" and
"Where is the man ... ?" Apparently the death edict has made so lit-

tle an impression on the king that Esther's quotation of it does not even ring a bell.

Although lost in English translation, the king's fury is effectively communicated in the Hebrew words, which sound like machine-gun fire when pronounced aloud. His honor is offended that someone would attempt injury to his queen and her people. The emotion and anger of Esther's reply are also lost in the bland English translation. In the Hebrew, her words ring out with staccato cadence. Esther answers both the "who" and the "where" with her succinct accusation: "A man hateful and hostile! This wicked Haman!" (pers. trans.).

Esther's words send Xerxes into an enraged quandary that drives him out of the banquet room and into the garden. In his commentary, M. Fox reads the questions circulating in Xerxes' mind: "Can he punish Haman for a plot he himself approved? If he does so, won't he have to admit his own role in the fiasco [and lose face]? Moreover, he has issued an irrevocable law; how then can he rescind it?"[1] The king's dilemma will soon be resolved by Haman's further folly.

Clearly Haman realizes that the king's fury is upon him. He also knows Xerxes well enough to realize that the king never made his own decision. It was the manipulative agenda of others that drove his actions, a ploy Haman himself had used so successfully in the past. Thus, his only chance of survival lies in the hands of Esther, whom he begs to intercede with the king for his life.

Harem protocol dictated that no one but the king could be left alone with a woman of the harem. Haman should have left Esther's presence when the king retreated to the garden, but where could he have gone? His choice was either to follow the king, who had bolted in anger from his presence, or to flee the room, suggesting guilt and inviting pursuit. Haman is trapped. Even in the presence of others, a man was not to approach a woman of the king's harem within seven steps.[2] That Haman should actually fall on the couch where Esther is reclining is unthinkable! Haman's untoward behavior is so unimaginable that in the Aramaic *Targum of Esther* he falls on the queen's couch only because the angel Gabriel has given him a firm shove, sealing his fate. It is Haman's final, fatal action.

---

1. Michael V. Fox, *Character and Ideology in the Book of Esther*, 86.
2. Edwin M. Yamauchi, *Persia and the Bible*, 262.

Precisely at this moment of impropriety Xerxes returns and finds his quandary about what to do with Haman resolved. It is unlikely that Haman is actually attempting to physically assault or sexually molest the queen, even though that seems to be the spin Xerxes conveniently puts on it. Regardless of intent, Haman has undeniably violated harem protocol, a serious affront to the king himself and reason enough to condemn him to death. When Harbona suggests that Haman be hanged on the gallows he had built for Mordecai—the Mordecai who, by the way, had saved the king from assassination—Xerxes concludes that Haman perhaps had secret sympathies with his attempted assassins. This fine point of court intrigue is amplified in the Greek version, which emphasizes that Haman, the king's closest advisor, will be executed in disgrace for treason.

The English word "gallows" connotes death by asphyxiation on a wooden stand with a rope noose around the neck. This word is chosen in the NIV because there is in English no exact equivalent for the form of execution practiced in ancient Persia. Both from the written witness of Herodotus and from excavated stone reliefs, we know that the Persians built "gallows" that were wooden stakes on which they impaled, not asphyxiated, their victims.[3] When the death of an enemy occurred by some other means, the bodies of the slain often would be impaled (i.e., "hung") on gallows for public display and further humiliation.

IRONY. THIS SCENE is about who gets life and who does not. Both Esther and Haman plead for their lives in this chapter. Neither is in control of their respective destinies. Both are caught up in a complicated web of intrigue that has taken on a life of its own. Esther's destiny lies with that of her people. Haman's destiny overtakes him like a thief in the night.

The scene is steeped in irony. Consider how the entire conflict between Haman and the Jewish people begins when Mordecai the Jew dishonors Haman the Agagite by refusing to fall before him. In his final scene, Haman falls before a Jew (and a Jewish woman at that!), whom he has unknowingly condemned to death, to plead with her for

---

3. LCL: *Herodotus* 3.125, 129; 4.43.

his life! On the couch of this Jewish queen he "falls" all the way from his exalted position as second over the empire to an ignominious death as a traitor. The enemy of the Jews is executed for being an enemy of the king. This sudden reversal of expected outcomes gives Haman's story a tragic irony. All of a person's best laid plans can in an instant be turned to produce the opposite of the intent. It is especially ironic when that person has all the power of a great empire behind him and when his downfall begins with something as insignificant as someone's night of insomnia.

Esther and holy war. Esther has been criticized for being hardhearted in not forgiving Haman and not interceding with the king on his behalf. After all, Haman did not know that the queen was Jewish when he sent out his decree of death because Esther herself had concealed her identity, so why should she take the decree so personally now? Moreover, she knew that he was not attempting to assault her when he fell upon her couch, so why did she let the king believe the worst? Surely she could have manipulated the clueless king to pardon Haman.

Apparently looking for an exemplary role model in Esther, L. B. Paton writes in his commentary:

> Esther has now a chance to intercede for Haman, but she does not take it. All his entreaties are in vain, and she looks on in silence while he is condemned to death ... it must be admitted that her character would have been more attractive if she had shown pity toward a fallen foe.[4]

The author gives us no insight into Queen Esther's mind at that moment, but is her lack of pity on Haman really the moral of the story? Is pity always a virtue? And is the lack of it always a character flaw (especially in a woman)? Perhaps it is in this very moment that Esther exhibits her greatest strength of character and fulfills her highest calling.

From chapter 5 onward, Esther is portrayed as queen of the world's mightiest empire. She comes into her own as queen only after she decides to align herself with God's covenant people. She is no longer a trophy wife, a queen in name only, but by putting on her royal robes in defense of her people she takes up the power of her position. Recall

---

4. L. B. Paton, *The Book of Esther*, 264.

Mordecai's words to Esther in 4:14, "And who knows but that you have come *to royal position* for such a time as this?" (emphasis added). Esther is portrayed by the author in her royal power, not in her personal character. Being queen of Persia made Esther the ruling monarch of the Jews, including those who had returned to Judah to rebuild the temple.

By designing the death of Haman the Agagite, Queen Esther has succeeded where her ancestor King Saul had failed, whether or not she was aware of it (see 1 Sam. 15; see also comments on 3:1). Esther is the Jews' queen during this time of holy war. Holy war is a troubling concept to modern readers, and the role of the monarch in holy war is unfamiliar to most.[5] In Scripture, holy war was initiated by God for his own purposes, and Israel's king was to be the leader of God's army and responsible to wage holy war according to the divine initiative.

The Amalekites had tried to destroy the infant nation of Israel shortly after they left the land of Egypt (Ex. 17:8–15). Because of this, God instructed Israel's first king, Saul, to attack and destroy the Amalekites, sparing not even women and children. The similarity of these words with those of the edict of Haman against the Jews in Persia, as well as the words of Mordecai's later counter-edict, is striking (cf. Est. 3:13; 8:11). Saul was to spare not even one of the Amalekites and to show no pity. But when Saul had the opportunity to kill their king, Agag, king of the enemies of God's people, he spared his life instead. This act of disobedience in holy war disqualified Saul from being Israel's king.

When Samuel heard of Saul's "mercy" on Agag, the enraged prophet killed Agag in obedience to God's command, but according to rabbinical tradition, not before Agag slept one last time with his wife. The son conceived in that union had a descendent generations later named Haman, who turned the power of Persia against the exiled nation of King Saul. Because of Saul's failure, the Amalekites continued to plague Israel throughout its history.

Haman the Agagite wore the signet ring that endowed him with the king's authority, and he effectively acted as the king of the enemies of God's people. In the Diaspora setting, God no longer fought holy war

---

5. See Tremper Longman III and Daniel Reid, *God Is a Warrior* (Grand Rapids: Zondervan, 1995), for a full discussion of holy war as a biblical-theological motif.

through Israel's king and army, for Israel no longer had either a king or an army. Would God's people still be protected by his covenant promises without holy war? The story of Esther demonstrates that God worked providentially through Mordecai and Esther to fulfill a promise of protection that previously would have been fulfilled through holy war. Queen Esther killed Haman with her cunning, as surely as King Saul could have, and should have, killed Agag with the sword. Commentators who criticize Esther for her lack of pity on Haman seem to have missed this connection to Israel's monarchy and its role in God's promise of destruction against those who oppose his redemptive work.

Esther's role as queen of the Jews in this story makes it inappropriate to use exemplary exegesis as the key to understanding this book. Esther is not portrayed as the ideal woman of God living out her relationship with the Lord as a direct example for women today. Her role as the Jewish queen of Persia in a specific stage of redemptive history and biblical theology means that no other woman can or should try to emulate directly her character or behavior, just as no Christian man today would emulate David when he killed two hundred Philistines for their foreskins as the bride price for Saul's daughter (1 Sam. 18:24–30).

Was Haman's death justified? Over time, Mordecai, not Esther, was understood in Jewish interpretation to be the hero who finally finished the job Saul had left undone. In fact, during the Hellenistic period Purim came to be called Mordecai's Day. Mordecai's role is certainly essential to the deliverance. The author of Esther introduces him as a second Saul by specifying both were Benjamites and descendants of Kish (see comments on 2:5). But although Mordecai's part was essential in the deliverance, it was Queen Esther who wore the crown of monarchy and who had the more direct part in Haman's death. The later Greek additions to this book portray Esther and Mordecai as partners in righteousness, together praying for and achieving God's redemptive purposes. On the other hand, the ancient Greek version, which was translated in Egypt during the reigns of a number of the Ptolemaic queens named Cleopatra, greatly diminishes Esther's overall role in the saga and magnifies Mordecai's.

This trend is also found in the Aramaic targums of Esther, which are amplified translations of the story. In an embellishment of this scene, one of the later targums explains that the king gave Mordecai the privilege of personally killing Haman. As Haman faces death, he begs Mordecai for mercy in words still dripping with pride:

> And Mordecai spoke to Haman, saying, Come with me, Haman, thou foe and wicked enemy and oppressor of the Jews, that we may hang thee upon the gallows which thou hast erected for thyself. Then the wicked Haman answered the righteous Mordecai, Before they bring me to the gallows, I beg thee, righteous Mordecai, that thou wilt not hang me as they hang common criminals. I have despised great men, and governors of provinces have waited upon me. I have made kings to tremble at the word of my mouth, and with the utterance of my lips I have frightened provinces. I am Haman; my name was called Viceroy of the King, Father of the King. I beg thee, righteous Mordecai, not to do to me as I thought to do to thee. . . . Do not remember against me the hatred of Agag, nor the jealousy of Amalek.[6]

When Haman appeals to "righteous" Mordecai for mercy, he implies that righteousness demands that Mordecai spare his life. But by his own admission, Haman's unwillingness to forgive Mordecai's affront to his honor and to spare Mordecai's people from death reveals Haman as being unmerciful himself and therefore unrighteous by his own definition. The interpreter(s) who wrote this targum clearly implies that in this particular case "righteousness" did not mean mercy for Haman, anymore than Saul's "mercy" on Agag was righteous. To be righteous meant being the agent of God's command of death to Amalek. Mordecai, the righteous one, ignores Haman's pleas and holds the "hatred" for Agag and the Amalekites against Haman because God had commanded they be destroyed, and Haman was one of them. To fulfill righteousness in this case Mordecai must kill Haman, not spare him.[7]

The irony of Haman's downfall in Esther is especially unsettling when one realizes that Haman indeed got what he deserved, but for crimes he did not actually commit. He did not plot to assassinate the queen, nor was he attempting to molest her, though Esther allowed the

---

6. Quoted in Paton, *The Book of Esther*, 265.

7. Interestingly, Paton, who criticizes Esther for her lack of pity on Haman, says not a word about Mordecai's similar hardness of heart when he discusses this scene from the targum.

king to conveniently take it that way. Yet the author does not allow us to feel sympathy for Haman, for at every step of the way, Haman's own fatal pride moves him toward his own destruction.

The first-century Jewish historian, Josephus, comments:

> And from hence I cannot forbear to admire God, and to learn hence his wisdom and justice, not only in punishing the wickedness of Haman, but in so disposing it, that he should undergo the very same punishment which he had contrived for another; as also, because thereby he teaches others this lesson, that what mischiefs any one prepares against another, he without knowing of it, first contrives it against himself.[8]

HUMAN EVIL AND **divine justice.** Who gets life and who does not? In this chapter both Esther and Haman face death and plead for life. When Esther reveals Haman as her mortal enemy, she at the same time reveals herself to be Jewish. In so doing, she not only indicts herself for living a lie in the harem of the king, she also brings herself under the irrevocable decree of death against the Jews. Although Haman himself is dead by the end of the chapter, Esther's plea for her life and for the life of her people remains unanswered. Despite the king's assurance, stated three times over, that he will certainly grant her request, has Esther asked for something not even the ruler of Persia's power and wealth can grant? The question remains to be answered.

The suddenness of Haman's death and his inability to prevent it is unnerving. One day he was on top of the world, with all the wealth and power that attends high political rank. He could boast to family and friends about his position and favor with the king and queen. The very next day, he is executed in disgrace. Overnight, the tables have turned, and he did not see it coming.

Driven by uncontrollable pride and arrogance, Haman had plotted to slaughter the Jewish people because his lust for power over others could not be satisfied as long as Mordecai the Jew refused to bow to him.

---

8. Josephus, *Antiquities of the Jews*, in *The Works of Josephus*, trans. W. Whiston (Lynn, Mass.: Hendrickson, repr. 1980), 241.

Given full reign, pride, like greed and lust, is insatiable. Haman does not appear to be anti-Semitic in the modern sense of the word, for he would probably have been willing to commit genocide against any population if it satisfied his megalomaniac pursuit of honor and power. His plan to take revenge on one man by annihilating his entire race was an evil of demonic proportions, regardless of who those people were. The enormous stature of Haman's evil is pictured in the seventy-five-foot height of the gallows he unknowingly constructed for himself. His sudden and unpreventable destruction was the just reward of such an evil mind.

But the story moves to a new plane of theological significance precisely because the people he picked on happened to be the Jews, the people Yahweh had chosen as his own. Speaking better than she knew, Haman's own wife, Zeresh, predicted that because Mordecai was Jewish, Haman could not stand before him, but would come to ruin (6:13). While inviting us to reflect on the question of who gets life and who does not, the author of Esther reveals the nature and destiny of human evil and the mysterious workings of divine justice.

Human evil, wherever it occurs and for whatever motivation, always sets itself against God, because God is the definition of goodness and righteousness. Divine justice inevitably and inextricably means the destruction of evil. The author of Esther shows that evil is personal. It is not some ethereal substance "out there"; evil does not exist apart from beings who are evil. Therefore, in order to deliver the Jewish people from annihilation as God promised in his covenant with them, God necessarily had to destroy the evil that threatened their existence. In this case that evil came in the person of Haman. Mercy on Haman would have been inconsistent with God's covenant.

Nevertheless, Haman's death illustrates that the divinely appointed path to destruction is a path that proceeds step-by-step from the will of the wicked person. There is perhaps no better biblical illustration than Haman of the truth stated by the great Christian theologian John Calvin, "Man falls according as God's providence ordains, but he falls by his own fault."[9]

If God's deliverance of his people in the book of Esther is by providence, so also is Haman's destruction. Deliverance of one and destruc-

---

9. Quoted in R. C. Sproul and Jerry Bridges, *The Providence of God Study Guide* (Orlando, Fla.: Ligonier, 1990), 69.

tion of the other are correlative in the book of Esther, shown as two sides of the same coin. Yet even though the deliverance providentially orchestrated by God necessarily implies the destruction of Haman, the author shows that Haman is responsible for each step that leads to his own death, even while mistakenly thinking he is safe in his power, wealth, and prestige.

Haman's example shows that human evil is self-deceptive. It allows evildoers to believe themselves justified in their evil actions and clever enough not to get caught in their own web. Haman had all the resources of the empire on his side as he schemed and plotted—power, prestige, wealth—but it all came to nothing because of that one unforeseen, unpredictable night of the king's insomnia. We have all read well-written mysteries of the "perfect" murder that is finally solved by some chance event the murderer could never have foreseen or prevented. People sin with the delusion that while others may get caught, they will not.

Evil is also self-deceptive because while it appears to provide well-being and safety, it feeds off impulses that blind us to the truth. Haman's true, precarious situation was veiled to him by the darkness of his own thinking. The truth he could not see was that while he thought he was prescribing his own honor, it was really Mordecai's (6:6–9). He constructed a gallows of colossal size, thinking it was for Mordecai, but in reality it turned out to be his own (5:14). Haman boasted to his friends of being honored by being invited alone to the queen's banquet, not realizing the truth that it was an invitation to his own execution. For Haman, things were actually not what they appeared to be, even while he himself was doing them. Suddenly, without warning, the true destiny of human evil is revealed: destruction by the long-promised justice of God. On the final judgment day when the truth is revealed, the condemned will finally realize that they have no one to blame but themselves.

Identification with a people. While reflecting on who gets life and who does not, the author of Esther reveals that life and death are determined by identification with a people. In that moment of horror when Haman finally sees the truth and realizes the import and consequences of what he has done, he begs for life, but to no avail. Haman is an Agagite, and his destiny is with this people whom God has already condemned to destruction. By virtue of his identity as an Agagite,

Haman comes to destruction, but is nevertheless a destruction he has built with his own hands as surely as he built the gallows.

Esther's destiny also is one with her people. If they perish, she will perish. By virtue of her identity with them, Esther shares in the destiny of God's people. Because God promised to deliver his people from the threat of Amalek, the destruction of Haman implies the salvation of the Jews. But at this point in the story, that deliverance is only implied and not realized.

In New Testament theology, life and death are also shown to be by identification with a people. The work of Jesus Christ is the consummation of God's covenant promises to ancient Israel (2 Cor. 1:20). Thus, the ultimate fulfillment of God's promise to his people for protection from death is found in Jesus Christ. Identification with him constitutes a people who will be delivered from death and live forever, just as Jesus was. In John 14:19 Jesus says to his disciples, "Because I live, you also will live." Conversely, to be outside of Christ is to be numbered among the people God has already condemned to death as defined in Genesis 3—humanity at large. The apostle Paul puts it this way: "As in Adam all die, so in Christ all will be made alive" (1 Cor. 15:22). Jesus Christ invites Jew and Gentile, people of all races, religions, and ethnic groups, to be born again into the people who will be saved by God's grace from destruction, the church.

Fallen human nature set itself against God in the Garden of Eden and was condemned to death by God. That fallen nature is embodied in the book of Esther as the Agagite nature of Haman, but it is the universal condition of all who have not been reconciled to God in Christ. Haman, the powerful, wealthy Agagite, pridefully sets out to live in a way that seems right to him, but in the end finds out only too late that he has actually set himself against God and his people. Sadly, so it will be with those who are not in Christ on their own day of judgment.

Esther 8:1–17

❧

THAT SAME DAY King Xerxes gave Queen Esther the estate of Haman, the enemy of the Jews. And Mordecai came into the presence of the king, for Esther had told how he was related to her. ²The king took off his signet ring, which he had reclaimed from Haman, and presented it to Mordecai. And Esther appointed him over Haman's estate.

³Esther again pleaded with the king, falling at his feet and weeping. She begged him to put an end to the evil plan of Haman the Agagite, which he had devised against the Jews. ⁴Then the king extended the gold scepter to Esther and she arose and stood before him.

⁵"If it pleases the king," she said, "and if he regards me with favor and thinks it the right thing to do, and if he is pleased with me, let an order be written overruling the dispatches that Haman son of Hammedatha, the Agagite, devised and wrote to destroy the Jews in all the king's provinces. ⁶For how can I bear to see disaster fall on my people? How can I bear to see the destruction of my family?"

⁷King Xerxes replied to Queen Esther and to Mordecai the Jew, "Because Haman attacked the Jews, I have given his estate to Esther, and they have hanged him on the gallows. ⁸Now write another decree in the king's name in behalf of the Jews as seems best to you, and seal it with the king's signet ring—for no document written in the king's name and sealed with his ring can be revoked."

⁹At once the royal secretaries were summoned—on the twenty-third day of the third month, the month of Sivan. They wrote out all Mordecai's orders to the Jews, and to the satraps, governors and nobles of the 127 provinces stretching from India to Cush. These orders were written in the script of each province and the language of each

people and also to the Jews in their own script and language. ¹⁰Mordecai wrote in the name of King Xerxes, sealed the dispatches with the king's signet ring, and sent them by mounted couriers, who rode fast horses especially bred for the king.

¹¹The king's edict granted the Jews in every city the right to assemble and protect themselves; to destroy, kill and annihilate any armed force of any nationality or province that might attack them and their women and children; and to plunder the property of their enemies. ¹²The day appointed for the Jews to do this in all the provinces of King Xerxes was the thirteenth day of the twelfth month, the month of Adar. ¹³A copy of the text of the edict was to be issued as law in every province and made known to the people of every nationality so that the Jews would be ready on that day to avenge themselves on their enemies.

¹⁴The couriers, riding the royal horses, raced out, spurred on by the king's command. And the edict was also issued in the citadel of Susa.

¹⁵Mordecai left the king's presence wearing royal garments of blue and white, a large crown of gold and a purple robe of fine linen. And the city of Susa held a joyous celebration. ¹⁶For the Jews it was a time of happiness and joy, gladness and honor. ¹⁷In every province and in every city, wherever the edict of the king went, there was joy and gladness among the Jews, with feasting and celebrating. And many people of other nationalities became Jews because fear of the Jews had seized them.

HAMAN IS GONE, but the evil he set in motion lives on in the decree of death against the Jewish people. The king's anger has subsided with Haman's execution. This suggests the ruthless king was not angry because Haman had plotted to annihilate a whole race of people in his empire, even if they were Esther's people, for that danger was still threatening. Apparently the king's pride had been hurt by Haman's affront to his honor, first by the decree against his queen's people and then by falling on her couch. Ironically, Haman's injured pride had driven him to plot the destruction of Mordecai and the Jews; the king's injured pride had driven him to execute Haman.[1] There is perhaps no better illustration of this in the Bible than "pride goes before destruction" (Prov. 16:18). The death of Haman sets a sequence of reversals into motion.

Because Haman was executed as a traitor to the throne, his property was confiscated. Herodotus reports an instance where the property of an executed traitor reverted to the king, who could dispose of it at will.[2] In this case because Esther was the person wronged by Haman, the king bestows Haman's estate on her.

Immediately, Esther summons Mordecai into Xerxes' presence, who gives to Mordecai, the man who had years before saved the king's life, the signet ring previously worn by Haman. In a great reversal Mordecai is vested with all the power and authority previously wielded by Haman (cf. 3:10). Having received Haman's estate, Esther in turn appoints Mordecai over all the wealth and property previously owned by Haman. Ironically, Haman's plot to destroy Mordecai leads to Mordecai's acquiring both Haman's position and property. As Fox points out, this scene restructures the relationship between Esther and Mordecai. "She now is a source and agent of wealth and empowerment for Mordecai."[3]

Esther pleads with Xerxes to "put an end to" Haman's evil death decree that still stands against her people (v. 3); but the king is unable to do so, for the decree of death is irrevocable. Xerxes' bravado that had previously assured granting Esther's request is now humiliated. All the power and wealth of the world cannot cancel death. Now, however, Esther and Mordecai have power and authority equal to Haman's. The only solution to their dilemma is to write another decree to counteract the first with equal force.

---

1. The dynamics of honor and shame in biblical cultures (and in the Middle East today) operated in ways unfamiliar to readers in modern Western culture. See L. R. Klein, "Honor and Shame in Esther," in *A Feminist Companion to Esther, Judith and Susanna*, ed. A. Brenner (Sheffield: Sheffield Academic Press, 1995); *Honor and Shame in the World of the Bible*, ed. V. H. Matthews and D. C. Benjamin, *Semeia* 6 (Atlanta: Scholars, 1996).

2. LCL: *Herodotus* 3.128–29.

3. Michael V. Fox, *Character and Ideology in the Book of Esther*, 202.

The royal secretaries are summoned, just as they had been previously summoned more than two months earlier by Haman (cf. 3:12). Just as they had done for Haman, the scribes write Mordecai's orders to "the satraps, governors and nobles" (v. 9). However, Mordecai's decree is addressed also to "the Jews," who are mentioned first in the list. The effect is to put the Jews of Persia on the same level as the rulers and to give them a distinct identity among the peoples of Persia. The people who were the helpless target of evil are now empowered.

As Haman had done, Mordecai writes in the name of King Xerxes. His message is that the Jews may take whatever measures are necessary to defend themselves. He seals the edict with the king's signet ring—the same one used by Haman to seal the decree of death against them—and sends out the edict by mounted couriers to every part of the empire (v. 10; cf. 3:12). Like Haman's edict, a copy of Mordecai's words was to be issued as law in every province and made known to the people of every nationality so that preparations could be made for that day (8:13; cf. 3:14).

In order to counteract Haman's decree, in other words, Mordecai has just effected a legalized war between the Jews of the Persian empire and any people of any nationality who might set themselves against the Jews. Just as Haman's edict had been posted publicly in Susa, Mordecai's edict was also to be posted in Susa (8:14; cf. 3:15). Civil war would be authorized even in the citadel of the king.

The author of Esther has constructed a contrast of reversals in chiastic order (see chart in comments on ch. 6). Haman's original edict had caused "great mourning among the Jews, with fasting, weeping and wailing. Many lay in sackcloth and ashes" (4:3). After that decree had gone out, Mordecai had clothed himself in sackcloth and ashes and went through the city, wailing loudly and bitterly. In such a state he could not enter the king's gate, much less the king's presence (see comments on 4:1). Now, as the counter-decree goes out, the reverse occurs. Mordecai comes from the very presence of the king "wearing royal garments of blue and white, a large crown of gold and a purple robe of fine linen," and he goes throughout the city in joyous procession (8:15; cf. 4:1–2). Mordecai, the Jew condemned to death, has risen from sackcloth and ashes to take the royal position of the one who had condemned him. His decree also brought "joy and gladness among the Jews, with feasting and celebrating" (8:17).

Haman's sudden death and Mordecai's rise to power brought such fear to "many people of other nationalities" that they "became Jews" (8:17). The Hebrew word translated "became Jews" occurs only here in the Old Testament, and its meaning is debated. How are we to understand this "conversion"? Some have argued that the Persians recognized the improbable series of events as the hand of God and thus responded in true, heartfelt conversion to the God of the Jews.

Frederic Bush expresses doubt whether this word denoted a sincere religious conversion.[4] As he points out, the people living throughout the empire would neither have known about nor seen the improbable series of events that led to Haman's downfall, especially since most of them occurred in the private quarters of the palace in Susa. They would have known only two things: They had a law written by Haman, who was now dead, and a second law written by Mordecai the Jew, who now held the reigns of power. Bush concludes:

> The enemies of the Jews might have been aware of an unnamed power ranged on the side of the Jews, but in the context it can hardly be some sense of the numinous that prompts the non-Jewish peoples to profess to be Jews, let alone a religious awe of the God of the Jews. It is surely, rather, the dread of the superior political and military power now wielded by Mordecai and the Jewish community that prompts their profession.[5]

Bridging Contexts

WITH THIS CHAPTER, as noted above, events leading to the deliverance of the Jews begin to reverse the previous events that initiated the conflict and threat. In almost identical words, Mordecai receives the signet ring once given to Haman, summons the royal scribes, and writes in the name of the king.

A translation issue. The decree of Mordecai echoes the words of Haman's decree. Haman effected as public law the order "to destroy, kill and annihilate all the Jews—young and old, women and little children—on a single day, the thirteenth day of the twelfth month, the month of Adar, and to plunder their goods" (3:13). Mordecai's decree

---

4. Frederic Bush, *Ruth/Esther*, 449.
5. Ibid., 449.

effected as public law the right of the Jews "to destroy, kill and anni-hilate any armed force of any nationality or province that might attack them and their women and children; and to plunder the property of their enemies ... [on] the thirteenth day of the twelfth month, the month of Adar" (8:11–12).

The extent of the parity between Haman's decree of death and Mordecai's counter-decree is obscured by the NIV translation. The NIV renders "women and children" as part of the compound direct object of the verb "attack," translating the decree as giving the Jews permis-sion to destroy any armed force that would "attack them [the Jews] and their women and children." This reading of the Hebrew is defended by J. Baldwin, a Christian commentator, as well as by R. Gordis, a Jew-ish exegete.[6] It is, however, a minority view among commentators and translators, who instead construe the Hebrew text of verse 11 to read: "... to destroy, kill, and annihilate any armed force and women and children of any nationality that might attack them."[7] In this reading of the Hebrew text, the Jews were given exactly the same terms of destruction that had been pronounced against them, their women, and their children.

Although she disagrees with this, Joyce Baldwin recognizes that commentators have been "almost unanimous" that, in fact, Mordecai's decree authorized the Jews to kill not only the men who attacked them, but the wives and children of those men as well. Those few commen-tators, like Baldwin, who have opposed this reading of the Hebrew have generally done so on the grounds that it seems to create a moral problem, for God's people should not be party to the same kind of mass slaughter that had been directed against their non-warring dependents. On her part, Baldwin explains that such interpreters and translators have misread the Hebrew because they understand the Esther story to be an example of "the retribution theme of the Old Testament by per-mitting, and even glorying in, the outworking of 'an eye for an eye and a tooth for a tooth' (Ex. 21:23–25), so proving its barbarity by com-

---

6. Joyce G. Baldwin, *Esther*, 97; Robert Gordis, "Studies in the Esther Narrative," *JBL* 95 (1976): 49–53.

7. Commentators who read permission for the Jews to kill the women and children of their attackers include F. Bush, *Ruth/Esther*, 443, 447; M. Fox, *Character and Ideology in the Book of Esther*, 99–100; Jon D. Levenson, *Esther: A Commentary*, 110–11; Carey A. Moore, *Esther*, 76, 80; L. B. Paton, *The Book of Esther*, 274. Major English translations that support this view include the NRSV, NASB, NKJV, NCV, and NAB. The NLT agrees with the NIV translation.

parison with the New."[8] In other words, she sees such interpreters to be motivated by a Christian agenda of amplifying the contrast between the Old and New Testaments on the issue of retributive violence.

However, not all interpreters who are offended by reading the decree as giving permission to the Jews to kill the women and children of their enemies are Christian. As already noted, Jewish scholar R. Gordis, like Baldwin, attempts to eliminate the perceived moral difficulty by reading "children" and "wives" in the Hebrew text as the third direct object of "attacking" ("... attacking them, [their] women and [their] children"), rather than in apposition with "armed force." His rendering, however, is criticized by M. Fox, also a Jewish scholar, who writes that Gordis's "valiant effort to eliminate the moral difficulty ... does not (regrettably) accord with the Hebrew, which lacks 'their' before 'children' and 'wives' ... even if the Jews did not carry out this aspect of Mordecai's decree, the decree does allow it."[9]

Christian scholar F. Bush criticizes the NIV reading endorsed by Baldwin by pointing out that the parallelism between Haman's decree in 3:13 and Mordecai's in 8:11 "clearly reveals" that the women and children of the attackers are to be destroyed:[10]

| 3:13 | to destroy | all the Jews ... | children and women | and to despoil them |
| 8:11 | to destroy | all the forces ... attacking them | children and women | and to despoil them |

It is the literary structure of reversals occurring throughout the book that favors the majority translation, not any agenda that contrasts the barbarity of the Old Testament in contrast to the New. If there is ambiguity in the Hebrew text of verse 11, the literary structure of reversals operating elsewhere throughout the book of Esther weighs in favor of translating verse 11 (against the NIV) as "to destroy, kill and annihilate any armed force, and their women and children, of any nationality or province that might attack them...." If this is indeed the wording of Mordecai's decree intended by the author, what then can be said to address the moral question of the Jews' being given permission to kill the children and wives of their enemies?

8. Baldwin, *Esther*, 97.
9. Fox, *Character and Ideology in the Book of Esther*, 99–100.
10. Bush, *Ruth/Esther*, 447.

A moral problem. One way to play down the moral question that surfaces with this translation is to note that even though the decree permitted the taking of plunder, the Jews did not in fact do so (9:10, 15–16). In a similar vein, therefore, as Fox's comments above suggest, even though the decree gave the Jews permission to kill the women and children of their enemies, it was not necessarily carried out. In fact, when the killing in Susa is reported, the body count refers only to "men" (9:6, 12). However, when the final count of 75,000 dead is given, the reference is more generally to the "enemies" (9:16).

Yet some interpreters see a moral problem even if the attack by the Jews was limited to Persian men, because such an attack seems to be unwarranted in light of what is perceived to be the Persian pro-Jewish sentiment after Mordecai comes to power. For instance, S. Goldman calls the attack "a massacre, a Jewish bloodbath against Persians."[11] But he does not see a Jewish bloodbath against Persians to be a "disservice" to the Jewish name, because

> the narrative of the Jewish attack on the Persians is an example of Jewish self-criticism, a bold questioning of the Jewish self-image.... Irony here produces a leveling effect: Jews behave like Persians, and Persians behave like Jews.... People turn out to be not so easily divisible as we have been led to think. Who is a Jew? Who is a Persian? The irony of a Jewish writer raising such questions is itself an ethical act. This irony means there is no superior race: "Jews in their actions, are not essentially different from the heathen."[12]

But a close reading of the text gives no reason to believe the Jews killed the Persians unprovoked, as Goldman suggests. The decree permitted the Jews only to defend themselves *against attackers*, making it a matter of self-defense. Presumably the Persians who were killed had in fact attacked the Jews, regardless of whatever pro-Jewish sentiment others held. If the Jews did attack their enemies indiscriminately, their actions exceeded the permission of the decree.

By Goldman's understanding, the book of Esther served as a self-criticism of the Jews in Persia, showing them to share in the violent human nature of their Gentile neighbors. This view is certainly consis-

---

11. Stan Goldman, "Narrative and Ethical Ironies in Esther," *JSOT* 47 (1990): 15–31.
12. Ibid., 24–25.

tent with the Lord's much earlier admonition to ancient Israel as they were about to enter the Promised Land (Deut. 9:4–6):

> After the LORD your God has driven them [the Anakites] out before you, do not say to yourself, "The LORD has brought me here to take possession of this land *because of my righteousness.*" No, it is on account of the wickedness of these nations that the LORD is going to drive them out before you. *It is not because of your righteousness or your integrity* that you are going in to take possession of their land; but on account of the wickedness of these nations, the LORD your God will drive them out before you, to accomplish what he swore to your fathers, to Abraham, Isaac and Jacob. Understand, then, that *it is not because of your righteousness* that the LORD your God is giving you this good land to possess, for you are a stiff-necked people. (emphasis added)

God's election of his people was not based on their own inherent moral superiority over the nations they would subdue. In fact, the reason the Jews had been later expelled from the Promised Land and were living in exile was because they and their kings had become as wicked as the Gentile nations. The Jews of Persia were capable of the same extent and decree of violence as their pagan neighbors.

The concept of holy war and its cessation. Perhaps this passage raises a moral question in the mind of modern readers that the original readers, and perhaps even the author, would not have recognized because they were familiar with the concept and practice of holy war.[13] Baldwin suggests an essential component in understanding the moral dimension of holy war when she writes that the decree as understood to give permission to kill the women and children of the Jews' enemies highlights its barbarity *"by comparison with the New* [Testament]" (emphasis added).[14] Why is it that retributive violence is found throughout the Old Testament but in the New Testament Jesus teaches us to love our enemies as ourselves (Matt. 5:44; Luke 6:27, 35)? How are these two contradictory ideas to be understood?

---

13. This is probably why Americans have difficulty understanding Middle Eastern politics, such as the intransigent position of Saddam Hussein, when they read headlines such as "Iraqis Are Told to Prepare for 'Holy War' on UN Sanctions," *New York Times* (January 19, 1998), A3.

14. Baldwin, *Esther*, 97.

The death of Jesus Christ, the Messiah of Israel, provides the only basis for the cessation of holy war, and the infilling of the Holy Spirit provides the only power by which one may love one's enemies as oneself. All of the vengeance God's people would like to wreak on those who practice evil has now been satisfied in the suffering and death of Jesus. He has taken the wages of sin, he has suffered the vengeance of evil. The vengeance due to us for our sins against others and due to them for their sins against us has been satisfied in Jesus' body on the cross. It is only on the basis of recognizing that the penalty has been paid by Jesus that we can forgive others as we have been forgiven. True holy war in human history has ceased because Jesus has fought its last episode on the cross.

It is no accident of history that the modern nations that still endorse the concept of holy war (Arabic, *jihad*) are nations that reject the gospel of Jesus Christ and the moral system he commands. The five phases of holy war spanning biblical history and its transformation by the death of Jesus are explained by T. Longman:[15]

(1) God fights for Israel
(2) God fights against Israel
(3) God gives hope for future reconciliation
(4) Jesus Christ is the divine warrior who ends holy war on the earth
(5) The coming day of Christ will destroy all evildoers.

The brutality of the Esther story that has so troubled interpreters and its relationship to the teachings of Jesus in the New Testament must be understood within the redemptive-historical context of holy war and Jesus' role in it.

As pointed out in the comments on 3:13, Haman's edict against the Jews of Persia echoed what was to be the fate of the Amalekites, whom Haman represents. Would God's people actually suffer the same fate as the wicked nations because of their disobedience to the covenant? Would God use Haman the Agagite to destroy the Jews exactly as their ancestors the Israelites had been commanded to destroy the Agagites? Such a reversal would have been more than tragically ironic. In historical hindsight, it would have ended God's redemptive

---

15. Tremper Longman III, "Our Divine Warrior," in *Bold Love*, Dan B. Allendar and Tremper Longman III (Colorado Springs: NavPress, 1992).

work in human history and signaled his abandonment to sin of not only his people Israel, but all humanity. In comparing the harsh terms of Mordecai's counter-edict to Haman's, both must be viewed in the greater context of biblical history.

Throughout Esther 8, the author has unfolded events in words that clearly echo but reverse events from the previous chapters. Therefore, Mordecai's decree is to be understood as the exact reversal of Haman's. This argues that the destiny plotted by Haman for the Jews is being turned back on the enemies of the Jews, including enemy wives and children. While the thought of Jewish-perpetrated mass killing may seem reprehensible by standards of modern morality (and probably even more so to readers of Esther on this side of the Nazi holocaust), the wording of Haman's decree (and subsequently, Mordecai's) actually echoes the Lord's words to King Saul given through the prophet Samuel (1 Sam. 15:2—3):

> This is what the LORD Almighty says: "I will punish the Amalekites for what they did to Israel when they waylaid them as they came up from Egypt. Now go, attack the Amalekites and totally destroy everything that belongs to them. Do not spare them; put to death *men and women, children and infants,* cattle and sheep, camels and donkeys." (emphasis added)

The Lord's words through the prophet Samuel in turn reflect his ancient promise in Exodus 17:8, 14—16, when the Amalekites were the first nation of the world who tried to destroy the Israelites:

> The Amalekites came and attacked the Israelites at Rephidim....
> Then the LORD said to Moses, "Write this on a scroll as something to be remembered and make sure that Joshua hears it, because I will completely blot out the memory of Amalek from under heaven."
> Moses built an altar and called it The LORD is my Banner. He said, "For hands were lifted up to the throne of the LORD. The LORD will be at war against the Amalekites from generation to generation."

The promise given by God at the time of the Exodus turned into a command of destruction in Deuteronomy 25:17—19, when the Lord said to his people as they were about to enter the Promised Land:

Remember what the Amalekites did to you along the way when you came out of Egypt. When you were weary and worn out, they met you on your journey and cut off all who were lagging behind; they had no fear of God. When the LORD your God gives you rest from all the enemies around you in the land he is giving you to possess as an inheritance, you shall blot out the memory of Amalek from under heaven. Do not forget!

The Amalekites as a people—men, women, and children—are paradigmatic in biblical theology as the enemies of God's people. God's double-edged promise turns into God's command as he sends Israel's army into battle against them.

Whether consciously or not, Haman has attempted by his decree of death against the Jews to reverse the destiny of destruction, which God promised to the Amalekites, bringing it against God's own people, the Jewish race. Mordecai's decree reverses Haman's and therefore turns that promise of destruction back onto the enemies of the Jews, who were seeking to destroy them. Mordecai's decree echoes the command of the Lord himself, who throughout the Old Testament declared holy war on the enemies of his people.[16] Because that promise of destruction included the wives and children of the Amalekites in 1 Samuel 15, so should the Hebrew be read in Mordecai's decree in Esther 8:11.

However, there are important differences between the mandate of 1 Samuel 15 and Mordecai's decree that must not be ignored. Unlike Israel's King Saul and his army, the Jews of Persia were not to initiate the attack, but only to take whatever measures necessary to defend themselves. The Jews of the Diaspora were to live in peace with their neighbors unless their own existence was threatened. They were then given the right to defend themselves by totally destroying anyone, regardless of nationality, who tried to destroy them. This broadens the definition of their enemy to include any attackers, and at the same time loosens the association of the mandate with its historical roots in the Promised Land. Perhaps the Esther story gave biblical justification for later Jewish writers to call their enemies Amalekites or Agagites, regardless of their nationality. Thus, both God's promise to

---

16. For an in-depth treatment of the biblical theme of holy war, see Tremper Longman III and Daniel Reid, *God Is a Warrior* (Grand Rapids: Zondervan, 1995).

protect his people and his command to destroy those who would destroy them are extended beyond the geographical borders of the Promised Land to wherever God's people are dwelling.

THE CONTEMPORARY SIGNIFICANCE derived from this passage depends on whether or not the reader views its meaning through the cross of Jesus Christ. If the reader does not, then it is indeed difficult to avoid using this text as a biblical rationale for some form of continued "holy" war, as Baruch Goldstein apparently did (see the Introduction). Christians who understand the hermeneutical implications of the cross of Jesus, however, must understand the significance of the passage quite differently.

The destruction of sin. If Haman's plot had succeeded and the Jewish nation had been annihilated during the reign of Persia, obviously Jesus would not have been born and God's plan of redemption would have been thwarted. The entire redemptive purpose and promise of God were inseparably bound to the lot of his covenant people. This fact alone, however, does not seem to demand the necessity of killing men, women, and children of other nations. Could not God preserve and protect Jesus' ancestors without resorting to the violence reported in Esther?

Whether we like it or not, the Old Testament is full of God's violence against the nations, who are portrayed as being such evil and sinful people that their destruction is the only remedy. Does this mean that there were no "good" people among those nations, people who did not deserve such judgment? This is the question Abraham asked the Lord before the destruction of Sodom and Gomorrah (Gen. 18:16–33). Far be it from God "to kill the righteous with the wicked, treating the righteous and the wicked alike." Abraham's understanding of God's justice prompted him to ask the Lord how many righteous people it would take to spare the cities of Sodom and Gomorrah. The Lord indicated a willingness to withhold destruction for the sake of the righteous—even just a handful among the city's population.

Apparently, however, not even ten righteous people, whether men, women, or children, could be found in Sodom and Gomorrah. Only Lot and his two daughters escaped the destruction of the cities, and that only by virtue of their relationship to Abraham (i.e., being a part of Abraham's people), not because of their own righteousness. The destruction of Sodom and Gomorrah and other nations in the Old Testament shows that in truth as only God can see it, there are no "good" people who by their own merit are undeserving of destruction. The Old Testament stories of death and destruction illustrate the New Testament teaching, "For all have sinned and fall short of the glory of God," and "the wages of sin is death" (Rom. 3:23; 6:23).

From the beginning of time God's war has been against sin and evil. It is easy to think wrongly of sin and evil as being abstractions apart from people. We seem to want God to destroy sin and evil but leave people alone. However, sin and evil do not exist apart from beings who sin and beings who do evil, whether angelic or human. Sin entered the world when Adam and Eve aligned themselves against God (Gen. 3). Because of their separation from God, he pronounced his irrevocable decree of death against them and all their descendants. The nature of sin (singular) is opposition to God, expressed as disobedience to his revealed will, i.e., various sins (plural). Because we are all sinners and evildoers, we all have God's irrevocable decree of death against us. God could have justly destroyed the earth and everyone on it, for none of us is "good" by God's high standards. Instead, he chose to issue a counter-decree to redeem a people out of sin and evil and into righteousness, removing them from the realm of his destruction to the realm of deliverance.

God's counter-decree. In Esther the irrevocable decree of death and the counter-decree of life both issue from one and the same authority— the king's signet ring sealed both. There has been much discussion in the commentaries whether it is historically true that the laws of Persian kings were irrevocable, since there is no extrabiblical attestation in Herodotus or other sources of this practice. It was not unreasonable for a monarch to refuse to rescind a law once publicly issued, for in doing so he would lose face and it would undermine his authority.[17]

Even if the author is using poetic license by introducing this element of irrevocability, perhaps he is making a theological point about human destiny. Just as Xerxes king of Persia could not simply rescind the first decree of death, God, King of the universe, cannot simply rescind the

---

17. Remember that a monarchy is not a democracy.

decree of death pronounced in the Garden of Eden against humanity. Instead, he issues a counter-decree of life, the gospel of Jesus Christ. Because God did not simply rescind the curse of death on humanity, his counter-decree of redemption necessarily resulted in the incarnation of his Son and in that Son's death on the cross.

This counter-decree of life was initiated in history long ago when Yahweh chose a people out of all the nations on earth through which he would achieve this purpose of redemption. He set aside a place for his redeemed people to live in peace and security, but it was a land already populated with wicked and sinful peoples. As he sent his people, ancient Israel, into the land, he promised to make a place a for them, which necessarily meant destroying the wicked population already occupying the land. But then he cautioned Israel that the reason why they were receiving the land was not because of their righteousness but because of his grace (see Deut. 9:4–6, quoted above). The Lord warned his people (8:19–20):

> If you ever forget the LORD your God and follow other gods and worship and bow down to them, I testify against you today that you will surely be destroyed. Like the nations the LORD destroyed before you, so you will be destroyed for not obeying the LORD your God.

Acting as Yahweh's agency on earth, Israel's kings were commanded to destroy completely peoples whose wickedness had reached such proportions that they were threatening the very existence of God's redemptive work through his people. As unsettling as it may be to reflect on the reality of God's wrath, divine wrath is a necessary complement to God's love and justice. Marcion, a Christian heretic of the second century, did not understand this, believing instead that the Father of Jesus Christ was too merciful and loving to be the same wrathful God of Old Testament Israel.

If, however, you or a loved one have been the victim of a horrible evil, your innate sense of justice demands that the wrong not simply be overlooked but that the perpetrator face appropriate consequences. To say that God is too loving to punish the wicked implicitly plays off God's love for the victim against God's love for the perpetrator. The full extent of God's love for all of us can be appreciated only by recognizing the full extent of his wrath poured out on Jesus for the sins of the world (John 3:16). It is on the Cross that God's love and his justice are reconciled.

The essence of holy war in the Old Testament is not about two nations in warfare, one of which happens to be Israel. Holy war is about God warring against sin and evil on the earth. His people were to live in the safety of holiness and righteousness. Their existence as God's redeemed people was threatened from the beginning by the rest of the world, of which the Amalekites became the paradigm nation. Therefore, the success of God's plan of redemption required the protection of his people in his war against evil, which required that those people take both offensive and defensive measures to assure their existence. This in turn meant that holy war became necessary whenever their existence was threatened until in the fullness of time, Jesus, the ultimate divine warrior and king of Israel, was born from and for God's people.

Salvation, in other words, necessarily implies destruction. Salvation's deepest significance is that people are actually saved from something both terrible and real, and that something is the wrath of God directed toward their sin and evil. Even in the Old Testament, God's wrath turned against his own people when they degenerated spiritually and morally to the point where they were as bad as the pagan peoples of the world. In judgment under God's wrath both Israel and Judah were destroyed, their cities burnt, and their people either killed by the sword or sent into a distant exile. Lamentations records Israel's understanding of God's wrath turned against his covenant nation (Lam. 2:5–6):

> The Lord is like an enemy;
> > he has swallowed up Israel.
> He has swallowed up all her palaces
> > and destroyed her strongholds.
> He has multiplied mourning and lamentation
> > for the Daughter of Judah.
> He has laid waste his dwelling like a garden;
> > he has destroyed his place of meeting.
> The LORD has made Zion forget
> > her appointed feasts and her Sabbaths;
> in his fierce anger he has spurned
> > both king and priest.

The destruction of God's chosen nation clearly demonstrates that God's violence is not directed against certain races or nations, but is against sin and evil wherever it is found. The army of ancient Israel was his agency, but when they failed to obey him, they found themselves under the same wrath he had for the nations. He shows no favoritism, regardless of nationality.

When God said in Deuteronomy 9:4, "Do not say to yourself, 'The LORD has brought me here to take possession of this land because of my righteousness,'" he declared that there are no inherently "good" people in any nation who by their merit are undeserving of death, including the people he had chosen to redeem. Yet God's promise and purpose were to save a people from his final destruction of the earth, and that purpose was inseparably bound to the people of his covenant. In his wrath he did not destroy Israel utterly when they turned to sin and evil, for to do so would have meant giving up on his plan to redeem humanity from destruction.

God's irrevocable decree of death and destruction has been countered by his decree that all who believe in his Son should not perish under his wrath but be delivered into eternal life. The violence of God against sin and evil can therefore be rightly understood only "in the shadow of the cross."[18] Jesus Christ is the ultimate divine warrior and king of Israel, who waged the final war against sin and evil on the cross on behalf of the people God will deliver from final destruction. As Reid and Longman explain,

> The paradox of the divine warrior is that while he fights off every effort to hijack Israel's destiny—whether from enemies without [e.g., Haman] or unfaithfulness within—he is also bearing the suffering of human history within himself. The God of battles carries sin and suffering with his own groans, and finally on the cross draws his sovereign wrath down upon himself.
>
> "Holy war" takes on new meaning in this light. The divine warrior, who formerly drove the sword of Assyria and Babylon into the heart of Israel and Judah, is himself pierced by the same sword, now in the hands of Rome.[19]

---

18. Daniel G. Reid and Tremper Longman III, "When God Declares War" *CT* (Oct. 28, 1996), 14—21. For a fuller treatment of the subject see their *God Is a Warrior*.

19. "When God Declares War," 20.

Today's war against sin and evil. Given Jesus' death and resurrection, is holy war still a legitimate concept for the way God works in the world today? Was Baruch Goldstein in any way justified for his assault on Purim in 1994 that killed fifty-five Palestinians and wounded 170 (see the Introduction)?

The church of Jesus Christ replaces the army of Israel as the agency of God that wars against sin and evil in the world, and the theater of the battle has moved to the human heart, where sin and evil reside. When the apostle Paul instructs Christians to "put on the full armor of God" (Eph. 6:11) in our fight against sin and evil, that armor is defined by the spiritual qualities of faith, righteousness, and truth. Each Christian faces an individual battle against the sin and evil in his or her own heart. Ultimate victory in this battle is guaranteed because of Jesus' victory over death and destruction when he rose from the grave and sent the Holy Spirit to empower those who are his to live righteously.

Are Christians now to wage holy war against unbelievers in the same way ancient Israel warred against the pagan peoples? In certain moments of Israel's history God commanded them to make war against the surrounding nations or they would not have survived. The church's survival today, however, does not depend on living securely within the boundaries of a particular geographical area. Our battle is "not against flesh and blood, but against the rulers, against the authorities, against the powers of this dark world and against the spiritual forces of evil in the heavenly realms" (Eph. 6:12). Jesus himself teaches that now our battle with our enemies is to be fought with weapons of love (Matt. 5:43), which is impossible without the power of the Holy Spirit. The marching orders of the army led by Jesus Christ are found in Matthew 28:19–20:

> Therefore go and make disciples of all nations, baptizing them
> in the name of the Father and of the Son and of the Holy Spirit,
> and teaching them to obey everything I have commanded you.
> And surely I am with you always, to the very end of the age.

It is through the conversion of people from the realm of evil and sin to the kingdom of the goodness and righteousness of Jesus Christ that the victory is now to be won.

Literal, physical holy war was once necessary for the survival of the Messiah's race until God's redemptive purposes were actualized in human history on the cross of Jesus Christ. This certainly does not mean that because Jesus has come, the Jewish people are now expendable! However, the Jewish people need Jesus the Messiah, the divine warrior and king, to deliver them from death no more or less than the people of other nations.

The biblical practice of holy war must not be confused with the legitimate right of Israel to exist as a modern nation today. Israel's existence today cannot be simply equated with the survival of God's covenant people in the ages before Christ, as if Jesus' death is irrelevant to the question. The right of Israel as a modern nation to use armed force to defend itself is as legitimate as the right of any other nation, but the continuing practice of holy war is not. Jesus Christ is the only Israelite righteous and just enough to wage holy war with clean hands and a pure heart. His cross is the only truly righteous theater of holy war. The cross of Jesus sanctifies all previous episodes of holy war in Israel's history and makes any subsequent episode carnal. After the Cross, the continuing practice of "holy war" is everything but holy.

Esther 9:1–19

❦

ON THE THIRTEENTH day of the twelfth month, the month of Adar, the edict commanded by the king was to be carried out. On this day the enemies of the Jews had hoped to overpower them, but now the tables were turned and the Jews got the upper hand over those who hated them. ²The Jews assembled in their cities in all the provinces of King Xerxes to attack those seeking their destruction. No one could stand against them, because the people of all the other nationalities were afraid of them. ³And all the nobles of the provinces, the satraps, the governors and the king's administrators helped the Jews, because fear of Mordecai had seized them. ⁴Mordecai was prominent in the palace; his reputation spread throughout the provinces, and he became more and more powerful.

⁵The Jews struck down all their enemies with the sword, killing and destroying them, and they did what they pleased to those who hated them. ⁶In the citadel of Susa, the Jews killed and destroyed five hundred men. ⁷They also killed Parshandatha, Dalphon, Aspatha, ⁸Poratha, Adalia, Aridatha, ⁹Parmashta, Arisai, Aridai and Vaizatha, ¹⁰the ten sons of Haman son of Hammedatha, the enemy of the Jews. But they did not lay their hands on the plunder.

¹¹The number of those slain in the citadel of Susa was reported to the king that same day. ¹²The king said to Queen Esther, "The Jews have killed and destroyed five hundred men and the ten sons of Haman in the citadel of Susa. What have they done in the rest of the king's provinces? Now what is your petition? It will be given you. What is your request? It will also be granted."

¹³"If it pleases the king," Esther answered, "give the Jews in Susa permission to carry out this day's edict tomorrow also, and let Haman's ten sons be hanged on gallows."

¹⁴So the king commanded that this be done. An edict was issued in Susa, and they hanged the ten sons of Haman. ¹⁵The Jews in Susa came together on the fourteenth day of the month of Adar, and they put to death in Susa three hundred men, but they did not lay their hands on the plunder.

¹⁶Meanwhile, the remainder of the Jews who were in the king's provinces also assembled to protect themselves and get relief from their enemies. They killed seventy-five thousand of them but did not lay their hands on the plunder. ¹⁷This happened on the thirteenth day of the month of Adar, and on the fourteenth they rested and made it a day of feasting and joy.

¹⁸The Jews in Susa, however, had assembled on the thirteenth and fourteenth, and then on the fifteenth they rested and made it a day of feasting and joy.

¹⁹That is why rural Jews—those living in villages—observe the fourteenth of the month of Adar as a day of joy and feasting, a day for giving presents to each other.

MORDECAI'S COUNTER-DECREE IMPLIED the survival of the Jewish people even before the thirteenth of Adar dawned. Eleven months after Haman had cast lots, the ill-fated day finally arrived. Before the author reports what happened that fateful day, he summarizes the significance of the events: "On this day the enemies of the Jews had hoped to overpower them, but now the tables were turned and the Jews got the upper hand over those who hated them" (v. 1). The outcome of the conflict had already been settled before it began because "the tables were turned." God's people would face the confrontation with the confidence that they would not be annihilated. In contrast, the people "of all the other nationalities" were living in fear of the Jews. The nobles, satraps, governors, and the king's officials helped the Jews in their defense, because they feared Mordecai, the man who had stood up to Haman and now ruled in his place.

In the armed conflict on Adar 13, the Jews struck down, killed, and destroyed those "who hated them." Five hundred men fell in Susa on the thirteenth and another three hundred the next day; seventy-five thousand died throughout the empire. The killing is reported in words that once again echo the Lord's command to Saul in 1 Samuel 15 (see comments on Bridging Contexts section of 8:1–17).

The author is careful to say three times that the Jews "did not lay their hands on the plunder" (vv. 10, 15, 16) even though Mordecai's decree allowed it. Mordecai's decree included the permission to plunder because he was reversing the exact terms that Haman's decree had previously established. However, unlike the Agagite's intent, the Jews understood the execution of Mordecai's decree as governed by the ancient command of holy war against the Amalekites.

One of the rules of ancient holy war was that plunder must not be taken. When Abram, for example, fought for Sodom because his nephew Lot had been taken captive, the king of Sodom offered him material reward. Abram, however, would accept nothing, lest that wicked city be the source of his prosperity (Gen. 14). This example set a precedent for God's people.

When the Lord commanded the conquest of the Promised Land, Joshua and the Israelites devoted whole cites to the Lord. This meant killing every living thing in it—men, women, children, cattle, sheep, donkeys—and burning the buildings to the ground. Any gold, silver, and precious articles found in the city were put in the treasury of the Lord's house (e.g., Josh. 6:20–24). The Hebrew word for such complete destruction was *ḥerem*, which means something devoted exclusively to God. There was to be no personal profit in holy war because the destroyers were acting not on their own behalf but as agents of God's wrath.

In actual fact, Israel's execution of holy war was often less than holy and tainted with their own sin. Immediately after crossing the Jordan, the twelve tribes were to conquer the land by waging holy war under Joshua's leadership. Jericho was the first city to be attacked with the orders that "the city and all that is in it are to be devoted to the LORD" (Josh. 6:17). The spectacular victory at Jericho was followed by the devastating Israelite defeat at Ai. Why was Israel defeated, even though their forces greatly outnumbered the men of Ai? The Lord said to Joshua in 7:11–12:

Israel has sinned; they have violated my covenant, which I commanded them to keep. They have taken some of the devoted things; they have stolen, they have lied, they have put them with their own possessions. That is why the Israelites cannot stand against their enemies; they turn their backs and run because they have been made liable to destruction. I will not be with you anymore unless you destroy whatever among you is devoted to destruction.

This disaster was caused by one man, Achan, who had taken a beautiful robe, two hundred shekels of silver, and fifty shekels of gold, all of which were to be destroyed. Achan's possession of them brought him and his family under the same ban of destruction as the things he had taken. Achan, the silver, the robe, the gold, his sons and daughters, his cattle, donkeys, and sheep, his tent, and all that he owned had to be killed and burned in order to satisfy the Lord's command concerning the complete destruction of Jericho.

Throughout its history, Israel took illicit plunder, trusted in the strength of its own army instead of waiting on the Lord, and generally lived no better than the wicked people they were to war against in God's holy name. Israel's first king, Saul, followed in Achan's way and violated the trust of holy war when he failed to destroy completely the Amalekites (see comments on Est. 8:1–16). Saul did not kill every living thing, and he plundered the best of their possessions. The confusion of his motives is revealed when he is confronted by the prophet Samuel (1 Sam. 15:18–19):

[The LORD] sent you on a mission, saying, "Go and completely destroy those wicked people, the Amalekites; make war on them until you have wiped them out." Why did you not obey the LORD? Why did you *pounce on the plunder* and do evil in the eyes of the LORD? (emphasis added)

Caught in disobedience, Saul tried to rationalize his actions, explaining that he was going to sacrifice all the plunder to the Lord later anyway. He tried to justify himself by claiming a deferred obedience. This is the context for Samuel's famous words, "To obey is better than sacrifice. . . . Because you have rejected the word of the LORD, he has rejected you as king" (1 Sam. 15:22–23).

Because King Saul failed to execute holy war properly in obedience to the Lord's command, he was disqualified as Israel's king and God's agent on earth. In Esther, the author's emphatic statement three times over that the Jews did not lay a hand on the plunder suggests that this episode against Haman and those who "hated" the Jews was understood as holy war, not as an opportunity for looting and personal gain. The Jews of Persia succeeded where Saul failed.

The ten sons of Haman were also killed that day, leaving no one to carry on their father's legacy of hateful pride. This is another practice in ancient warfare. When a leader was killed, so was his entire family so that no one would survive to mount a vengeful coup. The names of Haman's sons may reinforce the author's message that this is holy war. They are of special interest because they may be *daiva* names of ancient Persia.[1] *Daiva* names were once used of the gods in early Iranian and Hindu writings but later came to be associated with demonic powers in Eastern religions. If the names of Haman's sons do reflect this origin, the original readers would have probably recognized them as such. The author lists the names of Haman's sons possibly to show the allegiance of Haman and his family to the demonic powers of darkness and evil and, therefore, proper casualties of holy war.

In the Hebrew manuscripts and printed Hebrew edition (*BHS*) of Esther, the names of Haman's sons in verses 7—9 are written in margin-justified columns, set off from the rest of the text. The special significance of this unusual morphology is unknown. A similar arrangement is found in the list of names of the kings of Canaan conquered by Joshua and the Israelites in Joshua 12:9—24. Perhaps the practice of setting apart these names from the rest of the text visually expresses the idea that these enemies of Israel had been set apart for destruction. One of my Old Testament professors thought that the arrangement of their names on the page visually suggested their hanging.[2]

In the opinion of some scholars, the many Persian names found in the book of Esther provide striking evidence of the historical authenticity of the book's setting, since according to Yamauchi some of these names have also been found among the Persepolis texts.[3] However, this

---

1. Edwin M. Yamauchi, *Persia and the Bible*, 237—38.
2. The late Prof. Raymond Dillard, Westminster Theological Seminary, in classroom conversation.
3. Yamauchi, *Persia and the Bible*, 238.

argument is not completely compelling, because the linguistic difficulties of tracing these names in the Hebrew text of Esther back to their Old Persian origins are complex.[4] It appears that the author of Esther did have at least some knowledge of proper names from the Old Persian language, but what they meant and why he lists them so explicitly remains uncertain.

Esther requests that the bodies of Haman's sons be hung, that is, impaled, on gallows for public humiliation, just as their father had been. Though perhaps barbaric by modern standards, this also was a custom in ancient warfare. The bodies of King Saul and his sons—even Jonathan, whom David loved—were humiliated in this way by the Philistines on the city wall at Beth Shan (1 Sam. 31:1–13).

Echoes of Saul's failure resound throughout this episode of how the Jews got the upper hand and finally destroyed Haman the Agagite, who was effectively, if not formally, the "king" of their enemies. Thus, under the leadership of Esther and Mordecai, the Jews of Persia obeyed where King Saul had disobeyed and did to their enemies as the Lord had commanded so long before.

Mordecai's counter-decree legalized warfare throughout the empire on only Adar 13, but Queen Esther requested a second day of killing within the city of Susa on Adar 14. Her request delayed the subsequent celebration by the Jews in Susa until the fifteenth. At the time the book was written, Purim was celebrated in some places on two consecutive days, but in other places only one. The author feels constrained to explain not only the origin of the holiday but why it was celebrated on two consecutive days in some parts.

Some believe the details of the Esther story should be understood as myth with little or no historical basis, written to explain the significance of a Jewish festival whose true origin had been forgotten. However, an etiological reading of the story need not exclude the historical basis of the events it describes. Even if one rejects the story as history and reads it as myth, the author apparently had no problem with casting Esther as the initiator of a second day of bloodshed to explain the second day of Purim. From a literary perspective, the two days of killing are consistent with the other double events marking the rhetorical structure of the book.

---

4. L. B. Paton, *Esther*, 66–71.

Both Christian and Jewish interpreters have found Esther's request morally troubling and especially unbecoming a woman. In Paton's opinion, "for this horrible request no justification can be found."[5] C. A. Moore observes:

> It is Esther's request for the exposure of Haman's sons and an extension of the fighting, as well as her "failure" to intercede for Haman in vii 9, that has been primarily responsible for her reputation as a sophisticated Jael, i.e., a deceitful and bloodthirsty woman (see Judg. iv 17–22). Such a reputation certainly has some justification ... but unless one is willing to judge Esther's outward act in complete isolation, without any real knowledge of her inner motives and without full knowledge of the external circumstances, then one's judgment must be tentatively made. Then, as now, what the vanquished call "the villains" the victors regard as "the heroes."[6]

Michael Fox points out that given the stipulations of Haman's decree, the Jews' enemies could not lawfully have attacked them on a second day. Therefore, the Jews were safe and Esther's request was literally overkill. He evaluates Esther's action as "punitary and precautionary, eliminating opponents who might cause problems in the future."[7] While this might be considered the prudent act of a wise leader, Fox also notes that at this point Esther seems to turn vindictive. She no longer even attempts to justify ethically her request to the king and does not mention the welfare of her people. Mordecai is not mentioned as instigating the second day, and his decree does not compel it. Apparently Queen Esther has come into her own, acting not at Mordecai's urging, but on her own authority as a monarch. According to Fox, Esther's personality

> has evolved into the near-opposite of what it was at the start. Once sweet and compliant, she is now steely and unbending, even harsh. ... Literary values are here less important than liturgical purposes. Esther's request for a second day of fighting results more from the need to explain an existing practice than from any literary conception of her personality.[8]

---

5. Ibid., 287.
6. Carey A. Moore, *Esther*, 88.
7. Michael V. Fox, *Character and Ideology in the Book of Esther*, 112.
8. Ibid., 203.

Esther's apparent brutality does trouble modern sensibilities, as indicated in what is perhaps the most recent rendition of the story, Hugo Weisgall's new opera, *Esther*. In October 1993 the New York City Opera performed the premiere of *Esther*. At this scene the biblical story is supplemented when the heroine laments the slaying of the Gentiles and averts any perception of Jewish triumphalism with these words:[9]

> At last, there is a quiet, the horror long past.
> Yet, that that day could not have been avoided
> Fills me with grief, with regret.
> Yet I cannot forget, no one should forget,
> It must not be forgotten. It must not be repeated.
> So much blood, so many, so many dead.

The biblical Esther is evaluated almost universally in negative terms for requesting a second day of killing. The author makes no attempt to exonerate the queen or to justify her request. Yet it apparently served as a perfectly acceptable explanation of the two days of Purim in the mind of the author. If this episode in Israel's story has no basis in history, and if the author could have invented any reason to explain a second day of Purim, one wonders why he invented one that seems to impugn Esther and suggests that the Jews held their power as ruthlessly as did the pagan rulers. On the other hand, if it was widely known that Queen Esther was in fact responsible for the second day of killing in Susa, the author could not have easily avoided including it. If tradition is correct, it is perhaps after this incident that the people nicknamed their queen "Esther" alluding to Ishtar, the Babylonian goddess of love and war.

The Bible is remarkable in revealing the darker side of God's chosen leaders, often just at their shining moment. King David's adultery is a similar example of a story whose presence in the Bible is difficult to explain unless it was widely known to be true. His adultery occurred at the pinnacle of his remarkable military success and prosperity. Even today, many leaders fall at the height of their achievements. If the second day of killing happened because of a darker side to Esther's character, the author does not attempt to vindicate her. Perhaps he is

---

9. Quoted in Samuel Lipman's review of the opera *Esther* in *Commentary*, 97 (January 1994): 55.

suggesting that no one, Jew or Gentile, can handle power without yielding to its dark side. Perhaps Esther's request for a second day of killing shows that she herself had begun to feel the heady intoxication of the power she had so remarkably attained. Even as others in the court have manipulated Xerxes for their own agendas, Esther also has now learned to exercise her power over Xerxes for her own purposes.

On the other hand, Esther's reasons for the second day of killing in Susa may have been legitimate, even though they are unknown to us, and were also possibly unknown to the author. Haman was, after all, second only to the king, and he likely had many in Susa who were loyal to him and his decree. Esther's request is another instance of the disquieting moral ambiguity that characterizes this story. Rather than attempting to resolve it, we should reflect on it.

Whether or not Esther was justified in extending the killing a second day, the perennial failure of Israel's greatest leaders to war against moral and spiritual darkness without engaging in sin themselves suggests that no one is worthy to wage true holy war in God's name. God's strategy against sin and evil was awaiting the perfect warrior, who could execute divine justice with clean hands and a pure heart. His name is Jesus.

THE EFFICACY OF God's word. This final episode in the story of Esther brings the narrative to denouement. The victory implied by Mordecai's counter-decree has now been realized. The crisis is over, the danger is past. The story, though not the book, has come to an end. Literary critics have described this scene as anticlimactic. David Clines argues that the book of Esther once ended with chapter 8 and that this episode is a later addition by an author of lesser "narratival and logical skills."[10] Fox writes, "There is little doubt that in literary terms, the drama has fizzled out and been replaced by somewhat tedious reportage and analysis."[11]

It may be agreed that this episode is "reportage," lacking the vivid drama and action of previous scenes; however, the change in style is

---

10. David J. A. Clines, *The Esther Scroll: The Story of the Story*, 158.

11. Fox, *Character and Ideology in the Book of Esther*, 113.

purposeful. The meta-message is that once Mordecai's decree was issued, the deliverance on Adar 13 was a fait accompli. It remained only to report that, just as the decree implied, the Jews did have victory over their enemies and were in fact delivered from annihilation.

The motivation for this downshift in style is theological. Because Mordecai's decree expressed God's ancient decree of survival for his people and the destruction of their enemies, it was a done deal before the day dawned. The decree in effect guaranteed the outcome. The author is showing it is God's decree, his word, that assures the survival of his people; the rest is just detail. But it is important detail, because it shows that God's word is truly effective in the outworking of human history. God is capable of doing exactly what he says he will do, even centuries after he says it. This episode highlights the powerful efficacy of God's word as it is actualized in history through flawed, and even evil, people.

God in the affairs of Esther. The conflict between Mordecai the Jew and Haman the Agagite precipitated another episode of holy war between God's covenant people and the world that wanted to destroy them. Both sides of God's promise to Moses at Sinai—salvation and destruction—have been realized for the Jews and their enemies in Persia. The resolution of this episode of holy war invites the reader of Esther to consider not only *how* God has done it, but even *if* God has done it, since he is nowhere mentioned in the story. Even though the outcome of the story is consistent with God's ancient promise, what was God's role in these events?

In all other episodes of holy war in the Old Testament the text explicitly involves God. When the people of Israel first fought the Amalekites, Moses stood on the hill overlooking the battle, holding the staff of God raised to heaven (Ex. 17:8–16). During the period after the Conquest, the Lord raised up judges, who delivered Israel from oppression when the Spirit of the Lord came upon them (cf. Judg. 2:16–18). Saul and David were charismatic kings upon whom God's Spirit rested. Solomon received his wisdom from the Lord. God gave Daniel the ability to understand dreams and to discern wisdom. All of these people took their places in redemptive history as agents of God working to fulfill his covenant promise to his people.

In the book of Esther, the deliverance of the Jewish nation is connected to the same covenant that runs throughout the Old Testament.

Yet neither Esther nor Mordecai are described as devout Jews, nor are they described as empowered by the Spirit of God. As far as we know from the story, both of them seem either ignorant of, or indifferent to, the covenant God had made with their ancestors. Neither are shown to be living out the implications of that covenant in their individual lives. Yet it is through Esther and Mordecai that somehow God's covenant promise is fulfilled to the Jews scattered throughout the Persian empire. We cannot even be sure from the text that Esther and Mordecai themselves were fully aware of being essential links in redemptive history.

Indeed, M. Fox is not convinced that even the author of Esther is certain about God's role in the events he recounts. He considers the meta-message of the author's silence about God to be a "carefully crafted indeterminacy" that is

> an attempt to convey uncertainty about God's role in history. The author is not quite certain about God's role in these events (are you?) and does not conceal that uncertainty. By refusing to exclude either possibility, the author conveys his belief that there can be no definitive knowledge of the workings of God's hand in history. Not even a wonderful deliverance can prove that God was directing events; nor could threat and disaster prove his absence. The story's indeterminacy conveys the message that the Jews should not lose faith if they, too, are uncertain about where God is in a crisis. Israel will survive—that is the author's faith—but how this will happen he does not know.[12]

When the Bible states that the Spirit of the Lord is "upon" someone or that God has raised up someone for a special task, the reader knows to expect a story about the remarkable intervention of God in history. All biblical narratives (except prophetic narratives) were written after the events they describe had happened, as the author is reflecting back on and interpreting the significance of past events under divine inspiration. Since all history-telling is selective, the choice of events that are recognized in hindsight as significant contributes to the meta-message of the Bible as those events take their place in inscripturated redemptive history. It is, therefore, appropriate to interpret the book

---

12. Ibid., 247.

of Esther in this canonical context, with God as the invisible mover behind the deliverance of his people from the threat of annihilation.

However, as those events were unfolding day by day, even the individuals involved may not have recognized their significance in God's great plan and purpose. The author's deliberate silence on God's role as the story unfolds is also a part of his message. Fox's emphasis on the "indeterminacy" suggested by the author's silence should be allowed its full force. The fact is, God's "absence" in Esther is true to life as we experience it. Who could have been certain that God was positioning Esther to be an agent of his deliverance when she was taken to the bedroom of a lustful pagan king (and she pleased him in one night more than all the other virgins!)? In hindsight we may understand it to be so, but at that moment God truly was unseen and his intent concealed. It is therefore both appropriate and highly effective that the author of Esther has portrayed God as absent and his role in the story as uncertain, even though the outcome of the crisis itself seems assured when read within the larger biblical context.

When the Jews finally are delivered from destruction on Adar 13, consider the means by which it came. It stood as the terminus of a long sequence of improbable and even morally questionable events. When the deliverance was realized, it came about not through a miraculous showing of God's power or a great spiritual revival among the Persians. It came about through the natural outworking of all the ethical and political flaws inherent in the administration of the Persian empire. Just as the nobles, satraps, and governors had bowed down to Haman in fear of his power, they now helped the Jews only because "fear of Mordecai had seized them . . . his reputation spread throughout the provinces, and he became more and more powerful" (vv. 3–4).

There was nothing noble or admirable about the way this reversal of fortune occurred. God did not change the hearts and character of the people. They simply continued in the political intrigue and manipulations that characterized them. Even Esther manipulated the king for her purposes, just as others had done. Mordecai's increasing power caused others to fear him, suggesting that he was not meek and mild in his new eminence. As both Christian and Jewish interpreters have agreed, this episode of Israel's history in Persia is not one of impeccable morality and exemplary spiritual character. Even so, God's promise could not be frustrated.

Fox understands the book of Esther to link

> the issue of national salvation to human character. It raises the
> question of whether a person of dubious character strength and
> (initially) unclear self-definition can carry the burden of national
> salvation. Esther becomes a sort of judge (of the type we see in
> the book of Judges) without benefit of the Spirit of the Lord. She
> is a leader whose charisma comes not in a sudden divine impo-
> sition of spirit but as the result of a difficult process of inner
> development and self-realization.... In Esther, not miracles, but
> inner resources—intellectual as well as spiritual—even of peo-
> ple not naturally leaders, are to be relied upon in crisis.[13]

In other words, the book of Esther shows how God fulfilled his
covenant promise through providence instead of miraculous intervention. Divine providence means that God governs all creatures, actions,
and circumstances through the normal and ordinary course of human
life, without the intervention of the supernatural.[14] The biblical author's
view that the deliverance was a fait accompli on the basis of the ancient
decree given to Moses reflects deep confidence in God's ability to do
exactly what he says, regardless of how he chooses to do it.

The medieval Jewish exegete Abraham Saba understood the book
of Esther to indicate a maturing of Israel's faith. He takes this incident
in Israel's history to mark the time when the Jews finally came to accept
the Torah wholeheartedly as the basis of their faith.[15] Jewish midrash
suggests that until that time God's people followed him only because of
the mighty miracles he did, instead of believing him because of
who he is.[16] As miracles ceased, Israel's heart wandered to other gods,
no longer confident in Yahweh's power. Saba explains that this great
deliverance achieved without miracles was the reason the Jewish people finally came to rest their faith on the Torah, the Word of God,

---

13. Ibid., 205.

14. Miracles are another way God governs history, but by definition miracles are *supernatural* ("above nature") events that are distinct from the ways God usually controls history
through the established order of nature.

15. Barry Dov Walfish, *Esther in Medieval Garb* (Albany, N.Y.: SUNY Press, 1993), 93.

16. Note that some Christians today seem to have a similar understanding of God. They
come to Christ on the basis of what he can do for them and their loved ones right now,
rather than on the basis of who he is as Sovereign God and King of the universe.

rather than miraculous displays of his power. The story of Esther implies that what God's Word has decreed will happen, even without miracles. God's omnipotence is truly great.

GOD'S POWER AND presence in our lives. God works the same way today as he did in the book of Esther. We, too, live in an age when miraculous displays of God's might are not the usual way he does things, yet we are still expected to believe in his power and presence. A colleague recently told about an incident that spurred on his faith in God's power and presence in his life.[17]

One Sunday morning while Jeff was driving home from church, his five-year-old son, Nate, asked him to speed up so they would not be late for the start of Robin Hood on television. Jeff reminded Nate that the television had not been working because of a problem with the cable box. The repairman had been called, but since it was Sunday, he wasn't expected until sometime the next day. And even if he had shown up, the house was locked while they had been at church. After a few minutes of sullen silence, Nate suggested they pray that God would fix their TV in time for Robin Hood.

Jeff was about to remind Nate that we should not pray for things like that, because God is not at our beck and call, when he remembered the sermon text, 1 Peter 5:7, "Cast all your anxiety on him because he cares for you." The preacher had exhorted the congregation to pray about any matter that was on their heart, large or small, for if it troubled them, their heavenly Father cared about it. Jeff wanted his son to know he could turn to God with any troubling matter. A glance in the rearview mirror at Nate's pouting face clearly showed that missing Robin Hood was troubling to his son. Jeff pulled the car over and listened as Nate asked God to please fix their TV in time for Robin Hood. More concerned about his son's developing relationship with God than about the TV, Jeff asked the Lord to please hear Nate's prayer.

Soon they pulled into their driveway, and Nate bounded toward the front door as Jeff pulled the car into the garage. Jeff knew they had

---

17. With thanks to Dr. Jeffrey Schloss, professor of biology at Westmont College, for his permission to use this personal anecdote.

locked the front door before leaving for church and so was surprised to find the door standing open behind Nate. Jeff was flabbergasted when he entered the house and found Nate sitting in front of the TV watching Robin Hood! Just then a good family friend came down from upstairs. The friend was unexpectedly passing through town and, knowing where the outside key was hidden, had let himself in. Just a few minutes after he had arrived, the TV repairman arrived and quickly fixed the problem. Jeff says that now, more than a decade later, Nate barely remembers the incident. But Jeff vividly remembers it as an example of the extraordinary and completely unpredictable ways in which God can work.

However, are we certain that it was God at work? Certainly there was nothing miraculous about the repair of the TV. A more skeptical person might view this incident as merely an interesting confluence of improbable events. Reviewing the unusual sequence of events in hindsight, it's likely the TV was already working even at the moment Nate offered up his prayer, so it would have been repaired even if Nate had not prayed—or would it?

The relationship between petitioning prayer and divine providence is a deep mystery. Do our prayers move God to change the sequence of events? Does God anticipate our prayers and providentially arrange antecedent events to answer them even before we ask, as Nate's petition for the TV suggests (cf. Matt. 6:8, "... your Father knows what you need before you ask him")? If so, does God's foreknowledge of when we don't pray also have an analogous effect?[18] Was God at work in this extraordinary sequence of ordinary events or not? And if so, to what end? There is an unavoidable indeterminacy in understanding God's role in such events in life and history.

The author of Esther was reflecting on this kind of indeterminacy and inviting his readers to do so when he carefully crafted the story of the Jews' deliverance without explicitly mentioning God's role in the events. The book of Esther invites its readers to ponder the nature of faith in a world where God is unseen. Only people who entertain the possibility of God's interaction with human lives can discern the inde-

---

18. A full discussion of the relationship between prayers of petition and divine providence is beyond the scope of this commentary, especially since there are no prayers offered in the book of Esther. For a brief discussion of this topic, see the "Theological Postscript" at the end of this work.

terminacy in events that the author of Esther so eloquently expresses, for consistently atheistic rationalists will not admit even the possibility of an unseen reality.

Hebrews 11:1 defines faith as "being sure of what we hope for and *certain of what we do not see*" (emphasis added). In other words, the very definition of faith calls us to a certainty in the unseen reality lying behind, or beyond, the events we do see, even when, and perhaps especially when, the events are so incompatible with what we would expect given God's power and presence. Therefore, on what is our certainty to rest, if not on the visible events of history and life? It rests on the explanation God gives us of the unseen reality behind the visible events, that is, on God's Word. We move from indeterminacy to certainty only on the basis of God's Word. This means that the indeterminacy of Esther can be resolved only by reading the story in its wider canonical context. If this is done too quickly, however, the reader will miss the opportunity to reflect on the relationship between events and faith.

Events as historic as the deliverance of the Jews in Persia as well as those as private as a child's answered prayer are an encouragement to view all of life and history with the certainty of the unseen reality of God's presence and power. Such events reveal that God can and will do just as he has promised, even when we don't see how he possibly could. The awareness of God's power and presence should excite us to prayer that is full of anticipation. The answers to our prayers are already on their way, set in motion through a chain of previous events that might appear insignificant even if we somehow became aware of them.

God's redemptive plan. Our modern faith in God's promises rests on the texts of the Bible that are growing more ancient with each passing generation. We live at a time when there are no prophets of Yahweh bringing us his Word, so all that we know of God is found in his written Word and the promises it contains. The Bible contains selected events from times long ago and an explanation of the unseen reality that makes these events significant throughout all subsequent human history. Most centrally, it speaks of the crucifixion of Jesus, Israel's perfect warrior who with clean hands and a pure heart finally waged the ultimate holy war on the cross, conquering sin and death. But those words are two thousand years old, and many today fail to see their relevance for the troubling issues of modern life.

The Bible assures us that the full expanse of human history, including the days in which we now live, is encompassed by God's redemptive plan. At the moment he left, Jesus promised to be with us always, even to the end of history (Matt. 28:20). God is still working in this world, calling people into his kingdom and bringing all of history to its appointed end. One day God's redemptive work will be consummated when Israel's divine warrior and king returns and the world bows in submission to him. There is good reason to believe he is able to do just as he has said, even though he said it so long ago. Scripture warns of being skeptical about God's ability to fulfill his ancient promises (2 Peter 3:3–7):

> ... you must understand that in the last days scoffers will come, scoffing and following their own evil desires. They will say, "Where is this 'coming' he promised? Ever since our fathers died, everything goes on as it has since the beginning of creation." But they deliberately forget that long ago *by God's word* the heavens existed and the earth was formed out of water and by water. By these waters also the world of that time was deluged and destroyed. *By the same word* the present heavens and earth are reserved for fire, being kept for the day of judgment and destruction of ungodly men. (emphasis added)

The omnipotent word of God that created the universe justifies our certainty in the continuity of God's providential work in and through human lives to move his people from death to life as he moves history toward its end on the day of judgment. Our generation is no less a living link in God's work in history than were Esther and Mordecai's. Christ has come, but the gospel must still go out to all nations in every generation until he returns.

Even those whose sinful pride, like Haman's, pit them against God and the gospel are in the final analysis players in the universal plan of redemption. Perhaps in the end, they tragically will be what the apostle Paul refers to as "objects of his wrath," who like Haman (and Judas Iscariot) form dark links in a plan of salvation that nevertheless cannot be thwarted (Rom. 9:22–24). One would hope that before their end they will turn to Christ and become "objects of his mercy," counted among the people whom God has called out from both the Jews and Gentiles to be saved from his destruction of evil. For all who have come to know Christ have been saved from God's wrath, whether Jew or Gentile.

Walking by faith. As God brings his ancient promise of salvation to fulfillment in individual lives throughout history, we cannot at any moment know the significance of world events or even that of the ordinary events of our own private lives. The author of Esther calls us to trust in the power and presence of God even when, and perhaps especially when, he seems absent and we cannot imagine how he could possibly do what he has promised in his Word.

Reflection on the events described in Esther should make us more open to the creative and unexpected ways God works in us and through us. We are called to walk by faith, not by sight; however, that faith is a certainty in the unseen realities lying behind what we do see. We are to live with the knowledge that both our best moments and our worst are all a part of what God is doing in us and through us in the lives of others. We cannot see the end of the matter from the beginning or the middle. The story of Esther assures us that we do not have to.

Esther 9:20–28

MORDECAI RECORDED THESE events, and he sent letters to all the Jews throughout the provinces of King Xerxes, near and far, ²¹to have them celebrate annually the fourteenth and fifteenth days of the month of Adar ²²as the time when the Jews got relief from their enemies, and as the month when their sorrow was turned into joy and their mourning into a day of celebration. He wrote them to observe the days as days of feasting and joy and giving presents of food to one another and gifts to the poor.

²³So the Jews agreed to continue the celebration they had begun, doing what Mordecai had written to them. ²⁴For Haman son of Hammedatha, the Agagite, the enemy of all the Jews, had plotted against the Jews to destroy them and had cast the pur (that is, the lot) for their ruin and destruction. ²⁵But when the plot came to the king's attention, he issued written orders that the evil scheme Haman had devised against the Jews should come back onto his own head, and that he and his sons should be hanged on the gallows. ²⁶(Therefore these days were called Purim, from the word pur.) Because of everything written in this letter and because of what they had seen and what had happened to them, ²⁷the Jews took it upon themselves to establish the custom that they and their descendants and all who join them should without fail observe these two days every year, in the way prescribed and at the time appointed. ²⁸These days should be remembered and observed in every generation by every family, and in every province and in every city. And these days of Purim should never cease to be celebrated by the Jews, nor should the memory of them die out among their descendants.

WITH THIS CHAPTER the author returns his original readers to their own time, many years after the events in Persia had happened. Xerxes has been assassinated in his bedroom. Esther and Mordecai have lived out their days. Purim was becoming an annual celebration on the Jewish calendar. The author tells the story of Esther and Mordecai to say, "See, this is why we celebrate Purim as we do!" He explains that Mordecai "recorded these events, and . . . sent letters to all the Jews . . . to have them celebrate annually" so that future generations could commemorate the momentous deliverance of their ancestors that permitted each successive generation to exist.

It is fitting that the fulfillment of God's promise to the Jews in Persia should also be written down and commemorated. When the Lord promised to wipe out the memory of the Amalekites, he told Moses to write it down on a scroll "as something to be remembered" (Ex. 17:14). This gave the promise both divine authority and perpetuity. The events of the Esther story show a fulfillment of this promise many centuries later and far away from the place it was made, illustrating the efficacy of God's Word. In contrast to the empty bravado of the world's most powerful rulers, God is able to do just as he has said.

Purim joined the five Jewish feasts that were commanded by Moses in the Torah and celebrated miraculous events surrounding the formation of the nation of Israel as God's covenant people. Purim commemorates the survival of that covenant nation, even though it was dispersed in the judgment of the Exile centuries later. By the time of Jesus, the feast of Hanukkah had also been introduced into the Jewish calendar to mark the deliverance of the Jewish people from religious and cultural annihilation in their own homeland under the tyranny of Antiochus Epiphanies in the second century B.C. That deliverance, led by Judas Maccabeus, also came not by miraculous intervention, but by God's power working through ordinary events.

The authority on which Purim is based is unlike that of the feasts commanded by Moses in the Pentateuch. Mordecai was not a prophet or a miracle worker, nor did he rule as king in Jerusalem. He wore the signet ring of a Persian king, not the ephod of the high priest. Mordecai simply wrote letters to the Jews throughout Persia describing the remarkable events that had transpired in the palace at Susa, leading to the deliverance, and the people then responded collectively to their shared experience (see vv. 26–27):

> Because of everything written in this letter [Mordecai's] and because of what they had seen and what had happened to them, the Jews *took it upon themselves* to establish the custom that they and their descendants and all who join them should without fail observe these two days every year, in the way prescribed and at the time appointed (emphasis added).

The celebration of Purim is therefore different from the feasts prescribed by the Torah. Rather than being imposed on the people from above as God's commandment, Purim began as the spontaneous response of God's people to his omnipotent faithfulness to the promises of the covenant.

Once established, Purim was to be celebrated annually on two consecutive days. This can be understood in one of two ways. Either all Jewish people everywhere were to celebrate on both days, because originally a part of the community had celebrated on each day, or Jewish people should celebrate Purim on the one day appropriate to their location. Today Jews around the world celebrate Purim on one day, Adar 14, except those living in one of the cities traditionally considered walled at the time of Joshua, which include Jerusalem, Hebron, and Jericho, where Purim is celebrated on Adar 15.[1]

In explaining the origin of the holiday, the author of Esther also explains the origin of its name, Purim (v. 26). It is derived from the word *pur*, which was not originally a Hebrew word. *Pur* refers to the "lot" or "die" (singular of "dice") that Haman cast in divination to determine the day of death for the Jewish race (see comments on 2:19–3:15). This word occurs in the Old Testament only in the book of Esther and came into the Hebrew language as a loanword during the Persian period, with the Hebrew plural suffix *-im* added. The first time this foreign word is used (3:7), and again in 9:24, the author of Esther translates it into its Hebrew equivalent, *goral*, which the NIV renders "lot." This implies that when the book of Esther was written, the author

---

1. With thanks to Prof. Michael Fox, University of Wisconsin in Madison, for this information in personal communication. Adar roughly corresponds to March.

did not expect his readers to be familiar with the origin and meaning of either *pur* or *purim*.

Even though the word *pur* and its plural form *purim* occur only in the book of Esther, the equivalent Hebrew word, *goral*, occurs frequently throughout the Old Testament. Note, for example, Proverbs 16:33: "The lot [*goral*] is cast into the lap, but its every decision is from the LORD." In ancient times, the *goral* was the means used for divination to determine the will of the gods. When Haman cast lots, he was seeking guidance from the gods. Ancient Israel also used this method to seek Yahweh's will. For instance, Joshua used the lot to divide the Promised Land among the tribes, believing that in this way God would determine the allotment: "After you have written descriptions of the seven parts of the land, bring them here to me and I will cast lots [*goral*] for you in the presence of the LORD our God" (Josh. 18:6).

The Hebrew word *goral* has a second, related meaning, used to refer to the thing allotted by the roll of the dice. The English term *lot* happens to have a similar semantic range. The word can refer either to the means used to make chance selections (as in our word "lottery"), or to the share resulting from chance selection (as in the expression "my lot in life"). Continuing in Joshua 18:11, both the lots that are cast and the land allotted as the result of casting the lots are referred to with the word *goral*: "The lot [*goral*] came up for the tribe of Benjamin, clan by clan. Their allotted [*goralam*] territory lay between the tribes of Judah and Joseph" (Josh. 18:11).

In Psalm 16:5–6, David uses the word *goral* to refer to the circumstances of life that he recognized came from the Lord:

> LORD, you have assigned me my portion [Heb., *menoth*] and my cup;
>> you have made my lot [*goral*] secure.
> The boundary lines have fallen for me in pleasant places;
>> surely I have a delightful inheritance."

As king of Israel, David spoke not only of his own personal life, but also the national life of the people whom he ruled as a theocratic king and warrior of Israel. David recognized that the destiny of Israel was secure only because the Lord had secured it.

Therefore, the name of the feast, Purim, is a double entendre, signifying that the lot, or destiny, of God's people would not be determined by Haman's casting of lots before his gods. Only Yahweh determines the roll of the lot, and only Yahweh determines the lot of his people.

Furthermore, the custom of sending "presents of food" (Heb., *manot*) to friends and neighbors on Purim also symbolizes what God has destined for his people. The Hebrew word *manot* (sing., *manah*) translated "presents of food" in the NIV of 9:22 is the same word translated "portion" in Psalm 16:5 (see above). In the parallelism of this verse, *manah* in the first colon is used to refer to the same destiny as *goral* in the second. But the Hebrew word *manah* also has a second meaning, to refer to choice morsels of food. For instance, in 2 Chronicles 31:4, Hezekiah commands that portions of food be given to the priests and Levites so they can minister before the Lord without having to work the fields: "He ordered the people living in Jerusalem to give the portion [*manah*] due the priests and Levites so they could devote themselves to the Law of the LORD."

Therefore the use of the word *manah* in Esther 9:22 forms another double entendre, as the Jews send these "portions" of food (*manot*) to one another to celebrate their "portion" or destiny (*manah*) allotted by God.

Bridging Contexts

PURIM CONTINUES TO be celebrated by the Jewish people around the world today. For them the significance of the holiday and the book on which it is based have continued in unbroken tradition from generation to generation. However, the Holocaust of this century has for many Jews all but extinguished its joy. The book of Esther was treasured by Jews imprisoned in the Nazi death camps precisely because it promised the survival of their race despite Hitler's attempts to annihilate them. The hope of those who died in the death camps was realized. The Jewish people did survive, yet ironically many Jews of the subsequent generations have found it difficult to believe that God's presence and power are manifested in history as they grapple with the theological implications of Auschwitz. In *A History of God*, Karen Armstrong explains their unavoidable logic: "If this God is omnipotent, he could have prevented the Holocaust. If he was unable to stop it, he is impotent and useless; if he could have stopped it and chose not to, he is a monster."[2]

---

2. Karen Armstrong, *A History of God* (New York: Ballantine, 1993), 376.

Nevertheless, like the group of Jews in Auschwitz who put God on trial, found him inexcusably guilty and worthy of death, but still went to evening prayer, Jews continue to celebrate the significance of Purim year after year. This indictment of God is poignant, for when God did come into the world two thousand years ago, he *was* put on trial, judged guilty and worthy of death by human reasoning, and executed. The divine Messiah of the Jews took up the moral agony of Auschwitz and every other atrocity ever perpetrated against the human race. He agreed that God had to do something about such unimaginable evil and was willing to take it on himself so it could be destroyed on Calvary. Where is the evidence of his achievement? In Jesus' resurrection, which empties physical death of its power over everyone who takes refuge in him as the Messiah. The mortal has been clothed with immortality. Death has been emptied of its horror and swallowed up in victory (1 Cor. 15:54–55).

After the death and resurrection of Jesus Christ, the significance of Purim as a celebration of the power and presence of God extends beyond the boundaries of human history. The covenant promise that was expressed before Christ in the protection and survival of God's chosen nation is reexpressed after Christ's resurrection as protection and survival of the body of Christ (i.e., the universal church, including Jews who come to recognize that Jesus is the Messiah; see Matt. 16:18). God promises those who are in Christ not only protection and survival collectively as a people throughout the generations of human history, but individually after physical death and after the last day of history.

PURIM TODAY. PURIM is still celebrated joyously to commemorate the inviolability of the Jewish race by those who live only a generation or two from a modern expression of Haman's evil. There has perhaps been no other generation of readers who could so closely identify with those to whom the book of Esther was originally written. Today we read the book of Esther in the dark shadow of the Holocaust, deeply grieved that one-third of the Jews in the world were murdered during this century. One need not be Jewish to feel terror when such immense evil grasps the reins of a government.

One need not be Jewish to feel thankful that Hitler did not succeed. Both Jew and Christian should feel the same horror at the threat of genocide against other races in other parts of the world yet today. Jesus, the Messiah of the Jews, is Jesus, the Christ of all nations.

On Purim, joyful singing celebrates God's power to determine the destiny of those who are his:[3]

Song 1

He defeated the designs of heathen nations
    and set to naught their cunning plots,
when there rose against us wicked Haman
    the arrogant branch of Amalek's stock.
Glorying in his wealth he dug his own pit
    and his high position ensnared him.
He sought to trap and was trapped instead;
    he planned destruction but was himself destroyed.
Haman revealed his ancestors' hatred
    and stirred up his kinsmen's enmity of their brothers.
He remembered not the mercy of Saul,
    through whose compassion for Agag the foe was born.
The wicked planned to destroy the righteous,
    but the impure was caught in the pure one's hands.
Mordecai's merit overcame Saul's error,
    while Haman's transgression compounded Amalek's sin.
He hid his cunning schemes within,
    devoting himself to planning evil.
He stretched out his hands against God's holy ones,
    lending his wealth to blot out their memory.
When Mordecai saw that evil was abroad,
    and Haman's edicts were proclaimed in Shushan,[4]
he put on sackcloth and arranged for mourning,
    ordained a fast and sat in ashes.[5]
"Who will arise to atone for error
    and win forgiveness for our ancestors' sins?"

---

3. Robert Gordis, *Megillat Esther* (New York: Ktav, 1974), 93–97. Used by permission.
4. Heb. for Susa.
5. Notice that Mordecai is credited with "ordaining" a fast, although in Est. 4:16 Esther initiates the fast, and v. 17 reports that Mordecai carried out her instructions.

A flower blossomed from the palm tree,
> Hadassah [Esther] arose to stir those asleep.
Her servants hastened to give Haman wine
> that he might drink the venom of serpents.
He rose through his wealth and fell through his wickedness,
> upon the gallows he built himself was hanged.
All the world was struck with amazement
> when Haman's *pur* became our Purim.
The righteous escaped from the hands of the wicked,
> and instead the enemy was destroyed.
The Jews vowed to celebrate Purim each year
> for You, God, accepted Mordecai and Esther's prayer,
> while on the gallows Haman and his sons met their doom.

Song 2

The Rose of Jacob was radiant and joyful
> when men saw Mordecai arrayed in purple.
Their saviour You have been,
> their hope in every generation.
You have shown that all who hope in You
> will not be disappointed,
> and all who trust in You will never be put to shame.
Cursed be Haman, who sought to destroy me,[6]
> blessed be Mordecai the Jew.
Cursed be Zeresh, the wife of my foe,
> blessed be Esther, who was a shield for me,
and may Harbonah, too, be remembered for good!

Purim is still celebrated by sending gifts of food to friends and loved ones. The book of Esther in its entirety is read in the synagogue on Purim. During that reading, noisemakers are used; people cheer at Mordecai's name and boo and hiss at Haman's. The Talmud prescribes drinking and celebrating on Purim until one can no longer tell the difference between "Mordecai be blessed!" and "Haman be cursed!" (*Megillah* 7b). It is a holiday that the Jews continue to celebrate as a sign that they will never be destroyed as a people.

---

6. Notice the idea of personal solidarity with one's ancestors. Haman sought to destroy "me" because had his decree succeeded "I" would not have been born. Similarly, Esther was a shield for "me."

The significance of the holiday and the message of the Esther story were not lost on the Nazis, who would kill on the spot any Jew in the prison camps possessing a copy of the book of Esther. Yet the incarcerated Jews wrote copies of it from memory. The story of Esther was most precious to the Jews facing mass death, because in it they found assurance and hope that they, not their enemy, would triumph against all expectation.

The Christian's hope as seen in Esther. The book of Esther is part of the spiritual heritage of Christians bequeathed to us by Jesus Christ. Its significance has been transformed by his resurrection. Shortly before his death Jesus said, "Before long, the world will not see me anymore, but you will see me. *Because I live*, you also will live" (John 14:19, emphasis added). Because of his resurrection, Christians can face death with the assurance that we ourselves will not be defeated by the grave but will triumph over it against all human expectation. The deliverance of the Jews in Persia foreshadows the redemption of those from all nations who enter into God's covenant through Jesus the Messiah.

Throughout history the book of Esther has been read not as an isolated episode in Jewish history, but as symbolizing the final salvation of God's people at the end of time. The recurring forces of evil that first found expression in the Amalekites will ultimately and finally be eliminated by God as he has promised. The book of Esther forms a link between the covenant at Sinai, when Israel was formed as God's chosen nation, and the eschatological destiny of God's people.

Even the date on which Purim is celebrated hints at its eschatological significance. Holidays commemorating warfare and strife are celebrated on day of the battle itself (e.g., Bastille Day in France [July 14], Boston Massacre Day [March 5], Cinco de Mayo in Mexico [May 5], and Revolution Day in the former Soviet Union [Nov. 7]). Although the fateful day of the battle in Persia was Adar 13, Purim was to be celebrated not on Adar 13, but on Adar 14 and 15. As F. Bush points out,

> the festival does not celebrate victory in battle, and the joy prescribed is not malicious glee over the slaughter of their enemies. The festival commemorates, rather, the fact that they "gained relief from their enemies" and that life was "transformed for them from sadness to joy and from mourning to a holiday."[7]

---

7. Frederic Bush, *Ruth/Esther*, 328.

The first occurrence of Purim was a spontaneous celebration of the joy of finding oneself still standing on the day after an irrevocable death decree was executed. The day of death had come and gone and God's people were still alive! Thus, Purim is in this sense a Sabbath, a joyous rest after evil and the threat of death have passed. It symbolizes the eschatological joy of God's people, a *joie de vivre* in the most ultimate sense.

The eschatological reality of this joyful hope was first realized in the resurrection of Jesus Christ, who appeared to John with the words of a powerful victor, "Do not be afraid. I am the First and the Last. I am the Living One; I was dead, and behold I am alive for ever and ever! And I hold the keys of death and Hades" (Rev. 1:17–18). Jesus spoke these words at a moment in history when another mighty empire, Rome, had turned its force against the infant church in terrifying forms of persecution. Jesus assured his people through John's apocalyptic vision that the church would survive, against all odds. He encouraged with a promise, "Be faithful, even to the point of death, and I will give you the crown of life" (Rev. 2:10).

Christ reveals a new destiny, a destiny beyond death, where God "will wipe every tear from [our] eyes! There will be no more death or mourning or crying or pain, because the old order of things has passed away." The Lord then says, "I am making everything new! . . . Write this down, for these words are trustworthy and true" (Rev. 21:4–5).

Esther 9:29–10:3

S O QUEEN ESTHER, daughter of Abihail, along with Mordecai the Jew, wrote with full authority to confirm this second letter concerning Purim. ³⁰And Mordecai sent letters to all the Jews in the 127 provinces of the kingdom of Xerxes—words of good will and assurance—³¹to establish these days of Purim at their designated times, as Mordecai the Jew and Queen Esther had decreed for them, and as they had established for themselves and their descendants in regard to their times of fasting and lamentation. ³²Esther's decree confirmed these regulations about Purim, and it was written down in the records.

^{10:1}King Xerxes imposed tribute throughout the empire, to its distant shores. ²And all his acts of power and might, together with a full account of the greatness of Mordecai to which the king had raised him, are they not written in the book of the annals of the kings of Media and Persia? ³Mordecai the Jew was second in rank to King Xerxes, preeminent among the Jews, and held in high esteem by his many fellow Jews, because he worked for the good of his people and spoke up for the welfare of all the Jews.

QUEEN ESTHER WAS last mentioned in 9:13, when she requested the second day of killing and the humiliation of the bodies of Haman's sons. As the author reports it, she was the major player during the days of holy war; Mordecai was not mentioned as an active agent. Now Esther reappears to write "with full authority." At the beginning of her story she is referred to as "Esther (the girl Mordecai had adopted, the daughter of his uncle Abihail)" (2:15). At the end of her story her Jewish identity and Persian position are integrated in the reference to her as "Queen Esther, daughter of

Abihail," who writes "with full authority to confirm this second letter concerning Purim" (9:29). The Hebrew of this passage is obscure, making it difficult to know with certainty how many letters were written and which letter is the "second" one.

It is clear that the writing down of the events forms the authoritative basis on which future generations were to celebrate the holiday. This is consistent with the emphasis throughout this book on the written word. In Esther, written decrees are necessary to effect law, and once written in the king's name they are irrevocable. In a humorous parody of the notorious bureaucracy of the Persian court, one targum of Esther says that the women of the king's harem were summoned to his bed by written memo! (Can you imagine the king dictating *that* invitation to the royal scribes?) In Esther, the written word not only has authority, it has perpetuity. As Clines puts it, "In Esther, reality tends toward inscripturation, and attains its true quality only when it is written down. What is written is valid and permanent; what happens merely happens and is thereupon cast to the winds—unless it is recorded."[1]

It is therefore remarkable that Esther, Jewish woman and Persian queen, should write with full authority to confirm Mordecai's letter and establish Purim as something to be remembered and observed in perpetuity. The Hebrew is clear in using the third singular, feminine form of the verb "to write," making it certain that Esther is the one who writes this final confirmation of Purim. The phrase translated "along with Mordecai the Jew" is grammatically problematic in the Hebrew because of the gender and number of the verb; it is possibly a later addition. Mordecai first records the events and sends letters to the Jews to celebrate Purim annually (9:20). Then Esther writes "with full authority" to confirm the establishment of the feast.

In verse 32 it is "Esther's decree" that "confirmed" the regulations concerning Purim, which was written down in the archives. The form of the noun translated "decree" is the same word previously used in 1:15 to refer to the king's command to Vashti and in 2:20 to Mordecai's command to Esther. Apparently the author's use of this word invites the reader to consider Queen Esther's word to be on par with that of Xerxes and Mordecai.

---

1. David J. A. Clines, *The Esther Scroll: The Story of the Story*, 22.

Esther is remarkable in biblical history not only for her role in the deliverance of God's people, but for the authority she achieved to write—though she most likely used the scribes to record her words, just as Haman and Mordecai had done. Esther had initiated Mordecai's promotion and bestowed his wealth, and it was her authority that confirmed his previous letter. No other woman among God's people wrote with authority to confirm and establish a religious practice that still stands today. The importance of most biblical women, such as Sarah and Hannah, lies in their motherhood. Esther's importance to the covenant people is not as a mother, but as a queen.

Nevertheless, in chapter 10 it is Mordecai who gets the last word. When life returned to normal after the crisis, Mordecai continued to use his rank as second only to the king for the benefit of his people. When Haman had worn Xerxes' signet ring, he was effectively, though not formally, the king of the enemies of the Jews. Now Mordecai wears that same ring and is effectively, though not formally, king of the Jews. As the majority of Jews continued ever after to live in lands governed by pagan powers, Mordecai became the paradigm of a Jew who could achieve success in a pagan world and use that achievement for the protection and well-being of the Jewish people.

The ancient Greek version of the Esther story (LXX) was produced during the intertestamental period and reflects the high esteem in which Mordecai was held. The original Hebrew autograph is the divinely inspired text, but the subsequent Greek translation gives us insight into how the story was understood in the intertestamental period. There are two chapters inserted into the Greek version that envelop the book. Referred to as addition A and F, these two chapters contain, respectively, a dream of Mordecai and its interpretation.[2] The effect of these two additional chapters is to cast Mordecai as a prophetic dreamer similar to Joseph or Daniel.

The tale of Esther and Mordecai in the court of Xerxes is introduced in the Greek version with addition A, where Mordecai has a bizarre dream of two dragons prepared to fight, of a righteous nation about to perish, and of a little spring of water that becomes a great river. In addition F, which ends the LXX version of Esther, Mordecai remem-

---

2. There are four other additional chapters, referred to as B–E, inserted throughout the book.

bers the dream he had and interprets the events that had transpired as the fulfillment of his prophetic dream.

> These things have come from God. The little spring that became a river, Esther is that river.... The two dragons are I myself and Haman. The nations gathered to destroy the name of the Jews. But my people, this is Israel, who cried out to God and were saved. The Lord saved his people and the Lord delivered us from all these evil things.... Because of this he [God] made two lots, one for the people of God and one for all the nations. And these two lots came to the hour and day of judgment before God and for all the nations. (LXX Est. F:1–8, pers. trans.)

The eschatological significance of the events that had transpired in Persia and the explicit belief that they were controlled by God are revealed through Mordecai's interpretation of his dream in this Greek version of the story. The Jews of the Diaspora continued to face the threat of death brought by the changing winds of political intrigue under the Hellenistic kings. Without a king of their own, a Jewish man in high places in government was seen as the agent of God's covenant protection. Mordecai provided both a rationale and a role model for successive generations.

Bridging Contexts

THE MAIN CHARACTER in Esther. When students of mine reading the Hebrew text of Esther were asked to identify the main character, opinions were evenly divided between Esther and Mordecai. On literary grounds Esther is the main character of the story, but it is difficult to separate the roles of Esther and Mordecai in the story of this great deliverance.

- Had Mordecai not reported the assassination plot on Xerxes' life, he would not have later been due a reward from the king; but had Esther not been Xerxes' queen, Mordecai may not have been credited for his loyalty.
- Had Mordecai not refused to bow before Haman, the crisis would not have happened; but had Esther refused to please the king in his bedroom, there would have been no one to intercede for her people.

- Mordecai had persuaded Esther to go uninvited into the king's presence to plead for her people; but Esther had devised the strategy of forcing a confrontation between Haman and the king.
- Had Esther not identified Mordecai to the king as her close relative, Mordecai would not have worn the king's signet ring; but without Mordecai's decree, Haman's decree of death would have prevailed.
- Because Mordecai had come to power, the fear of him reversed the Jews' fate; but had Esther not interceded for her people, they would have perished.

Even at the very end of the book, in 9:29–32, it is difficult to completely separate Mordecai's role and authority from Esther's in writing the documents that established Purim. As Fox observes,

> the author depicts a successful relationship of power-sharing between male and female, in which both attain prestige and influence in the community. In the pivotal scene in chapter 4, man and woman give each other mutual obedience.[3]

The ancient Greek version magnifies Mordecai's prominence in the story and diminishes Esther's. One easily quantifiable illustration of this is found by counting the number of occurrences of Esther's name compared to Mordecai's. In the Hebrew text each is mentioned by name an almost equal number of times (Esther, fifty-five times; Mordecai, fifty-two). In the LXX, including the six additional chapters, Esther is mentioned by name forty-six times and Mordecai, fifty-four.[4] Perhaps this reflects the esteem with which Mordecai was so highly regarded at the time the Greek translation was made. It may also reflect a possible desire for Jews of the Ptolemaic era to distance themselves from a female queen during the time of a succession of Ptolemaic queens named Cleopatra, who ruled over them in Egypt when the Greek translation is believed to have been made.

---

3. Michael V. Fox, *Character and Ideology in the Book of Esther*, 210.

4. In fact, the number of occurrences of the names of both Esther and Vashti are reduced significantly in the Greek version, but the number of occurrences of the names of Haman and Xerxes, as well as that of Mordecai, are increased. See Karen H. Jobes, *The Alpha-Text of Esther: Its Character and Relationship to the Masoretic Text*, 120.

Nevertheless, in the scene when Esther calls a fast in preparation for her uninvited audience with Xerxes, the Greek version includes the prayers of both Esther and Mordecai that are not found in the Hebrew (and therefore, neither are they found in the NIV).[5] These prayers introduce a strong religious element to the Greek version that moves the story into the mainstream of biblical tradition. In their prayers Mordecai and Esther mention Abraham, the Exodus, circumcision, and the temple. They plead with God to deliver them even as he had delivered their ancestors from Egypt. However, in this case, Esther and Mordecai were pleading for a people in exile, standing under the judgment of God. Was their annihilation to be the final and ultimate execution of his severe justice? Was there any point in pleading with God?

In their plea, Mordecai and Esther echo words and phrases from the Greek version of Moses' prayer as he intercedes for God's people in Deuteronomy 9:26–29. Neither Mordecai alone nor Esther alone is portrayed as the intercessor and agent of deliverance. It is the combination of their two independent prayers that echoes the ancient plea of their ancestor, Moses.[6] In the LXX version, Esther and Mordecai together succeed as the spiritual leaders of God's people.

Esther and Mordecai as partners. The Lord instructed Moses to write his words on a scroll because God's promise to defeat the Amalekites was "something to be remembered" (Ex. 17:14). Just as the independent prayers of Esther and Mordecai in the Greek version together echo Moses' prayer, so in the canonical Hebrew book the writings of Mordecai and Esther together establish Purim as something to be remembered. In prayer, in concert of action, and in writing, Esther and Mordecai together reenact Moses' leadership of the covenant people.

The meta-message of what is implied by the Hebrew and amplified in its Greek translation is that *both* Esther and Mordecai were indispensable as God worked providentially to fulfill his covenant to his people exiled for their sin in Persia. Esther was not and, because of her gender, could not have been a religious leader of the Jews. But then neither was Mordecai. He was not a prophet, priest, or king in Israel.

---

5. The Greek version of Esther including the six additional chapters can be found in English translation in the *New Oxford Annotated Bible with the Apocrypha* (New York: Oxford Univ. Press, 1994).

6. Jobes, *The Alpha-Text of Esther*, 176–83.

Esther was both queen and Jewish, effectively making her the queen of the Jews during this crisis period. Because Esther willingly shared her power with Mordecai, he wore the signet ring of the Persian king, effectively making him king of the Jews. Mordecai was the highest-ranking Jewish man at that moment in history, bearing the authority of a pagan monarch. Esther and Mordecai together functioned as Israel's monarchy in the Persian exile. Together they accomplished what had previously been entrusted to the theocratic monarchy when God's people lived within the borders of the Promised Land—successfully leading holy war, assuring the survival and safety of the covenant people, and exercising authority over the religious practices of the people.

Neither Esther nor Mordecai had the power or position alone to deliver their people. It was only as they acted in concerted power and authority that they were able to lead God's people through the crisis of death and into deliverance. Neither of them aspired to the role; perhaps neither of them deserved it. It was thrust on them by a series of improbable circumstances largely beyond their control. Nevertheless, their unlikely partnership accomplished God's ancient promise, and the Jewish race was preserved until in the fullness of time, God entered history through this people as the Messiah. How marvelous are God's inscrutable ways!

BEYOND MOTHERHOOD AND **ordination.** Because the book of Esther has eschatological significance, it endows eternal purpose to the partnership of women and men in roles other than marriage and childbearing. Moreover, it endows the laity of the church with that same eternal purpose. God has placed Christian women and men not only in marriage relationship, but in community with one another in the church. The sound marriage and family structure is essential for the well-being of both society and church, but it is not the only way in which women and men may effectively relate to each other for the glory of God. Christian men are not only husbands and fathers, nor are Christian women only wives and mothers. Both have a wider range of interests, talents, gifts, and calling from the Lord.

Consider the words of Jesus in Luke 18:29–30, which suggest that family relationships and responsibilities do not exhaust our service to God:

> "I tell you the truth," Jesus said to them, "no one who has left home or wife or brothers or parents or children for the sake of the kingdom of God will fail to receive many times as much in this age and, in the age to come, eternal life."

Since the time of Christ both men and women have a responsibility beyond the confines of the home. In our society women and men receive the same education in the classroom, fill the same positions in the workplace, and worship side by side in the church. Scripture affirms that both women and men bear the image of God (Gen. 1:27) and have equal standing in Christ (Gal. 3:28). The relationship of men and women in community outside the family should work for the glory of God and the fulfillment of his redemptive purposes.

Unfortunately, the question of woman's role in the church has been too narrowly focused on the question of ordination. In fact, relatively few Christians—either men or women—are heading for ordination, and so the discussion completely overlooks the reality of life for most members of the church. Nevertheless, the evangelical church unfortunately has made the question of ordination the central one in its discussion of women's roles and, worse yet, in many places a litmus test of orthodoxy (regardless of whether one defines "orthodoxy" as favoring or opposing women's ordination). Judging from the state of the discussion, one would think that the church has no vision for the significance of a woman's life in Christ other than motherhood or ordination. Can no other calling be affirmed?

Not only the focus of the discussion of a woman's role in the church, but also the format has been unproductive. In many churches discussions work toward a negative summary of what women cannot do, regardless of how the given church body defines the role. Women need a positive statement from the church validating their roles as other than wives and mothers and affirming their calling as responsible adults living and working for the glory of God.

The role of the laity. The story of how Esther and Mordecai share responsibility in a mutually dependent way is a story that dignifies the role of the laity. It affords the church the opportunity to reflect on the part the laity have to play in the larger picture of life and redemptive history. Neither Esther nor Mordecai held "ordained" positions in the community of faith, yet it is they, and not the "ordained clergy" of that period (to use modern terms), who find a place in redemptive history. It is by their "lay leadership" (to use another modern expression) that Purim was instituted and still stands. Moreover, it was through their "secular" vocations—Mordecai as a court official and Esther as queen of a pagan empire—that God worked.

In other words, the story of Esther and Mordecai is an example of how the laity of the church has also been vested with an essential place in God's plan of redemption. While Christians might debate whether the ordained clergy may or may not be both male and female, there is no escaping the fact that the body of Christ is certainly both.

The story of Esther and Mordecai endows the "secular" roles of God's people with eternal significance. As a young Christian I was once taught that every Christian should reach a point of spiritual maturity that takes them into "full-time Christian work" as a pastor, missionary, evangelist, or Bible teacher. In retrospect, I believe that well-intentioned teaching had a deficient theology of the laity, as the "holy priesthood" chosen by God (1 Peter 2:4–5). I also suspect that the teaching was actually intended, perhaps unconsciously, for the men of the congregation, because the women who seriously responded to it met resistance and suspicion whereas the men were applauded and affirmed. The point, however, is that the church must not forget the spiritual significance of *vocation*, of God calling women and men to "secular" positions where their work glorifies him no less than the work of those called to be ordained clergy in the church.

Redemptive history and "secular" history. The story of Esther and Mordecai shows how God fulfills his covenant promise from age to age through divine providence in the lives of both women and men. In the book of Esther we see the inseparable relationship between God's redemptive covenant and his providential rule of history. God rules not only redemptive history, but by his power all of history serves his redemptive purposes. Redemptive history and secular history are not two separate streams of human existence, but one. Redemptive history is united to and is one with "secular" history. The events that define redemptive history emerge from the stream of "secular" history only by being so identified and interpreted through Scripture.

The union of redemptive history and "secular" history under God's sovereign rule implies a synergistic relationship between the clergy and the laity as the body of Christ fulfills its role in the world today. The Reformation principle of the "priesthood of all believers" was developed in opposition to a clergy that was withdrawn and separated from the unordained believer both in life and liturgy. The "holy" and the "secular" were deliberately kept apart. The laity participated in God's redemptive work only by receiving the sacraments from the ordained clergy, who stood between them and Christ. The medieval clergy had in effect taken Christ hostage, and in their human weakness used their power to abuse God's grace. The Reformation put God's Word into the language of the people and the Bible into the hands of the laity. The Reformers saw salvation as a living relationship with the Lord, embracing every aspect of life.

Leadership of the church and administration of the sacraments are rightly the responsibility of the ordained clergy, but God's redemptive work in the world is not confined to those who are ordained. The apostle Paul writes in Ephesians 4:12 that those holding the offices of the church are to equip God's people, both women and men, for the work of ministry so that the body of Christ might reach its goal in him. The ordained officers of the church do not alone carry the work of the Lord from generation to generation. Both clergy and laity have a role in the ministry of the gospel. The work of the laity is shown both in Scripture and history to be essential for actualizing God's redemptive plan and bringing it to its culmination in Christ. The significance of Esther and Mordecai as agents of God's providential rule encourage all of us to live for Christ as we live out the calling God has given to us, both men and women, whatever that calling may be.

As we continue to live faithfully in Christ, we can be sure that whatever happens to us—the decisions we make, the mistakes we regret, and even the sins that shame us—are all links in God's plan not only for our individual lives but for his greater work in history. Through his inscrutable ways, along paths that are sometimes dark and treacherous, he brings his people to that day when all creation will rejoice that our sorrow has been turned into joy and our mourning into celebration.

A Theological Postscript:
The Doctrine of Divine Providence

ALTHOUGH THERE IS NOT one tiny miracle found in the book of Esther, the cumulative result of a series of improbable events leads one to ponder the miraculous quality of the ordinary. As it has been said, "a coincidence is a miracle in which God prefers to remain anonymous."[1] If, as the book of Esther implies, God interacts with individuals in such a way as to move history to the goal ordained by his eternal purposes, surely even the ordinary takes on a miraculous luster. In some ineffable way, ordinary human decisions cooperate with the divine plan.

It seems stunning that God interacts with the physical universe at all, whether by occasional miracles or continuously through the laws of nature. When one tries to imagine by what mechanism that interaction could occur, any contact of God with the universe is in some sense miraculous.[2] We most associate God's presence and power with miracles that are by definition supernatural, such as the virgin birth and resurrection of Jesus Christ. But Scripture teaches the continuous power and presence of God in relation to his creation. Theologians refer to God's continuous sovereign control over the universe, usually working through the ordinary laws of physical and human nature, as divine providence. Of course, God has also intervened miraculously at times, working in ways that defy the established natural order. Events such as the virgin birth and resurrection of Jesus Christ are by definition supernatural.

It is not always apparent, however, whether a biblical event was the supernatural suspension of the laws described by physics, chemistry, and biology, or natural events occurring with extraordinary timing. Some biblical miracles would have been clearly supernatural, such as the floating axhead (2 Kings 6) or the changing of water into wine

---

1. Quoted in Jon D. Levenson, *Esther: A Commentary*, 19.

2. For a collection of provocative articles on this subject, see *Chaos and Complexity: Scientific Perspectives on Divine Action*, R. J. Russell, N. Murphy, and A. Peacocke, eds. (Vatican City State: Vatican Observatory Publications, 1995).

(John 2). Other "miracles" may have been the result of ordinary events occurring with extraordinary timing or intensity, such as the parting of the Red Sea at the time of the Exodus, which may be understood as the result of a rare, but not unknown, meteorological event.

The book of Esther is perhaps the most striking biblical example of the doctrine of divine providence. It invites us to reflect on God's continual superintendence of history and, therefore, his superintendence of human decisions and actions. Without any observable miracle or any detectable intervention by God, human decisions led to an outcome that God had promised many centuries before. This outcome was not only against all human expectation, but was the exact reversal of the expected outcome. This means that to whatever extent we wish to credit God for directing the events of the story, we must recognize that he was to that extent influencing the minds of those involved.

It seems easier and less problematic to conceive of God as directing the paths of the galaxies than the thoughts and decisions of the human mind. However, we cannot take seriously the New Testament teaching that all history is moving toward an appointed end unless we also take seriously God's sovereignty over the decisions of billions of people, both those who know and honor him and those whose hearts and minds are far from him. To say that God controls history is to say that God ultimately controls the human beings who make it. This of course brings us immediately to that age-old question of the relationship between God's sovereignty and human free will.

Most religions have a concept of how God interacts with the universe. Christian and Jewish theology have as their most fundamental principle that God is distinct and separate from the universe, which he created from nothing. The alternative is some form of pantheism, the belief that God and the universe are coextensive and coeternal. Pantheism conceives of God not as a personal Creator, but as the soul of the universe, who is one with it, just as the human body and soul form a complete being. Whatever laws govern the operation of the universe directly represent the action of the divine spirit. Christianity and Judaism reject this conception of God, yet believe that God is omnipresent within the universe, is omniscient of everything that happens in the universe, and is omnipotent over the universe and everything in it. The creator-creation distinction gives rise to the most profoundly interesting, and in some ways most disturbing, theological questions.

Using what the Bible teaches about God's relationship to and inter-action with the universe, Christian theologians identify the three elements of divine providence as (1) the preservation of the existence of the universe and all life within it, (2) divine concurrence in human action, and (3) divine concurrence that moves history toward a planned end.[3] The story of Esther illustrates all three of these elements to some extent, but especially draws our attention to the latter two.

(1) *The preservation of the existence of the universe and all life within it.* The Bible teaches that not only did God initially speak the universe into existence, but that its continuing existence is also directly dependent on him. A deistic concept of a God, who creates a self-sustaining universe as a watchmaker would build a watch, does not square with biblical teaching but grows out of the scientific empiricism of the eighteenth century. The New Testament assigns the role of sustaining the universe to Jesus Christ, the Son of God, who "is the radiance of God's glory and the exact representation of his being, *sustaining all things by his powerful word*" (Heb. 1:3, emphasis added).

The continuing dependence on God for the existence of the universe is not a *prima facie* theme in the book of Esther. However, the preservation of a redeemed humanity necessitated the preservation of the Jewish people under the Persian regime. Indirectly, this reflects the concept that God sustains all things to their appointed end through ongoing involvement with his creation. This is more clearly discerned by remembering that the Jewish people of Persia were God's covenant nation, though they are not identified as such in Esther. They are faced with two possible destinies: annihilation and destruction or preservation and continued existence in the flow of redemptive history. Because God's covenant people embody God's promise to redeem humanity to the final destiny of new creation, the survival and continued existence of God's people implies his involvement in sustaining all things until the appointed consummation.

Moreover, the concept that God sustains all things "by his power-ful word" is also reflected in the story of Esther. It is God's ancient promise to Moses—that is, God's word to Moses—that guarantees the survival and continued existence of his chosen people. This guarantee

---

3. See the annotated bibliography at the end of the Introduction for writings of Christian theologians and biblical scholars on the topic of divine providence.

of survival is reflected in Esther in the written decree of Mordecai, which reexpresses the intent of God's ancient promise in that particular historical moment. The words of the king of Persia are emphasized as irrevocably effective in Esther, but are shown to be ultimately ineffectual, in contrast to the truly irrevocable words of the King of the universe, which define reality.

The universe was created and structured by God's spoken word. The expression "God said, 'Let there be ... and it was so'" is the repeated refrain in Genesis 1 that calls the universe into existence and orders its structure. After its creation the universe continues to be sustained by God's irrevocable and efficacious word. The course of redemptive history is defined by God's irrevocable and efficacious word as documented in the Bible. Therefore, reality described by Scripture and reality as experienced in creation are both rooted in the same authoritative speech of God.

(2) *Divine concurrence in (every?) human action*. The Reformed theologian Louis Berkhof defines concurrence as "the cooperation of the divine power with all subordinate powers, according to the preestablished laws of their operation, causing them to act precisely as they do."[4] The theme of divine concurrence in human action is necessarily implied by the Esther story if we understand the deliverance of the Jews to be the outworking of God's covenant promise through the decisions of Xerxes, Haman, Esther, and Mordecai. Divine concurrence with human thought has been both an intriguing and morally troubling concept for theologians through all ages.

The Bible presents divine concurrence as operating in such a way as to leave human beings responsible for evil, yet to show God's using the effect of their evil for his good purpose. For instance, Joseph, whose life was ruined when his brothers sold him into slavery in Egypt, recognizes God's concurrence in that heinous act and the greater good God accomplished by it: "You intended to harm me, but *God intended it* for good to accomplish what is now being done" (Gen. 50:20, emphasis added).

Does this imply that God is concurrently involved with every human decision, or does divine concurrence operate selectively in certain people or in only occasional instances? The book of Esther suggests that divine concurrence operates in *every* human decision and

---

4. Louis Berkhof, *Systematic Theology* (Grand Rapids: Eerdmans, 1941; repr. 1986), 171.

action to move history to its appointed end. The author of Esther begins his story with the worldly and unreligious events of Xerxes' lavish war council and Vashti's refusal to obey him. Neither of these people worshiped Yahweh, nor were they aware of his involvement, yet without Xerxes' pride and Vashti's defiance, Esther would not have come to a royal position "for such a time as this." God was apparently orchestrating antecedent events, which involved him concurrently in the decisions of Xerxes and Vashti.

Does divine concurrence operate only in those human decisions that are in accordance with his revealed will? Consider that although Esther was born into Yahweh's covenant nation, her marriage to a pagan king was not the conscious choice of a covenant man and woman seeking to establish a godly family, but the result of Esther's winning what was basically a sex contest. It may be difficult or troubling to think of God's concurrence in such questionable human conduct as occurs in the book of Esther, but it is impossible to separate events in Esther in which we can identify divine concurrence operating from those in which it did not. In the mix of good and evil within the human heart, God's involvement is nevertheless concurrent.

The Bible does not wince at God's involvement with human evil, though his involvement must be distinguished from his moral responsibility for it. Through the prophet Isaiah (Isa. 45:7) the Lord claims control over all things:

I form the light and create darkness,
> I bring prosperity and create disaster;
> I, the LORD, do all these things.

Note too the words written in the wake of Jerusalem's destruction: "Is it not from *the mouth* of the Most High that both calamities and good things come?" (Lam. 3:38, emphasis added).[5] While admitting divine concurrence in every event, Christian theologians have been careful to also protect the biblical teaching that God does not violate his holiness by his concurrent involvement with evil human actions and that human beings remain morally responsible for themselves. The Westminster Confession 5.4 states this distinction:

---

5. Notice the allusion to God's word, i.e., "mouth," as determining both calamities and good things.

God's power, unsearchable wisdom, and infinite goodness are so manifested in providence that it [providence] does extend to even the first fall into sin, and all other sins of angels and people, not by bare permission, but by his ordering and governing, yet so as the sinfulness pertains only to the creature, and not to God, who is neither the author nor approver of sin.

Berkhof explains how some theologians conceptualize the relationship between divine concurrence and human free will.[6] God arranges and groups events and objects around people in such a way as to place each person at every step in those circumstances that he knows will be a sufficient inducement for that person to do, by his or her own free will, the very thing called for in God's plan. This explanation is an interesting way to think about the relationship of God's action and human will, but it is not completely satisfying. To modern ears it may sound like what law enforcement would call entrapment.

Theologians have provided many intriguing discussions of this topic, but have offered no logically satisfying resolution of the tension between God's sovereignty and human will and responsibility. As Christians we accept that tension and believe both that God is sovereign and that humans are responsible for themselves because the Bible teaches both.

The story of Esther provides a concrete example that affords rich reflection on the mysterious interplay between God's sovereignty and human free will. If we interpret this story as unfolding according to God's purposes, then Haman is surely an example of someone who falls by divine providence, yet falls by his own fault. Haman's pride-driven evil at every step led him toward what turned out to be his own destruction in the reversal of destiny called for by God's covenant promise. He had plotted for God's people what God had intended for the Amalekites, and at every step Haman willfully and deliberately pressed toward what he wanted. Tragically, his pride blinded him to the truth, and he did not realize until it was too late that his willfulness had led him to death and destruction (see the Contemporary Significance section of 7:1–10).

The apostles of Jesus Christ were not troubled by the idea that God is concurrently involved in all human actions, including that greatest evil, the unjust execution of the morally perfect Jesus. The apostles and earliest Christians who witnessed the death of Jesus rec-

---

6. Berkhof, *Systematic Theology*, 174–75.

ognized that "Herod and Pontius Pilate . . . with the Gentiles and the people of Israel . . . did [to Jesus] what your [God's] power and will *had decided beforehand* should happen" (Acts 4:27–28, emphasis added). This realization of God's involvement in the death of Jesus did not cause them to doubt either God's goodness or his omnipotence. To the contrary, the recognition of God's concurrent involvement in all human action was of great comfort to them.

This realization also provided the courage they needed to pray further: "Now, Lord, consider their threats and enable your servants to speak your word with great boldness" (Acts 4:29). The apostles and earliest Christians were emboldened to face even the greatest threats because they understood divine concurrence, knowing that everything they would experience, including persecution, suffering, and even death, would work for God's greatest good.

Here in Acts 4:23–31 we find the almost surprising association of fervent prayer in response to the recognition of divine providence. This association is surprising because the modern understanding of divine providence has often seemed to dull, if not eliminate, the motivation for prayer. Divine providence is often misunderstood today as an almost fatalistic determinism. If God has already determined what must happen, then of what good is it to pray?

Throughout the ages of the church various theologians and apologists have answered that question in different ways. C. S. Lewis understood prayer to be efficacious because the prayer of God's people was itself an integral part of divine action:

> Prayer is not a machine. It is not magic. It is not advice offered to God. Our act, when we pray, must not, any more than all our other acts, be separated from the continuous act of God Himself, in which alone all finite causes operate.[7]

Systematic theologian Donald Bloesch explains that while "God's ultimate purposes are unchangeable . . . his immediate will is flexible and open to change through the prayers of his people."[8] Others have

---

7. Quoted in R. C. Sproul, *The Providence of God Study Guide*, for the video or audio series, written by Jerry Bridges (Orlando: Ligonier Ministries, 1990), 105.

8. Quoted by Jack A. Keller, in "On Providence and Prayer," *The Christian Century*, 104 (Nov. 4, 1987): 967.

observed that not all prayers for God to overcome evil and suffering are answered as we would expect them to be, given God's goodness and omnipotence; they have argued that God's power in the world is mitigated by agents of evil, but his will will be ultimately accomplished.[9] In other words, "God's power is not irresistible in the short run, but it is inexhaustible in the long run."[10] Therefore, we should continue to pray in cooperation with the divine will, knowing that ultimately God will prevail. But surely the parable of the wheat and weeds in Matthew 13:24–43 teaches that it is by no lack of God's power that evil continues to exist but by his deliberate decision he allows it to exist for now. To destroy evil would mean nothing less than the end of history, since evil is so deeply rooted in human existence.

Still others, who reject the biblical teaching that prayer changes things but who value religion for its psychological benefit, recommend prayer as a means of changing our own attitude toward the circumstances that trouble us. We can find peace of mind through prayer when we are convinced that whatever happens is actually a part of God's greater good. Scripture teaches that God will keep in perfect peace those whose minds are focused on him (e.g., Isa. 26:3; Phil. 4:8–9). That peace is found, however, in God's power and presence, not in any self-deception as unbelieving pop psychologists imply by recommending prayer as mantra.

It is no doubt beyond human comprehension to understand logically the relationship between God's divine action in the world and the prayers of his people, but passages such as Acts 4:23–31 teach that prayer is to be the Christian's response to the recognition that God sovereignly directs all things. If there is divine concurrence in all human action, then prayer is no exception. As Charles Spurgeon put it, "Prayer prompted by the Holy Spirit is the footfall of the divine decree."[11]

The earliest Christians who prayed the bold prayer of Acts 4:24–30 were unafraid to recognize that God's power and will had decided beforehand that Herod and Pontius Pilate, along with the Gentiles and the people of Israel, would kill Jesus Christ (Acts 4:27). God's involvement in this great evil did not cause them, as it apparently

---

9. This is an approach popularly taken, for instance, in Rabbi Harold Kushner's *When Bad Things Happen to Good People* (New York: G. K. Hall and Co., 1982).

10. Keller, "On Providence and Prayer," 968.

11. Quoted in R. C. Sproul's, *The Providence of God Study Guide*, 100.

causes many today, to doubt God's goodness in having his only begotten Son crucified. Instead, they saw Jesus' crucifixion as greater than any evil that could befall themselves. Correlatively, they understood that the greatest good, salvation, had been worked through the greatest evil, Christ's crucifixion, and that God's greater good would result also from any suffering and evil that they might experience as they lived out this good news. Rather than dull their motivation for prayer, this recognition of God's sovereignty over evil fueled their confidence that whatever might befall them was indeed a part of this greater plan; such knowledge drew them to worship God in fervent prayer. Were God not in control of bringing a greater good out of evil, redemption by any definition would be impossible.

(3) *Divine concurrence that moves history toward a planned end.* Throughout the Bible, God's involvement in human action is always described as being purposeful. The treachery of Joseph's brothers served a purpose far beyond their knowing. When they felt the guilt of their evil, Joseph comforted them with these words (Gen. 45:5–8):

> And now, do not be distressed and do not be angry with yourselves for selling me here, because it was to save lives that God sent me ahead of you.... But *God sent me* ahead of you to preserve for you a remnant on earth and to save your lives by a great deliverance.
>
> So then, *it was not you who sent me here, but God.* (emphasis added)

Divine concurrence in human action is purposeful toward a divinely appointed end. Such concurrence in the decisions of Pilate, Herod, and all the others that led Jesus to the cross accomplished an ultimate good that no one involved could ever have imagined: "Once you were alienated from God and were enemies in your minds because of your evil behavior. But now he has reconciled you by Christ's physical body through death to present you holy in his sight, without blemish and free from accusation" (Col. 1:21–22). Furthermore, the New Testament teaches that all of history is still moving toward the final point of God's plan, when Christ returns.

This necessarily implies that today, even as you read this page, God is working concurrently in human action. For where do private, insignificant, ordinary acts end and monumental, historic events begin? Do not great, history-making people emerge out of ordinary antecedent events, such as the first meeting of the couple who would eventually give them birth? For God to accomplish the great acts of redemption, such as the Exodus or the crucifixion of Jesus, the lives of many players had to be brought into confluence. What chain of ordinary events brought Herod and Pontius Pilate together to conspire in Jerusalem against the Son of God? How do we separate redemptive history from the web of events of all of history? The book of Esther suggests that God has dignified all of history, even its seemingly most insignificant events, with his power and presence working through providence to fulfill his covenant promises.

According to Scripture, God's involvement with the universe is not capricious. Neither is God waiting to see what we all decide to do so he can then intervene if things are not going as planned. God governs the universe toward a goal, and that goal is inseparably bound to the people he has chosen to bring into covenant with himself in Jesus Christ.

The author of Esther skillfully highlights God's kingship over the affairs of the world in comparison to the foibles and follies of the great and powerful King Xerxes. Despite Xerxes' great power and wealth, the true King of the universe moved history onward right under Xerxes' nose as the Persian king reveled in his illusion of being in control. And God wasn't even "there"—a thought that should humble professing atheists, who see no evidence of God in the world! Perhaps the author of Esther shows Xerxes making not even one decision of his own in order to underscore the fact that even one of Persia's greatest kings was not really in control of events despite the outward appearance of majesty and power. The book of Esther pokes fun at the earthly powers-that-be and the prince of darkness, who finagles them in the spiritual realm.

There is no way to understand the events told in the book of Esther as being of God without affirming the three elements of divine providence just outlined. If the book of Esther is understood as communicating truth about human nature and redemptive destiny in the form of story, surely the truth it communicates demands the claims of divine providence. How omnipotent is our God in all the earth!

Scripture Index

General Index

Bring ancient truth to modern life with the
NIV Application Commentary series

Covering both the Old and New Testaments, the NIV Application Commentary series is a staple reference for pastors seeking to bring the Bible's timeless message into a modern context. It explains not only what the Bible means but also how that meaning impacts the lives of believers today.

Daniel
Tremper Longman III reveals how the practical stories and spellbinding apocalyptic imagery of Daniel contain principles that are as relevant now as they were in the days of the Babylonian Captivity.

Tremper Longman III
ISBN: 0-310-20608-1

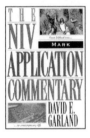

Mark
Learn how the challenging Gospel of Mark can leave recipients with the same powerful questions and answers it did when it was written.

David E. Garland
ISBN: 0-310-49350-1

Luke
Focus on the most important application of all: "the person of Jesus and the nature of God's work through him to deliver humanity."

Darrell L. Bock
ISBN: 0-310-49330-7

Available at your local Christian bookstore

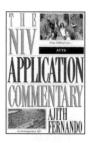

Acts

Study the first portraits of the church in action around the world with someone whose ministry mirrors many of the events in Acts. Biblical scholar and worldwide evangelist Ajith Fernando applies the story of the church's early development to the global mission of believers today.

Ajith Fernando
ISBN: 0-310-49410-9

1 Corinthians

Is your church struggling with the problem of divisiveness and fragmentation? See the solution Paul gave the Corinthian Christians over 2,000 years ago. It still works today!

Craig Blomberg
ISBN: 0-310-48490-1

Galatians

A pastor's message is true not because of his preaching or people-management skills, but because of Christ. Learn how to apply Paul's example of visionary church leadership to your own congregation.

Scot McKnight
ISBN: 0-310-48470-1

Ephesians

Explore what the author calls "a surprisingly comprehensive statement about God and his work, about Christ and the gospel, about life with God's Spirit, and about the right way to live."

Klyne Snodgrass
ISBN: 0-310-49340-4

Available at your local Christian bookstore

ZONDERVAN®
.com

Philippians
The best lesson Philippians provides is how to encourage people who actually are doing quite well. Learn why not all the New Testament letters are reactions to theological crises.

Frank Thielman
ISBN: 0-310-49 340-4

1&2 Thessalonians
Paul's letters to the Thessalonians say as much to us today about Christ's return and our resurrection as they did in the early church. This volume skillfully reveals Paul's answers to these questions and how they address the needs of contemporary Christians.

Michael W. Holmes
ISBN: 0-310-49380-3

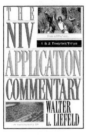

1&2 Timothy, Titus
Take the Pastoral Letters from their early-church context and accurately apply them to contemporary ministry.

Walter L. Liefeld
ISBN: 0-310-50110-5

Hebrews
The message of Hebrews can be summed up in a single phrase: "God speaks effectively to us through Jesus." Unpack the theological meaning of those seven words and learn why the gospel still demands a hearing today.

George H. Guthrie
ISBN: 0-310-49390-0

Available at your local Christian bookstore

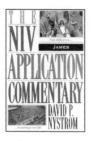

James

Give your church the best antidote for a culture of people who say they believe one thing but act in ways that either ignore or contradict their belief. More than just saying, "Practice what you preach," James gives solid reasons why faith and action must coexist.

David P. Nystrom
ISBN: 0-310-49360-9

1 Peter

The issue of the church's relationship to the state hits the news media in some form nearly every day. Learn how Peter answered the question for Christians surviving under Roman rule and how it applies similarly to believers living amid the secular institutions of the modern world.

Scot McKnight
ISBN: 0-310-49290-4

2 Peter, Jude

Introduce your modern audience to letters they may not be familiar with and show why they'll want to get to know them.

Douglas J. Moo
ISBN: 0-310-20104-7

Letters of John

Like the community in John's time, which faced disputes over erroneous "secret knowledge," today's church needs discernment in affirming new ideas supported by Scripture and weeding out harmful notions. This volume will help you show today's Christians how to use John's example.

Gary M. Burge
ISBN: 0-310-486420-3

Available at your local Christian bookstore

ZONDERVAN®
.com

We want to hear from you. Please send your comments about this book to us in care of zreview@zondervan.com. Thank you.

ZONDERVAN.com/
AUTHORTRACKER
follow your favorite authors